Exporting American Architecture, 1870–2000

Planning, History and the Environment series

Editor:

Professor Dennis Hardy, Middlesex University, UK

Editorial Board:

Professor Arturo Almandoz, Universidad Simón Bolívar, Caracas, Venezuela

Professor Nezar AlSayyad, University of California, Berkeley, USA

Professor Eugenie L. Birch, University of Pennsylvania, Philadelphia, USA

Professor Robert Bruegmann, University of Illinois at Chicago, USA

Professor Jeffrey W. Cody, Chinese University of Hong Kong, Hong Kong

Professor Robert Freestone, University of New South Wales, Sydney, Australia

Professor David Gordon, Queen's University, Kingston, Ontario, Canada

Professor Sir Peter Hall, University College London, UK

Dr Peter Larkham, University of Central England, Birmingham, UK

Professor Anthony Sutcliffe, Nottingham University, UK

Technical Editor

Ann Rudkin, Alexandrine Press, Oxford, UK

Exporting American Architecture, 1870–2000

Jeffrey W. Cody

3 March 2003

For Paula,

with warm regards,

Jeff Cody

 Routledge
Taylor & Francis Group

LONDON AND NEW YORK

First published 2003 by Routledge
11 New Fetter Lane, London EC4P 4EE

Simultaneously published in the USA and Canada
by Routledge, 29 West 35th Street, New York, NY 10001

Routledge is an imprint of the Taylor & Francis Group

© 2003 Jeffrey W. Cody

Typeset in Palatino and Humanist by PNR Design, Didcot, Oxfordshire
Printed and bound in Great Britain by St Edmundsbury Press, Bury St Edmunds, Suffolk

This book was commissioned and edited by Alexandrine Press, Oxford

British Library Cataloguing in Publication Data

A catalogue record for this book is available from the British Library

Library of Congress Cataloging in Publication Data

A catalog record for this book has been requested

ISBN 0–419–24690–8 (hb)   0–415–29915–2 (pb)

Contents

Preface

Although I did not know it then, this book began in Shiraz, Iran in Fall 1978 when my companion (and later wife) Mary and I – both Americans – were teaching English to finance our 3-year odyssey through Europe and Asia. Mary had been hired to tutor a dentist's wife who lived next to the American Consulate. Having left the U.S. in 1976 as wandering backpackers, we were stunned 2 years later to find ourselves surrounded by American-style, split-level houses – towering above opaque walls – in a patrician neighborhood on the outskirts of a historic city. The suburb was on its way to becoming a gated community. Ribbons of sidewalks snaked between houses and streets. The exteriors of the lavish residences were decorated with Western architectural details. The houses were separated by green lawns that were nourished with precious water from the southern Iranian desert.

When the dentist's wife greeted us at the front door, she proudly gave us a tour of the house. We were surprised by the American-ness of the house's interior, an emotion further fuelled by what we witnessed in the kitchen. There, seated on the floor next to a gigantic American refrigerator that dispensed ice cubes from its door were two women in shawls (i.e., in *chador*) bent over and plucking feathers from several dead chickens. They were lost in conversation and oblivious to our presence as they cut up the birds' bloody flesh in the centre of the floor. The contrast between the suburban American nature of the kitchen and the activities of the old women, which might have just as easily taken place in the dirt outside a tent, could not have been starker. Six months later, when Mary and I fled Iran after revolutionary zealots torched the school where we taught, the image of those women – and the dentist's wife – remained vivid in our memories of Shiraz, as the city experienced the Islamic Revolution. Swept in the vortex of the Iranian Revolution, we were witnesses to a critical political shift that would reach into the early twenty-first century. However, it was only much later that I realized that I had also witnessed a fascinating example of the exporting of American architecture.

A North American suburban residence had been transplanted and yet had 'morphed' into something distinctly non-American. Where had it come from? Who had designed and marketed it, and when had it made its appearance in Shiraz? I remember being curious about these questions but I was too rapidly whisked up in the prelude of revolution to set about answering them. I now realize that, judging by its gleaming condition, probably the dentist's house was a 1970s import/export, a testimony to the oil-rich infusion of American influence throughout Iran fuelled by Mohammed Reza Shah Pahlavi, toppled by an aged ayatollah in early 1979. But my experience with this example of American architectural exporting caught me off-guard. Then I had had little training as an architectural historian. It was only by gaining a fuller perspective that I came to see that American suburban offshoot with greater historical clarity. This book seeks to provide readers, too, with a richer context for their understanding of the spatial, cultural and technological aspects of globalization concerned with U.S. architecture, planning and construction.

In addition to my vagabonding in the late-1970s, this book also grew out of a research paper I wrote at Cornell University (Cody, 1983) and more fundamentally out of PhD research I conducted during 1987–88 in Shanghai. As I investigated the career of Henry K. Murphy, an American architect who practiced in China from 1914 to 1935 (Cody, 2001), I was surprised to find evidence of so many other American companies engaged in the drama of construction. When had they arrived in East Asia and why were they there? And if they were anchored in Shanghai, where else did they (or other Americans like them) settle? In the early 1990s, as I began asking how I might learn more about these largely-phantom designers, builders and planners, I also began sharing my observations and questions with friends and colleagues at Cornell University, where I was then

teaching. For their helpful nudging and nurturing at that time, I warmly thank Professors Michael Tomlan, Sherman Cochran, John Reps and Michael Kammen. I also am grateful to several students from Cornell's Graduate Program in Historic Preservation Planning who periodically assisted me in my research sleuthing. I am especially indebted to many of Cornell's Olin Library Reference staff, who so tirelessly and efficiently helped me find and then consult largely forgotten sources attesting to American architectural exportation.

Several scholars beyond Cornell also assisted me at key junctures: Olivier Zunz at the University of Virginia, David Van Zanten at Northwestern University, Isabelle Gournay at the University of Maryland, Paula Lupkin at Washington University, Fabio Grementieri of the Ministry of Culture in Buenos Aires, Jane Loeffler of Washington, D.C., Tom Peters at Lehigh University and Tunney Lee, now retired from MIT and the Chinese University of Hong Kong. For several years Anthony Sutcliffe, Special Professor, University of Nottingham, has been a keen supporter, encouraging me to publish with Routledge and introducing me to Ann Rudkin, a patient and helpful editor who has helped me sculpt this work in important ways. In 2001 Bill Logan at Deakin University (Melbourne) kindly arranged for me to spend a brief but useful time as a visiting scholar down under. The Chinese University of Hong Kong, where I have taught since 1995, has provided me with several Direct Grants for Research, which greatly assisted me in the course of my investigations. Several colleagues and students at the Chinese University have also come to my aid at critical times: Professors Tsou Jin-yeu and Andrew Li, Benny Chow Ka-ming, Kathleen Feagin, Rosetta Kwong and Gabrielle Kwok.

As my understanding of American architectural exporting has evolved, I have presented preliminary results of my research at several conferences. The most important were those organized by the Society of Architectural Historians, the Society for the History of Technology, the International Planning History Society, the Association of Collegiate Schools of Architecture, the University of Paris-VII, the Institut d'Asie Orientale at the University of Lyon-III, the Chinese University of Hong Kong and the University of Hawaii. I have also published earlier versions of my research in *Architectural Research Quarterly* [*ARQ*], *Planning Perspectives* and *Construction History*. Writing for these journals and attending these professional meetings helped me enormously to focus my attention on particular dimensions of my topic, and I thank all those associated with these publications and conferences who challenged me to be clearer and more probing.

Practitioners actively engaged in American architectural exporting have also kindly shared their knowledge and reminiscences: Scott Kilbourn and Kent Muirhead of RTKL, Leslie Robertson of LERA Associates, Cameron Hestler of HOK, Paul Katz of KPF, Fred Matthies and Ray Zee of Leo A. Daly, Dana Low of TAMS, Tom Fridstein of SOM, Lyndon Neri of Michael Graves Associates, Allan Morris of Llewellyn-Davies and Alex Lui of Lee Hysan Development Company, Hong Kong. Other friends have also provided warm support, most notably Nancy and Charlie Trautmann, Libby and Tony Nelson, Karen and Dave Smith, John and Alice Berninghausen, Spencer and Mike Leineweber, Tom Campanella, Jack Sidener, Nelson Chen, Zofia Rybkowski, Ric Richardson and Jeff Howarth. Nancy Wolf, whose

artwork graces the cover and chapter openings, has kindly allowed her stimulating visions to complement my words, for which I am very grateful.

Above all, however, I rest on the shoulders of my family. In the first decade of the twentieth century my grandfather, an electrician, played amateur baseball in Puerto Rico while he was engaged in a construction project there, and in the early-1950s my father was an export trader, working from New York with clients in Latin America. In the late-1960s, a decade after my father's early death, my mother had the wisdom to let me join a high-school exchange programme to Chile where, as I began to travel, I took the first steps that have led to this book. Although sadly none of these relatives has lived to see this book's birth, they unknowingly helped plant its seeds. In a more immediate sense my daughter Maura and my son Aaron have been exported from, and then re-imported back into the U.S. many times in their short lives and, in the process, they have given me more strength, joy and inspiration than they can imagine. My brother Jerry and my aunt Alice and uncle Bob have also lovingly urged me on as this book has taken shape. My wife Mary, though, has been my staunchest and most steadfast companion through all the vicissitudes related to this venture, from Iran to Shanghai, and in myriad places before and after. Without her love and faith this book would never have become a reality. However, despite all this assistance from so many, I alone am responsible for all the weaknesses that inevitably remain.

Jeff Cody
Hong Kong, November 2002

Acknowledgements

I would like to thank all those who have granted permission for reproduction of illustrations. Particularly, as noted in the Preface, I thank Nancy Wolf for allowing me to include her drawings. Details of these are as follows:

Cover: 'The Dragon and the Highrise', 2000, pencil on paper, 22 in x 15 in. By courtesy of the Marsha Mateyka Gallery, Washington. (Photo credit Tony Holmes)

Introduction: 'Who Are We?', 1985, pencil on paper, 12 in x 15 in. Collection James and Marsha Mateyka. (Photo credit Charles Rumph)

Chapter 1: 'The Gods Cried Again From the Hut In Me', 1983, pencil on paper, 22 in x 15 in. Collection Karen A. Franck. (Photo credit Charles Rumph)

Chapter 2: 'Lost City', 1988, pencil on paper, 12 in x 16 in. Collection Linda Joy Goldner and Robert J. Segal. (Photo credit Tony Holmes)

Chapter 3: 'Perfect Order', 1988, 22 x 33 in, pencil on paper. Collection of John Fondersmith. (Photo credit eeva-inkeri)

Chapter 4: 'The First Circle', 1992, pencil on paper, 26.5 in x 37.5 in. Collection Sallie Mae, Student Loan Marketing Associate. (Photo credit D. James Dee)

Chapter 5: 'California Coastline'. 1975, pencil on paper, 23 in x 29 in. Private collection. (Photo credit Nancy Wolf)

Chapter 6: 'Wheel of Fortune', 1991, pencil on paper, 30.5 x 22 in. Collection Gina Kennedy. (Photo credit D. James Dee)

Every effort has been made to identify and contact copyright owners of other illustrations in the text and sources are noted in the captions. However, if any errors or oversights have occurred, we would wish these to be corrected at a later printing. Please contact the publisher, c/o Routledge.

Introduction

When the World Trade Center towers were pulverized and the Pentagon blasted in September 2001, and as thousands lost their lives, the damages wrought to these iconic symbols of American architecture and 'neocolonial power' were palpable and immediate (Wright, 2002, p. 126). Images of the architectural devastation were transmitted instantaneously; the human catastrophes reverberating from that devastation were global in scale. Buildings that served myriad functions and held fragile lives became spaces of memory and meaning that transcended steel and concrete. The exporting of American power, commodities and values were

inevitably linked to these tangible symbols of the United States. Mohammed Atta, one of those who plotted the attacks, reportedly believed that 'high-rise buildings had desecrated [Egypt]' where, in the 1960s and 1970s 'ugly apartment blocks [became] shabby symbols of Egypt's haphazard attempts to modernize' (Ruthven, 2002, p. 260, quoting from *Newsweek*, 7 January 2002). The United States was inextricably linked to that tendency to modernize, and similarly the exporting of American architecture – as an ideal, or simply a mass of building materials – reflected one dimension of a confused mosaic. This book examines that dimension in finer detail, seeking to place the exporting of American architecture in a broader historical context, and in so doing helping to clarify that mosaic.[1]

The mosaic is composed of two kinds of architectures, one related to spaces of consumption and the second to technologies of production. In the early twenty-first century, as the United States has become a political and military superpower, it also sits at the center of global popular culture and corporate capitalism (Gitlin, 1992; Rockwell, 1994; Farhi and Rosenfeld, 1998; Trueheart, 1998; Waxman, 1998; Wagnleitner and May, 2000; Friedman, 2000). U.S. entrepreneurs have exported American landscapes of consumption to virtually every corner of the globe, from fast food franchises, theme parks, cinemas and other versions of entertainment to shopping centres, high-rise corporate icons and suburban gated communities (Watson, 1997; Hannigan, 1998; Heikkila and Pizarro, 2002). 'America leads the world in all dimensions of power – military, economic, cultural, scientific – by a margin out of all proportion to its population' (*Economist*, 29 June 2002, special section, p. 3). Therefore, some Americans have argued, the U.S. should embrace its leadership position and assume an 'imperial' role (Judis, 1992; Ricks, 2001). As the U.S. journalist Charles Krauthammer has expressed this sentiment, 'People are now coming out of the closet on the word "empire" . . . The fact is no country has been as dominant culturally, economically, technologically and militarily in the history of the world since the Roman Empire' (Eakin, 2002). 'American empire' has increasingly become a phrase either to characterize or to label the complex sets of conditions that result in U.S.-related places of consumption (Kaplan, 2001; Bacevich, 2002). However, even when the word 'empire' is not directly linked to the United States, its implicit association with capitalism, power and the U.S. as the country at the centre of that power is found in intellectual commentaries about recent cultural trends, most notably in the book *Empire* (Hardt and Negri, 2000).

Exported technologies of U.S. production have received far less attention by scholars. The research of Lougheed and Kenwood (1982), Headrick (1988), Marx and Smith (1994) and Nye (1996), as well as the commentary by Marlin (1975) argue compelling about the need to trace the connections between American technological prowess and historical trends. Several contemporary U.S. scholars assert that one of the chief selling points of American architecture abroad concerns building technology and the efficient ways in which U.S. designers and builders and architectural practitioners can help clients achieve a high-quality spatial and formal solution (Katz, 1999; Lui, 1999). This point was borne out in a 1997 survey conducted by the Continental Europe branch of the American Institute of Architects, which canvassed an unspecified number of European architects in thirteen countries, asking what words best summed up American architects. The survey found that American architects were efficient (59 per cent), aggressive (37 per cent), successful (34 per cent), business-oriented (25 per cent), turf-conscious (20 per cent) and wealthy (17 per cent), but it also elicited a prevalent opinion among European architects that what Americans build is 'bizarre, boring, formal, conservative and environmentally wanting' (Vonier, 1997). It would have been fascinating to hear the assessments of architects from other regions about their American peers, but unfortunately no such survey has been conducted.

To be more fully understood, the confused mosaic related to U.S. design and construction abroad needs to be pencilled in with finer lines. Without more substantive historical understanding, the ongoing exportation of American architectural ideals, designs and building technologies might mistakenly be seen as relatively recent phenomena associated with U.S. foreign trade, military power or globalization. In reality, that exportation has a broad and deep history, which this book seeks to illuminate. Without confronting that history, we might well become lost in the present. My main argument is that crucial, historical U.S. foundations underpin early twenty-first century, globalizing trends in built environments worldwide. I suggest that those foundations begin to be set in place in the 1870s and that they shift over time and place. To get a glimpse of those foundations I have operated at a fine grain of empirical investigation, unearthing evidence largely from contemporary trade journals, but also from other sources. As one critic has asserted, 'History's indispensable to shape our understanding but it needs to be there at the takeoff, not the landing. To find our voice and tools of choice in shaping human futures, we need to nurse that vision not with scalpels, but with sutures' (Tipson, 1997, p. 169). I have worked with both scalpels and sutures, carefully cutting through fine details, but also stitching together disparate events, people, places and works of architecture and city planning. Simultaneously, I have tried to maintain both a micro- and macro-perspective. As the novelist John Irving observed, 'Any good book is always in motion – from the general to the specific, from the particular to the whole, and back again. Good reading . . . moves the same way' (Irving, 1989, p. 324).

At the micro level I have found 'smoking guns' that demonstrate key architectural connections between the United States and non-U.S. contexts. Some of those connections naturally involve individuals: architects, contractors, engineers, developers, planners and others involved with the built environment. Others relate to either private companies or public agencies: building material suppliers, construction firms, architectural or planning partnerships, government bureaus and others whose commercial or institutional reach extended beyond U.S. borders. One of my challenges has been how to find these people and companies. Where did they operate, when, how, and why? Other connections have clearly related to sites: city plans, buildings, complexes and tangible technological

relics. By retaining in part a place-based focus, I have sought to heighten the significance of the site and, in so doing, let the site illuminate the significance of broader trends. Although several scholars have usefully preceded me in researching 'spaces and places' in the context of globalization (Alsayyad, 1992, 2001; Zukin, 1993; Jacobs, 1996; Oncu and Weyland, 1997; Cox, 1997; Olwig and Hastings, 1997; Ellin, 1999; Smith, 2001), none has scrutinized the precise, trans-national details associated with American architectural exportation. Because U.S. construction technologies and building forms influenced so many places worldwide since the late-nineteenth century, it is crucial to trace the dynamics of that change, in part by exploring which U.S. companies and individuals were engaged in the exporting, as well as when, where and why they did so. As I have asked these questions, I have found other 'smoking guns' about these firms and individuals in the form of fleeting glimpses, vague references and obscure examples published in contemporary American trade journals, whose editors and writers paid careful attention to the exporting of architecture as a set of constituent parts that were bought and sold as technologies and materials. Curiously, most of the American architectural journals did not often heed this trend until after World War II, which is one reason why some have assumed that the exporting of American architecture only began in conjunction with Henry Luce's famous phrase, 'the American Century', which he introduced in *Life* magazine in February 1941.

For a macro-level perspective I have adopted an approach derived from several current, sometimes overlapping positions about historic globalization. One of these positions is related to 'world history' (sometimes called 'global history'), which seeks to move beyond limited geographical and temporal domains in order to clarify overarching historical themes (Frank, 1998; Pomeranz, 2001; Tignor *et al.*, 2002). To place specific cases in sensible context,

I have followed trails blazed worldwide by U.S. dollars, which have led me to look beyond the confines of a limited geographic region, and instead to follow where the money took those who were actually engaged in architectural exporting. These money trails have also compelled me to look behind the forms (i.e., the architectural works) to see the economic and social incentives suffusing those forms. Economic historians ascribing to 'world systems theory' have been conducting research in this vein for at least the past quarter century (Wallerstein, 1974, 1980). Other scholars have enriched the theory by examining the dynamics of information technology transfer (Castells, 1996, 1997, 1998; Yeung, 2000), postmodernist economics (Harvey, 1989), regional competition (Scott, 1998), and 'new geographies of centrality' (Sassen, 2000, p. 5).

Another set of intellectual positions that relates directly to the dynamics of American architectural exportation is concerned with postcolonialism. For the past quarter-century, Edward Said's work (Said, 1978 and 1993) has inspired many historians and cultural theorists to re-examine conventional assumptions about the implications of colonialism in a range of cultural contexts. In this regard, because of their strong empirical focus – relating theories to both architectural practice and product – the work of Wright (1991), Alsayyad (1992), Dirks (1992), Thomas (1994), Crinson (1996), and Çelik (1997) is particularly helpful. As will be shown below, especially in the first two chapters, the neocolonial reach of the United States in the early 1900s, and beyond, fits well within the theoretical paradigms and actual cases discussed by this group of inspiring scholars.

A third body of scholarship that relates directly to the topics I broach here centres around questions of cultural globalization and cultural imperialism. John Tomlinson's work is particularly helpful (Tomlinson, 1991 and 1999), as is that of Atherton (1985), Russett (1985), Bowen (1985), De Grazia (1985), Wagnleitner (1986), Featherstone, Lash and Robertson (1995),

Appadurai (1996), and King (1997). Scholarship about either 'social imperialism' (Schoonover, 1991) or 'informal imperialism' (McCormick, 1967; Bickers, 1999) also provides useful frames of reference for comprehending the cultural reach of imperialism in its myriad guises. With a sharp focus on the United States, research by Davis (1981), Horwitz (1993), Kaplan and Pease (1993), Pells (1997), Watson (1997), Wagnleitner and May (2000) and Trumpbour (2002) is especially illuminating. However, as Kalb (2002, pp. 1–3) explains, the burgeoning scholarship devoted to globalization ('the grand narrative of our time', as he calls it) has become so voluminous that to summarize even the work only published within the past decade would not only require enormous space, but would be largely repetitive (Lechner and Boli, 2000). When I embarked on this research in the early 1990s, the word 'globalization' was virtually never uttered. Now it appears in world headlines practically on a daily basis.

What appears with much less frequency, however, is a well-defined historical perspective about issues melded to 'globalization'. Clearly there have been architectural transfers of know-how and design throughout most of human history. For centuries, if not for millennia, the military and cultural reach of Greek, Roman, Mayan and other empires had crucial implications for architecture and city construction. Scholars have begun to plumb the depths of these implications, but much more research needs to be conducted before the 'confused mosaics' related to these cases just mentioned, and many others, can be clarified. This book is but one step in this long and meandering series of directions that will bring to light the rich dimensions of architectural change from imperial centres to controlled dominions, and vice versa. The book centres around the transplanting of American architecture during what Luce and others have called 'the American Century' (Judis, 1992; Cantor, 1997; Zunz, 1998; White, 1999). It explains how, why and where American architects, contractors, realtors, planners or building materials exporters have marketed American architecture overseas. In part they have profited because American standards have often been the norm by which other places have been judged to be 'modern', 'progressive' or 'developed'. International clients have emulated American buildings such as skyscrapers, they have followed patterns of American urbanism such as suburban residences, and they have adopted American concepts of form and space for eating and shopping such as fast-food restaurants and shopping malls. The book asks how we should understand the dynamics of these trends and what lessons we should learn from them.

Below, I reach three major conclusions. First, as the transplanting of American architecture occurred, it did so in more complex ways than some might assume. Rather than being characterized as strictly a direct, equivalent transplantation, I have seen the exporting of American architecture more as a hybrid transformation, with a spectrum of results from nearly direct imitation to barely discernible architectural genes. James Watson's research about McDonalds in East Asia is particularly illuminating in this regard (Watson, 1997), as are the conclusions of John Atherton, who maintained that where culture meets differing contexts, 'the shift in context deteriorates meaning' (Atherton, 1985, p. 221). Second, if it is true, as Atherton has asserted that the 'U.S. continues to function as a freewheeling symbol factory for the world' (Atherton, 1985, p. 222) then it is also true that the freewheeling began much earlier than many assume. The evidence demonstrates loud smoking guns as early as a century ago. As will be clear below, the strands of construction linking the U.S. to other regions and social contexts were sometimes long, at other times tangled, but often intriguing. Finally, the more sustained examples of American architectural exporting suggest a need on the part of both the exporter and the receiver of the exported architecture to be sensitive to the cultural integrity of any given

place, investing time to understand how best to meld exported architectural technologies with pre-existing, enduring practices.

To reach these conclusions I trace a narrative and weave an analysis that begins in the 1870s, when the Philadelphia Centennial Exhibition sparked the exporting of American architecture. In 1898 American military victories helped shape the United States' confident political and economic stance *vis-à-vis* other imperial powers. In Chapter 1, therefore, I lay the foundation for exporting American architecture, looking at the important role played by exhibitions, railroads, bridge building and the steel frame in late-nineteenth century exporting. Chapter 2 moves beyond steel to examine one of its main technological complements, concrete, and explores how both these materials provided a firm foundation for creating a system of contracting abroad in the first two decades of the twentieth century. In Chapter 3 I focus on some of the crucial dynamics of early-twentieth-century architectural exporting, associated with adjustments that American architects, builders and engineers either chose to make or decided to avoid making, as they sought linkages abroad. Chapter 4 examines the American city as a new paradigm of either 'efficient' and/or 'scientific' modernity between the two world wars. American architects, engineers, planners and other 'experts' became some of the main transmitters of this U.S.-infused paradigm to non-American contexts. I argue that some of these projects were isolated ventures, while others were part of conscious efforts aided by private and public organizations such as the U.S. Department of Commerce and the Export-Import Bank of the United States. The thrust of Chapter 5 concerns the 30 years after World War II, when American architectural exporting was tied to the provision of what I term 'architectural tools of war and peace'. During this period the U.S. government assumed a more significant role in fuelling the flames of architectural exporting. Finally, in Chapter 6, I examine some recent trends in American architectural exportation, using the historical context I have created throughout the book to understand more immediate events and developments with greater depth, clarity and perspective.

Some of the most significant, initial events related to my analysis of American architectural exporting occurred in Philadelphia, a city located roughly at the epicentre of the three pivotal sites associated with September 11, 2001: Manhattan, Washington, D.C. and Shanksville, Pennsylvania. This geographic coincidence – associated with U.S. tragedy, power,

culture and architecture – is a reminder of how history and the present fuse into a continuum. Regarding the exporting of American architecture, that fusion begins by considering what occurred in Philadelphia and elsewhere during the 1870s.

NOTE

1. In this book, the word 'America' will sometimes be used as a shorthand version of the United States of America. In those cases where other 'Americas' are referred to (e.g., Latin America, South America), I will use the appropriate adjective.

1

Exporting Steel-framed Skeletons of American Modernity

The exporting of American architecture began in the mid-nineteenth century as a disjointed set of personal adventures and commercial initiatives. Some of the adventurers were entrepreneurs selling either building components or prefabricated structures, such as slave structures, windmills and wharf buildings. Others were daring individualists with a flair for the unknown. Still others were building and planning consultants who were either lured abroad by new kinds of clients or propelled overseas by their U.S.-based headquarters. The scope of activities associated with this small and disparate cast of architectural exporters is easier to chart after 1876,

when visitors from overseas marvelled at examples of American industrial technology displayed at the Philadelphia Centennial Exhibition. Roughly two decades later, after the Chicago Columbian Exposition in 1893, both architectural episodes and building personalities received even greater notoriety abroad, particularly in Europe but also further afield (Lewis, 1997). However, it was not until the waning gasp of the nineteenth century that Americans awoke more fully to the possibilities of exporting their construction knowledge to commercial and cultural contexts so much further afield. 'By 1900 the United States had successfully constructed one

Figure 1.1. China and the U.S. clinging to the same globe. In this 1870s advertisement for an American-made rock drill, China is depicted by a man wearing a conical hat, next to his drill, with a pagoda in the background. The U.S. is caricatured as Uncle Sam beside a similar drill, with a four-storey office building nearby. The business connections between the two distant nations (implied here by a drill that could cut magically through the centre of the earth) became more of a reality in the late-nineteenth and early twentieth centuries. (*Source*: *Chinese Scientific Magazine*, 1877, **2**(9), figure 9)

kind of empire – territorial across the continent – and was building another – economic as well as territorial – overseas' (Twombly, 1995, p. 22).

From a building material standpoint, these exporting activities were frequently related first to timber, iron and steel (a focus of attention in this first chapter), and then to concrete (scrutinized more fully in Chapter 2). Economically, these activities should be seen in the context of the 1893 depression, which provided an incentive for American entrepreneurs to engage in the broader range of foreign trade in order to produce a profit. In a political context, American exporting activities followed the U.S. annexation of

Hawaii in 1898 and other major military victories secured by the United States in the Philippines and Cuba, when U.S. President Theodore Roosevelt and others began to demonstrate a staggering imperialistic stance. Some historians have seen these victories and the trade associated with them as the onset of a 'new empire' (LaFeber, 1963), and others as the trade associated with an American 'informal empire' (Hays, 1995, p. 208; Ricard, 1990). It was in this imperial context that American planners, architects and constructors in several allied professions began to ride on the political coat-tails created by those victories. They began to plan new communities, erect structures using U.S. technologies, fashion commercial and residential landscapes befitting American capitalistic enterprise and ship American-based building technologies to far-flung shores that most Americans could barely locate on a globe.

As will be shown more comprehensively in Chapter 2, by World War I these ventures began to coalesce into more rationalized processes and organizations and they began to reflect a particularly American brand of modernity. Other historians, who have previously probed the dynamics of what some have termed that 'landscape of modernity', have examined the relationships between pluralism and the American Century (Ward and Zunz, 1992, p. 4, and Zunz, 1998), between foreign politics and American pop culture (Wagnleitner and May, 2000), between Canadian and U.S. architectural practices in the late-nineteenth and early-twentieth century (Gournay 1998), or between high-rise construction and *'américanisme'* (Cohen and Damisch, 1993 and Cohen, 1995). This scholarship is 'part of a growing literature on the influence of American culture abroad' (Kaplan and Pease, 1993; Pells, 1997; Appy, 2000; Wagnleitner and May, 2000, p. 4). However, despite this proliferating scholarship, what might be called the architectural/technological DNA of that modernity – the strands of construction-branded

Figure 1.2. Uncle Sam gazing at a world atlas. As U.S. foreign trade swelled in the late-nineteenth and early twentieth centuries, many Americans engaged in that trade were compelled (for reasons of profit as well as curiosity) to learn more about the nations, cultures and peoples touched by U.S. corporate interests. (*Source: Export American Industries*, 1914, **13**(4), p. 53)

genes that comprise an architectural personality that many the world over recognized as 'American' in the early twentieth century – remains unclear.

These genes (primarily made of timber, iron, steel and concrete) were the progenitors of the architectural forms and spaces that designers, contractors and suppliers were marketing between 1876 and 1914, when business entrepreneurs, engineers, planners, contractors, and architects began to forge a first crucial portion of the foundation for the exporting of American architecture. Already by the 1860s American investors and U.S. federal institutions had begun snaking new commercial passages across that globe – Secretary Seward's 'folly' of acquiring Alaska from Russia was in 1867, the same year that the U.S. acquired the Midway Islands in the Pacific. Soon thereafter Americans involved in many aspects of the building trades began to respond to the new opportunities implied by those ventures. Probably the best example of

that trend was how one of the nineteenth century's major construction-related swan songs – the Panama Canal – afforded American engineers and builders the possibility of demonstrating their skills in construction to a more global audience than had occurred in the years preceding the American Civil War (1860–1865). 'By the 1890s the possibilities of foreign trade had come to excite the imagination of many American business and political leaders' (Hays, 1995, p. 208). As many businesses began to feel the effects of the 1893 depression, the imagination of foreign trade was tied to the hope for greater profits. By the outbreak of World War I in 1914 – the same year that the Panama Canal became fully operational – American architectural expertise was becoming increasingly noteworthy, not only in Europe but also in regions under either formal or informal imperial reach. Americans associated with building – in all its forms – transmitted construction knowledge more rapidly than many now realize, from cities such as New York to Buenos Aires, or from Detroit to Shanghai. Information passed either through cables and published journals, or through conversation and actions in the field after the arrival of steamship and train travel. By the early years of the twentieth century, therefore, the first building blocks of a foundation for exporting American architectural know-how were in place. But how and when, precisely, did that transference occur and who or what was responsible for the actual laying of those blocks? What was the mortar binding them together? To analyse the dynamics and implications associated with exporting American architecture, it is critical to understand that foundation with greater clarity.

One way to achieve that clarity is to set a proper context in which the activities of crucial personalities and companies point to salient and meaningful trends. Before the 1880s those personalities and firms were few in number. Two American architects who exemplified the wandering, inquisitive nature of certain American architectural adventurers were

Ithiel Town and Jacob Wrey Mould. During the late 1820s Town travelled in Europe on the kind of journey that countless other American architects have taken since, curious to see firsthand the architectural realities he had only read or heard about (Liscombe, 1991). A half-century later, after a career in New York, the 'eccentric, ill-mannered' Jacob Wrey Mould was employed by the railroad contractor Henry Meiggs to be the architect-in-chief of the Department of Public Works in Lima, Peru (Placzek, 1982, vol. 3, p. 247; Van Zanten, 1969). Town's curiosity and Mould's work for a government department presaged the activities of many American, construction-oriented professionals. Some of the key American designers of the later nineteenth century whose work began to be recognized overseas were even more well-known in their own country than Town and Mould. For example, several scholars have shown how, in the 1880s, the work of architectural geniuses such as Henry Hobson Richardson began to attract the attention of European critics who marvelled at buildings such as Trinity Church in Boston and the Allegheny County Courthouse in Pittsburgh (Reinink, 1970; Tselos, 1970; Eaton, 1972). Australian architects were similarly impressed with Richardson's Romanesque-style adaptations (Orth, 1975), and some Australian engineers in the 1880s were likewise so enthralled with the ways American builders were constructing viaducts to support railroads that they copied those solutions in the Australian outback (Crimes, 1991, p. 101). At the threshold of the twentieth century Louis Sullivan and Frank Lloyd Wright followed Richardson's lead in attracting the wide-eyed attention of many European observers. Moving beyond the scale of either the individual or the single work of architecture, recently some historians have begun to cast appropriate light on the powerful sway held by the American city itself, as well as the architects and planners associated with its dramatic rise, over many European urbanists in the late-nineteenth century and beyond (Cohen and

Damisch, 1993; Gournay, 1998 and 2002; Zevi, 1981; Koch, 1959).

Other architectural designers from the U.S. attracted attention not so much by their finished buildings as by their formative presence in European schools of architecture. For example, in the last quarter of the nineteenth century increasing numbers of U.S. architectural students followed the pioneering lead of Richard Morris Hunt to the École des Beaux-Arts in Paris, the mecca of architectural education, where they began to interact professionally with largely European peers (Baker, 1980). These examples were meaningful not only because of what they implied for the development of American architecture domestically, but also because they set key precedents for U.S. architects commanding stronger respect among their European counterparts.

Other precedents, although much less well known to later observers because their existence was often only documented in either newspapers or trade journals, were also fundamentally important in laying the foundation for American architectural exportation. For example, some of the earliest cases of that exportation were related to slavery, seen in how West Indies plantation owners purchased

Figure 1.3. American-made plantation buildings shipped to the West Indies in the 1860s. (*Source*: D.N. Skillings & D.B. Flint, 1861, *Illustrated Catalogue of Portable and Sectional Buildings*. Boston: the authors)

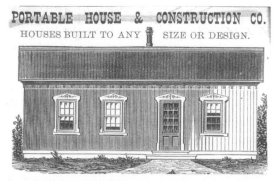

Figure 1.4. Portable timber-frame house sold to foreign clients in the late 1870s by the Ayer Company of Chicago. By the turn of the twentieth century, other kinds of prefabricated buildings followed the precedent set by these timber structures in being shipped as a kit of parts that could be assembled upon delivery. (*Source*: *American Exporter*, 1879, **3**(6), p. 35)

ALADDIN HOUSES

Figure 1.5. Prefabricated bungalows marketed abroad by the Aladdin Company, Bay City, Michigan in the early twentieth century. Aladdin boasted that 'we fell the standing timber, finish it and cut each part to fit exactly in its required place so that any unskilled laborer can erect it as well as the most expert carpenter'. (*Source*: *American Exporter*, 1913, **73**(6), p. 137)

designs from Boston or New York as early as the 1860s to house slaves (Skillings and Flint, 1861) (see figure 1.3).

This example of exporting slave structures resonates with what the historian John Blair has learned about how some of the earliest exports of American popular culture – Jim Crow variety shows and Buffalo Bill Cody's Wild West show were similarly rooted in racism (Blair, 2000, p. 17). Many of the designs for slave dwellings were for one-storey, rectilinear structures whose uncomplicated joinery made them easy to erect, probably by those very slaves who lived in them. Flexibility, economy and ease of construction were significant factors that attracted potential buyers. Such was the case, for instance, of the wooden but 'warm as brick houses built to any size or design' that the Ayer's Portable House and Construction Company shipped abroad from Chicago in 1879 (figure 1.4).

Relative to European exports, which were sometimes elaborate kits in parts, the first American examples of exporting 'portable buildings' were small-scale operations initiated by timber merchants who specialized in satisfying clients' desires for

cheap, quickly-transported, low-rise, boxy spaces where either slaves or others could reside, or where a variety of simple functions could be performed (Lewis, 1993). In the early twentieth century, several American companies were still exporting 'knocked-down' houses; one of the most significant was the Aladdin Company (figure 1.5) (*American Exporter*, 1913, **73**(7), p. 135; *American Exporter*, 1914, **74**(1), p. 119). Larger wood-framed 'portable houses' were also being shipped abroad, particularly to Central and South America, by the turn of the century (*American Mail and Export Journal*, 1894, **21**(9), p. 132).

At the end of the nineteenth century, however, American designers of exported structures began employing a range of building materials that surpassed timber. They began to use iron, followed by steel and concrete, to create higher, broader and more flexible spaces in more far-flung markets. Below, the implications of American innovations concerning these materials and the technologies associated with them will provide a more complete tableau of American architectural exporting at the beginning of the twentieth century. But before delving into the salient case study examples that relate to these issues, it is necessary to examine the fuller social and political context in which those examples thrived, and part of that context derives from two significant exhibitions in late-nineteenth century America.

Expositions of 1876 and 1893: Initial Catalysts for Exporting American Architecture

Because so many U.S. architects, engineers and builders were culturally tethered to Europe, it is tempting to see the cross-fertilization of architectural knowledge prior to the 1870s as largely a one-way street from Europe to the former British colony of the United States. However, this Eurocentric assumption is called into question when one considers how the economy of the former colony was also so intermeshed with those of non-European regions. For example, during the eighteenth century, because of the sugar, molasses and rum trade with Europe and the Caribbean, many North American entrepreneurs were active throughout Central America. As historians have shown, that trade was directly related to the importation of slave labour from Africa (Meinig, 1986). In the mid-nineteenth century, American railway promoters enticed male workers from southern China to help construct the transcontinental railroad, completed in 1869 (Takaki, 1993). Architectural historians have shown how some of the building traditions of these cultures left a variety of influences throughout the U.S. (Upton and Vlach, 1986; Oszuscik, 1988; Upton, 1998). Some scholars have also demonstrated the architectural influence from (what became) the United States to cultural 'hearths' outside continental North America – particularly the West Indies – in the period prior to the mid-nineteenth century (Crain, 1995). However, scholarship is relatively scant about this influence, often limited to descriptions of domestic high-style examples rather than investigations of either hybrid, Creole residences or other building types influenced by the North American mainland. Nonetheless, this

research also suggests that the nature and scope of architectural influence between either Europe and the U.S. mainland, or between that mainland and other hinterlands was far more complicated and dynamic than many have previously assumed (Chapman, 1995).

The cross-fertilization of U.S./non-U.S. architectural influence intensified and became even more variegated after 1876, when the exporting of American architecture became disseminated well beyond Europe and the rarefied atmosphere of the professional architectural *atelier*. The year 1876 was a watershed because of the Centennial International Exhibition in Philadelphia which, in addition to the hubris of patriotism it engendered in Americans, also became a spark that demonstrated to knowledgeable observers worldwide that U.S. technology was advancing significantly and, therefore, that it was going to be a force to be reckoned with (Greenhalgh, 2001; Giberti, 2002). Exhibitors demonstrated this force with products such as pumps, engines and other heavy machinery related to steel, which attracted large crowds at the Exhibition (Rydell, 1984;

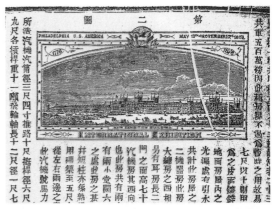

Figure 1.6. Engraving of the Main Exhibition Building, Philadelphia Centennial Exhibition, 1876, reproduced in a Chinese journal within months of the Exhibition. This figure, and the text accompanying it, reflect how attentive some foreign audiences were to the Exhibition and the technological innovations it displayed. (*Source*: *Chinese Scientific Magazine*, 1877, **2**(3), figure 2)

Rydell, Findling and Pelle, 2000). Foreign journalists who wrote about the Exhibition for diverse audiences worldwide also helped disseminate knowledge of the American exhibits to far-flung corners of the globe (figure 1.6).

New steel-related technologies – assisted by innovations such as Bessemer open-hearth smelting processes – were linked to improvements in American urban infrastructure, architecture and the burgeoning U.S. railway industry (Crimes, 1991, p. 131; Misa, 1995, especially chapters 1 and 2). These technologies not only intrigued potential foreign clients, but they also inspired confidence in American exporters. As the historian Samuel Hays has shown, that 'force' grew in the context of American post-Civil War industrialization. 'The rapidly expanding iron and steel industry, stimulated enormously by the railroads, became the foundation of industrial America. Far outstripping the domestic supply, the demand for iron and steel constantly encouraged expansion of American mills' (Hays, 1995, p. 11). Hand in glove with railroad expansion was American industrialists' embracing of mass production, which 'depended upon improved manufacturing techniques, of which standardization of parts and processes was especially significant' (Ibid., p. 12). Regarding its railways, the United States was following the lead of the United Kingdom, which 'exported the railway to many parts of the world, as a concept and in component form' (Atterbury, 2001, p. 159). The first significant phase of American architectural exporting similarly was linked to both developments in construction-related metals such as iron or steel, and in the standardization of components manufactured from those metals, such as I-beams or trusses.

One measure of the celebration associated with the 1876 Centennial Exhibition came in a journalistic form when, in 1877, Charles Root and Franklin Tinker established the *American Exporter* (figure 1.7). In *c.* 1896 that journal absorbed the *American Mail and Export Journal*.

The young publishers had been deeply impressed by all they had seen, heard and inferred at the Philadelphia exposition, and it was this fact more than any other which impelled them, when choosing a new sphere of publishing activity, to select the subject of American exporting, which they firmly believed was destined to an expansion to which there were no assignable limits. (*American Exporter*, 1928, 102(1), p. 46)

One of the publication's early editors re-affirmed the importance of the Philadelphia Exhibition when he said that

the searching study of foreign trade conditions which [the Exposition] prompted gave a tremendous impetus to our export trade, for then began that organized, aggressive movement on the part of our Government and our people which has since won for American manufacturers the deserved and enviable position which they now hold in the world's commerce. (*Ibid.*, p. 48)

'Export is the flywheel of production', Root and Tinker proclaimed (*American Exporter*, 1912, **70**(5), pp. 75–83), and American exporters began to be lured successfully into adapting their production for foreign markets. That flywheel, made of steel, drove American manufacturers to meet the needs of foreign clients. Within a quarter century they competed successfully with British and, to a lesser extent, German manufacturers, who had been predominant in the iron and steel trades for most of the nineteenth century. The *American Exporter* became a major source of information for domestic and overseas commercial

Figure 1.7. Masthead of the inaugural issue of the *American Exporter*, the most popular trade journal for U.S. exporters in the late-nineteenth and early twentieth centuries, which encouraged its readers (among them building materials exporters) to expand their markets and increase production. (*Source*: *American Exporter*, 1877, **1**(1))

entrepreneurs as they sought assistance from both private and public sectors in fostering the exporting of American industry, as well as its products, including those related to architecture.

Historians have demonstrated that U.S. exporting in the late nineteenth century was characterized by marked regional variation, but data also show that overall the U.S. reflected a 255 per cent growth in aggregate exports between 1870 and 1900, much of that (especially in the north-eastern U.S.) in manufactured goods, particularly agricultural implements, iron and steel, leather and refined petroleum products (Hutchinson, 1986, p. 141). Advertisements and articles in the *American Exporter* and other trade journals flesh out these statistics with specific examples. Shortly after 1876, eastern U.S. building material suppliers shipped roofing slates to Europe, Midwestern entrepreneurs exported windmills to remote regions of South America and Asia, and companies specializing in iron and steel began to discover that many clients across the globe highly valued the products they began purchasing from U.S. agents.[1]

One of the earliest companies to ship U.S. iron components overseas was the Edge Moor

Figure 1.8. Windmills near Buenos Aires, Argentina constructed in the 1890s using materials exported from the United States. Wooden structures like these were among the first exported by U.S. producers after the Philadelphia Centennial Exhibition of 1876. They were especially popular in South America. (*Source: American Mail and Export Journal*, 1895, **32**(10), p. 147)

Iron Company of Wilmington, Delaware, which specialized in railway bridge and viaduct construction. By 1881 the company had secured the contract, 'with very great opposition' from local manufacturers, for the erection of three kinds of bridges in South Australia and Victoria, 'each an example of elegance and simplicity, combined with a maximum of strength and affording a monument of American skill and enterprise' (*American Mail and Export Journal* 1881, **7**(6), p. 274).[2] Because of what occurred subsequently regarding the appeal of American construction technology, the diffusion of those kinds of iron and steel 'monuments' – beyond Australia to Africa, Southeast Asia and South America – was one of the important trends of the pre-World War I period in the saga of the exporting of American architecture. The fact that local manufacturers objected strenuously to Edge Moor's presence was also significant – and indicative of later challenges in American architectural exporting, as will be shown below – because it indicates how American architectural form and technology sometimes sparked economic and social ferment.

Although the Philadelphia Exhibition was critically important in opening the door to overseas markets more widely for American exporters, it was the Columbian Exposition of 1893 in Chicago, celebrating the 400th anniversary of Columbus's 'discovery' of America, which boosted American architectural exports even more substantially. Some of this came in the form of actual material goods, such as steel and concrete. However, the impact of this Exposition – the 'White City' as it was dubbed – went beyond the exportation of either components or whole buildings. Its more fundamental influence stemmed from the fact that many European architects began to focus more assiduously upon American architecture, urbanism and technology as exemplars of modernity. In the past decade several scholars have begun to quantify and qualify the architectural/theoretical effects of this Exposition beyond the boundaries of the

United States (Cohen, 1995). Their research focuses in part upon the skyscraper as either a 'heroic deed (or misdeed, as it was for some)', upon America as a 'scene of future life' (Cohen and Damisch, 1993, pp. 11–13), and upon 'the global structures and thematic strategies that buttressed the formal influences of Richardson, Sullivan, Wright, Neutra and Fuller' (Cohen, 1995, p. 15). Cohen has perceptively documented the extent to which French, German, Russian and other European architects were attracted and subsequently influenced by the White City. He has also explained how, both before and after the Fair, European architects and planners such as Sir Patrick Geddes, Ebenezer Howard, Werner Hegemann, Adolf Loos and others were stimulated by the horizontal, vertical and otherwise three-dimensional, social qualities of American places.

Ever since the Chicago Fair in 1893, then, American cities have intrigued a broad palette of architects/urbanists worldwide. After experiencing American architecture and cities, either first- or second-hand through naturally distinctive lenses, these people have subsequently either remained in the U.S. to become American citizens or have left and interpreted what they experienced in other cultural contexts. Similarly, American architects, engineers, contractors or other kinds of commercial entrepreneurs advertised their services to clients in far-flung markets. This might appropriately be termed the 'supply side' of the architectural export equation, although the precise variables of that supply side are still murky. What is even less clear is the 'demand side' of that equation, which demonstrated either a variable thirst for, or distaste of American architectural know-how, and it is that dimension of the dynamic that also merits further attention. John Blair, examining cases of nineteenth-century exports of American entertainment forms, expressed this point when he argued that

cultural exports of this sort are not simply shipped out at random; they arrive in specific cultures at specific times.

Bi-national factors that may vary profoundly from one time and place to another affect the ways and the degrees to which any given cultural product takes hold and why. (Blair, 2000, p. 17)

Masako Notoji, researching how American popular culture has been integrated into a Japanese variant, has discovered the same reality.

American popular culture products, from music to fast food to theme parks, appeal to standardized tastes and lifestyles around the world. But, in actuality, the values and meanings attached to such exports are often reconstructed and redefined within the contexts of the importing societies. (Notoji, 2000, p. 219)

The 'copying' of American technology led, inherently, to hybrid results in form and substance. Either an intangible American idea about architecture, or a more tangible tectonic element of that architecture thus became the impetus for other kinds of architectural form that had roots in the U.S., but then rapidly reached worldwide proportions, albeit at first in isolated cases. If Blair and Notoji are correct, that American cultural products are necessarily transformed when they are transplanted, then it is appropriate to characterize that transplantation as cross-fertilization. But one of the critical questions, then, is what critical examples of architecture as a cultural product – besides the Chicago Fair and the notoriety of a few notable American architects – demonstrate how Americans were exporting their construction knowledge in the final quarter of the nineteenth century? Three such cultural products were the iron and steel railway bridge, the steel-framed skyscraper, and the U.S.-configured, industrial workplace.

The Atbara Bridge: U.S. Engineers trump U.K. Competitors in Africa

As suggested above by the Edge Moor Iron Company's operations in Australia, one significant example of American architecture as an exported cultural product was the railway bridge.

Americans offered several advantages to purchasers of steel bridges in foreign countries, in spite of that prejudice which naturally favors one's own countrymen . . . Americans are twenty years in advance of other nations (except Canada) in the art of bridge design and construction. (Clarke, 1901, p. 43)

By the late nineteenth century, steel was being manufactured in the U.S. 'at much less cost than in any other country' (*Ibid*.). Furthermore, 'the market for bridges [was] far greater in the U.S. than elsewhere . . . [There was] an average of one span of metallic bridge for every three miles of railway' and by 1900 the U.S. was laced with approximately 190,000 miles of rail (*Ibid*). From 1870 to 1900, as American trains roughly doubled in weight to carry significantly more freight, older bridges needed to be strengthened. This demand for bridge-building sparked a boom in companies specializing in this kind of construction, which supplied 'themselves with the best labor-saving and accurate-working machinery' (*Ibid*.). In Europe, trains did not get heavier, 'old bridges answer their purpose, and the demand has been chiefly confined to new ones. Bridge building is merely an adjunct to other business' (*Ibid*.). As a result, European bridge-building companies began to lag behind their American counterparts.

Furthermore, by the early twentieth century three commercial and technological breakthroughs related to steel elevated the formal attractiveness and spatial flexibility of American architecture. The first was related to the speed and efficiency with which American steel producers began to meet potential clients' demands. This breakthrough, in turn, was aided by American advances regarding electricity.

The electric traveling crane is, without doubt, the most potent individual factor in the success of American shops, next to which [is] the application of electric motors for driving . . . machines, doing away with shafting and belts, which . . . enable tools to be placed in such positions that long pieces can generally be kept parallel with the direction of the general shop travel. (*Ibid*., pp. 50–52)

The second breakthrough was the ability to export the components of the characteristically American high-rise, steel-framed building. The third was the merging of steel with concrete to create new technologies for reinforcement that began to rival those of the French, who were pre-eminent in this domain until the early twentieth century. One of the best examples demonstrating the first innovation – speed and efficiency in delivering prefabricated bridges – occurred in 1899, when an American ironworks firm outbid a British company to construct the Atbara Bridge over a tributary of the Nile River, north of Khartoum, then in Egypt and today in Sudan.

By the middle of the nineteenth century Britain was a pre-eminent exporter of iron technologies, both to its colonies and other markets. However, in the waning half of the century Britain experienced

Figure 1.9. The Atbara Bridge near Khartoum, Sudan. This structure, erected in 1899 by African labourers working with U.S. supervisors from the Pencoyd Iron Works in Pennsylvania, was pivotal for American exporters. It was the first time that U.S. bridge building contractors successfully outbid U.K. competitors who, until this commission, many in the bridge building and steel manufacturing businesses assumed to be supreme. (*Source: American Exporter*, 1901, **47**(6), p. 38)

increasing competition, first from Germany and then more surprisingly from the United States (Atterbury, 2001). Lord Kitchener, the Sirdar of Khartoum, summarized the mood of some observers when, at the inauguration of the Atbara Bridge on 27 August 1899, he said:

The construction of this magnificent bridge, I think, may fairly be considered a record achievement. So far as the failure of the efforts to place the construction order in England is concerned, I think that it demonstrates that the relations between labour and capital there are not sufficient to give confidence to the capitalist and to induce him to take the risk of establishing up-to-date workshops that would enable Great Britain to maintain its position as the first constructing nation of the world. But as Englishmen failed, I am delighted that our cousins across the Atlantic stepped in. This bridge is due to their energy, ability and power to turn out work of magnitude in less time than anybody else. I congratulate the Americans on their success in the erection of a bridge in the heart to Africa. They have shown real grit far from home, in the hottest month of the year and depending upon the labour of foreigners. (*American Exporter*, 1899, **44**(4), p. 30)

Kitchener was referring to Americans working for the Pencoyd Iron Works, whose main offices were in Philadelphia but whose manufacturing plant was in Pencoyd, Pennsylvania (Pencoyd Iron Works, 1900) (figure 1.10). In terms of its operating capacity at the turn of the century, Pencoyd was the largest of the twenty-three bridge-building companies then doing business in Pennsylvania (Darnell, 1984, pp. 79–80). The 'foreigners' Kitchener referred to were convicts who were assigned by the Egyptian War Office to help a team of eight, skilled, American ironworkers (*New York Times*, 1899, 7 October, p. 8).

Figure 1.10. Pencoyd Iron Works, Pennsylvania, where the steel components of the Atbara Bridge were manufactured in 1899 before being shipped to East Africa for assembly. (*Source*: Pencoyd Iron Works, 1900)

In January 1899 Pencoyd bid for the contract to erect the Atbara Bridge, a single-track railway bridge commissioned by the Egyptian War Office, but also related to Lord Kitchener's military campaign against the Dervishes. Kitchener's success

was due mainly to the fact that he opened a line of railway communication as he went, and was able to concentrate his forces with full supplies . . . in the heart of the far-distant Soudan [*sic*] country. In order to continue his campaign against the Dervishes, the General found it necessary to complete a railway line as far south as Khartoum, and this involved bridging the Atbara River. (*Scientific American*, 1902, 15 March, p. 104)

The 1,100 feet-wide site was dry for much of the year but it became a raging torrent in late June, and British army engineers were reticent about designing the bridge over that torrent. In Fall 1898, when Kitchener inquired in London how long it would take to build the bridge, the reply was two years. Kitchener was impatient. He sent tenders to two American and five British firms, specifying a cantilever bridge. Baron Crotner, the British Consul General in Egypt, oversaw the contract bidding. Initially, the Maryland Steel Company (U.S.) and Horsley (U.K.) seemed to be most favoured, but each proposed using falsework (i.e., temporary wooden framework structures) to erect the bridge, which would have meant waiting for construction to begin after the summer floods. Therefore, Crotner asked for new bids, specifying that 'the bridge should be built by overhang, from pier to pier' (*Ibid.*). Crotner then decided to award it to Pencoyd not only because the Americans' bid was 40 per cent cheaper, but also because Pencoyd promised to deliver it in seven weeks, one-quarter of the time promised by Rigby & Westwood (U.K.), and in half the time proposed by the Patent Shaft and Axle Company (U.K.).

In April 1899, when he learned about Pencoyd's successful bid, Mr. Westwood reacted angrily. He believed that his tender was higher than the Americans' because 'special girders were required, which were dropped in the case of the Americans, who were allowed to supply a pin-bridge, which good English engineers have utterly discarded because it makes a weak bridge' (*New York Times*, 6 April, 1899, p. 3). The other partner, Mr. Rigby, grumbled that

I simply do not believe that any firm in the world can turn out a bridge of that size in the time mentioned . . . I decline to believe that the work on it was commenced on February 8. The American firm either had the specifications before or adapted a standard bridge to suit the requirements of the case . . . The general feeling is that the British firms have been unjustly treated. (*New York Times*, 4 April, 1899, p. 5)

London's *Evening News*, taking the British side, offered another explanation.

Scandalous! It is only explicable if one remembers the habitual animosity shown by the Khedive and his Government to their habitual protectors. If the bitter antipathy to British engineers, revealed in these proceedings, cannot be traced to the Khedive and is the result of foolish prejudice and unpatriotic preferences on the part of his English advisors, the sooner these advisors are brought to book the better. (quoted in the *New York Times*, 1899, 6 April, p. 3)

Countering these charges, Pencoyd's spokesman asserted that

of course the English firms feel vexed at our successful bid for the work in what they regard as their own territory. Nevertheless, I am surprised at the view taken by Mr. Rigby, and it shows great ignorance of American resources. I scarcely need say that there was nothing underhanded about our securing the contract. We assuredly had not specifications in advance or any advantage over English firms. But Mr. Rigby's remark that no firm could turn out a bridge of the size needed in the time we have will make American bridge builders smile. Instead of preparing the work in seven weeks, we could have done it in seven days if absolutely necessary. (*New York Times*, 1899, 4 April, p. 5)

The spokesman chided that 'Englishmen require too much time for thinking in the bridge building business' (*Ibid.*).

In contrast, Pencoyd acted. Beginning in early

February 1899 Douglas Fox, one of Pencoyd's chief engineers, designed the bridge and workers began manufacturing the components of the bridge's superstructure: trusses, chords, pier-caps, and rivets. Despite losing a week's work because of a fierce blizzard, Pencoyd shipped the material and its building crew from New York on April 22; they arrived in Atbara on June 16. The blustery remarks of Pencoyd's spokesman about only needing seven days to prepare the work in Pennsylvania contrasted with the harsh reality of the construction work the Pencoyd team encountered in the East African desert, where Pencoyd's superintendent contended with sweltering heat, frequent delays, gruelling sandstorms, and 'provokingly slow' gangs of six convicts each, who were only able to drive 100 rivets a day, instead of the 150 a day that American four-man riveting crews usually drove. Pencoyd's bridge had seven Pratt trusses, each 147 feet long and 16 feet wide.

One span was erected temporarily on shore to serve as a holdback anchorage for the first span over the river. The inshore end of this temporary span was loaded with 60,000 pounds of steel rails; a steel traveling derrick was erected on the top chords, and a temporary connection was made between the two spans . . . After the connection over the pier had been made the erection proceeded continuously across the river, while the overhang method, which is customary in the erection of cantilever bridges, was used. (*Scientific American*, 1902, 15 March, p. 184)

By October 1899 the Pencoyd crew was back in Pennsylvania, where they were greeted as heroes (*New York Times*, 1899, 7 October, p. 8).

However, as some Americans celebrated, other English engineers fretted. The Secretary of the U.K. Engineers' Society lamented that 'we certainly regret the transference of work essentially belonging to our market, and it would be affectation to deny that there is indignation and much comment on the state of affairs. We hope it will prove only a temporary transference, but you know the danger' (*New York*

Times, 1899, 9 April, p. 7). Ironically, though, it was an English metallurgical chemist, Benjamin Talbot, who helped boost Pencoyd's notoriety. While working on the Atbara project, Pencoyd hired Talbot, who for ten years had been developing a continuous, open-hearth Bessemer process for producing steel at the Southern Iron Company in Chattanooga, Tennessee (Misa, 1995, p. 152). The 'danger' feared by the Secretary of the U.K. Engineers' Society was that the Atbara Bridge project would set a precedent for American contractors. That is precisely what occurred, as several American bridge-building companies began undercutting their European competitors, from Africa to Southeast Asia (*American Exporter*, 1900, **46**(4), p. 30; *American Exporter*, 1903, **51**(10), p. 24; Shannahan, 1908). Within a few years of Pencoyd's triumph, both the Pennsylvania Steel Company and the American Bridge Company had used designs by the engineer Sir Arthur Rendel to build viaducts in Burma and Uganda, respectively (Clarke, 1901). These were followed by bridges in Australia, New Zealand, Taiwan, Southern Manchuria, Japan, Mexico and South America erected by the United States Steel Products Export Company (*Far Eastern Review*, 1911, **8**(2), pp. 49–52).

Low domestic prices and intense industrial activity abroad facilitated a dramatic surge in a full range of American iron and steel products for export, from nails and spikes to rods and sheets (*American Exporter*, 1899, **43**(2), p. 17). Some companies retained shed designs and replaced wooden members with steel (*American Exporter*, 1895, **35**(3), p. 45). The metal products not only signalled a material shift from the earlier wood products, but they also implied that wider spans could be created by using arches and trusses. As new spaces were created using these prefabricated materials, some contemporaries marvelled at the industrial progress those spaces seemed to bring with them. But other contemporaries, particularly in regions such as the upper Nile that were under the political and economic control of more industrialized, colonial powers, were less optimistic.

More than any other technological innovation, the railway embodied the great material advances associated with the first Industrial Revolution and dramatized the gap which that process had created between the Europeans and non-Western peoples. Powered by the steam engines that were the core invention of the industrial transformation, locomotives boldly exhibited the latest advances in metallurgy and machine-tooling. Running on tracks that reshaped the landscape across vast swaths of Europe and later the Americas, Africa and Asia; crossing great bridges that were themselves marvels of engineering skill;

AMERICAN FOREMEN AND NATIVE RIVETTERS AT WORK ON THE GOKTEIK VIADUCT.

Figures 1.11 and 1.12. The Goktiek Viaduct, Burma, erected by 'native riveters and American foremen'. Designed by the Pennsylvania Steel Company in 1900–01, this viaduct demonstrates how American skill in erecting long-span structures was making its mark by the turn of the nineteenth to twentieth centuries. (*Sources: Book-keeper*, 1908, **21**(1); Clarke, 1901, p. 57)

. . . railways were at once 'the most characteristic and the most efficient form of the new technics'. (Adas, 1989, pp. 221–222)

By the late 1890s the efficiency of American construction was inevitably bringing American builders into the cultural and economic entanglements implied by colonial dominance. The media of steel arches and trusses became the messages of social and economic change.

An Abortive American High-Rise for London's Strand

A second key product that exemplified American construction in the late nineteenth century was the skyscraper, which American entrepreneurs began to market and construct overseas at the end of the nineteenth century. As Chicago, New York and many other U.S. cities began to see their skylines change due to innovations in steel-framing for high-rise towers, some Americans realized that these structures could be packaged as a set of discrete, stackable components to be assembled abroad, in principle if not always in practice, as easily as in America. The time seemed ripe for such forays, especially in Europe, because several designers from the Old World by the 1890s were being awed in Chicago or New York by the birth of the 'American Century' christened in the form of the skyscraper (Cohen, 1995, pp. 19–37). Not all were thrilled, however. In 1901, when the first American-style skyscraper was being planned for the Strand in London, some critics feared that by exporting the skyscraper, building syndicates were planning 'an American invasion of London' (*London Times*, 1901, 20 November, p. 8).[3]

The genesis for this 'invasion' was the creation in 1900 of a new main street from the Strand to Holborn with an extension to Russell Square; it became a project 'which most caught the public imagination in 1900' (Service, 1979, p. 7; Schubert and Sutcliffe,

1996). The avenue, with the crescent of the Aldwych at its southern end,

was the pride of the young London County Council, which directed a committee to make plans soon after its creation in 1889. The plan was published in 1898 and demolition of the infamous rookery on the site started in August 1900. Countless suggestions were made about the style to be adopted in the buildings that would grow along it. (*Ibid.*)

While the Council was debating the best name for the new avenue (which in 1905 became Kingsway, in honour of King Edward VII) several entrepreneurs created an English-American syndicate to erect:

an office building on American lines, which will be the largest and handsomest structure of the kind in the world . . . Along American lines means, of course, that the building will be a gigantic structure of steel faced with stone, and will be abundantly supplied with [30] lifts, as well as with heating and lighting arrangements worked from a common source in the basement. (*London Times*, 1901, 20 November, p. 9)

In 1900 'gigantic' meant ten storeys, which was how high the proposed building would have risen, encompassing 900,000 square feet and occupying a frontage of three-eighths of a mile. The syndicate's directors were Frederic Esler, a N.Y. entrepreneur who 'represented large American interests' and he was joined by Sir Richard Farrant, Earl Grey; Sir C. Rivers Wilson, the Earl of Kintore; and George Cornwallis West, the new Director of the British Electric Traction Company. The syndicate hired an unnamed 'well-known' British architect to revise plans that Esler made in New York, and the directors proposed that British workmen would erect the skyscraper using British building materials. The American director, Esler, saw the enterprise as a 'forerunner of the inevitable rebuilding of the whole of London on American lines'. 'With the increasing taxation', Esler maintained, 'property owners cannot long subsist from the small buildings which distinguish London' (*New York Times*, 1901, 21 November, p. 7). However, others saw the situation differently. Not only did the proposed tower contravene existing building laws, but some worried that 'the mammoth building would deform the new thoroughfare' and be a hideous 'addition to that conglomeration of architectural chaos which is modern London' (*New York Times*, 1901, 21 November, p. 7).

The leading article in the *Times* of London was more positive:

What concerns Londoners is that we have here practically a new departure in the way of providing business accommodation, and helping to solve the problem of getting elbow-room in proximity to business centres. This scheme will . . . be an object-lesson, of which we stand very much in need. We are far too slow in meeting the wants of an enormous population, and far too much given to muddling along with timid extensions of methods essentially antiquated. There is needless alarm in some quarters over the American invasion. It is forgotten that we are always invading other people in just the same way. In every corner of the globe British capital is invested and British enterprise is directing all sorts of industries. But we forget to be equally enterprising at home, and the Americans have found it out . . . They are really doing very well just now. They are setting up a magnificent electrical factory in the north; they are pushing that electrification of the Underground which has been promised so long; they are interesting themselves in 'tubes'; and [American ideas and methods] are largely recognized in the new telephone service. (*London Times*, 1901, 20 November, p. 9)

Ultimately, those on the Council enforcing the building laws did not permit the building's construction. However, as suggested above, there were other ways in which American architectural influences were beginning to be exerted in London during the first few years of the twentieth century. 'Innovations of a decidedly American character have been introduced in the newest buildings, and it is said that the American influence is making itself felt' (*American Exporter*, 1905, August, p. 68). By 1912, one of the ways that influence was manifested was in how one American version of the department store was 'capturing the British public by [its] open air methods of doing business'. This was Selfridge & Company, which opened successfully on Oxford Street (*American Exporter*, 1912, **70**(1), p. 9).

None of the journalists writing about these corporate manifestations of 'American invasion' in London wrote about the irony that shortly after American engineers were trumping British competitors in rural Africa by so efficiently erecting railway bridges, American investors were challenging British building laws in central London by attempting to scrape the sky with a corporate tower. This little-known precedent provides a curious context to the debates occurring a century later in London between English Heritage, arguing for the conservation of London's townscape, and realty developers urging that Canary Wharf-like developments be permitted to spread throughout the city.

Shipping American Skyscrapers Abroad: Milliken Brothers

At the turn of the century, if there was an American skyscraper 'invasion', it was not restricted to Europe. By 1910 high-rises erected with American components were soaring from East Asia to South Africa to Central America.

There is a steady development of demand for steel buildings of American design throughout the world . . . In the early stages of the development of the American skyscraper, American methods of steel building construction were not regarded with favor by foreigners. Many of the most notable examples of the new style of construction . . . were a type of architecture so unsightly that it would not have been tolerated in the old cities of the world. Foreign architects . . . viewed with distrust the comparatively light skeleton designs of American steel work. Time has, however, demonstrated the strength and safety of this form of construction, and the constant increase in the value of land in the large cities of the world has compelled an increase in the height of buildings, thus removing one of the principal obstacles to the development of American steel construction, and the pioneer work of American architects and engineers in foreign countries is beginning to yield substantial returns. (*Far Eastern Review*, 1911, **9**(2), p. 49)

One of the first American companies that understood how profitable it might be to capitalize overseas upon the three innovations associated with the steel frame (i.e., its links to efficiency, the high-rise building and concrete) was the Milliken Brothers Company, established in New York City in 1887.[4] In the early 1890s Milliken secured contracts for both bridges and high-rises in several U.S. cities. In 1890–1891, for example, Milliken was the contractor for Louis Sullivan's Wainwright Building in St. Louis, and in 1907–1908 Milliken erected Ernest Flagg's Singer Building in New York as well as several other high-rise buildings, especially in New York.[5] What distinguished the company was its foresight in disseminating the American steel-frame building as a viable building technology overseas by the turn of the century. At the turn of the century the Milliken Brothers Company was one of the earliest multi-national American construction firms. The company thought it was desirable 'to find an outlet in foreign countries for [American] iron and steel' (*Milliken Brothers Catalogue*, 1899, p. 7) and it outlined three reasons why foreign clients sought American producers over English, German or French competitors: first, because of speed (five to six weeks for finished buildings from the date of the order); second, because the finished products were precision-manufactured by first creating wooden templates to avoid costly errors in later stages of production; and third, because of the efficiency in marking and shipping the goods, which made it easier to 'pick out the pieces and properly assemble the structure after it [was] received' (*Ibid.*, p. 8).[6]

At Milliken's main office, over 150 engineers and draftsmen were employed to fill foreign and domestic orders. The company established branch offices in London, to serve European markets; in Mexico City and Havana, to gain access more easily to Central and South American locations; in Capetown and Johannesburg, South Africa,[7] to market themselves on that continent (Picton-Seymour, 1989; Greig, 1971); and in Honolulu, Hawaii and Sydney, Australia, to handle Asian clients. By 1907 Milliken had erected

eight mills in Hawaii for the Oahu Sugar Company, a cable station on Midway Island and several prefabricated steel buildings on Guam, Taiwan and in northern China.

If a client desired, Milliken was pleased not only to provide a design but also erect from scratch 'distinctively American, fire-proof buildings using

Figure 1.13. Roberto Boker Building (also known as 'Casa Boker'), Mexico City, the first American steel frame building in Mexico, 1899–1900. The three-storey department store was erected in less than a year using materials and instructions from the Milliken Brothers Company in Brooklyn, New York. (*Source*: Milliken Brothers *Catalogue*, 1899, p. 117)

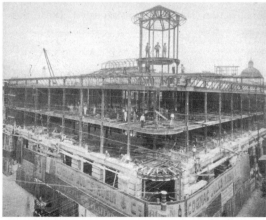

Figure 1.14. Warehouse of the Roberto Boker Department Store, built using similar technologies as the main store it serviced. (*Source*: Milliken Brothers *Catalogue*, 1899, p. 121)

Figure 1.15. Interior of the Roberto Boker Department Store. U.S. technologies tied to the building's form were complemented by U.S.-derived models for displaying consumer goods, thus creating spaces of consumption geared towards Mexican middle and upper class clients. (*Source*: *American Exporter*, 1901, **47**(5))

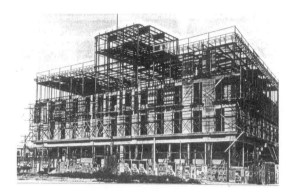

Figures 1.16, 1.17 and 1.18. Havana Cigar Factory, Cuba, built *c*. 1904–05 using American steel framing techniques of the Milliken Brothers Company. Once the structural frame was erected, the building was clad in stone, masking its steel skeleton. (*Source*: Milliken Brothers *Catalogue*, 1905, pp. 120–127)

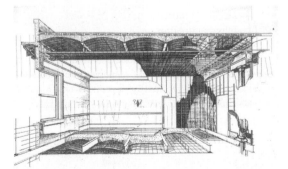

Figure 1.19. Section of a typical Milliken Brothers building, which shows how its steel frame was complemented by other building materials such as hollow tile, concrete, wood and plasterboard. (*Source*: Milliken Brothers *Catalogue*, 1905, plate 44)

Figure 1.20. Sugar mill building, Elizalda, Cuba. Milliken buildings were not just shipped to urban contexts; they also were purchased by rural industrialists who liked their flexible layouts as well as the speed and efficiency with which they could be constructed. (*Source*: Milliken Brothers *Catalogue*, 1899, p. 141)

Figure 1.21. Bridge in Costa Rica, built with Milliken parts. Bridges were among the earliest kinds of structures exemplifying the exporting of American architecture. (*Source*: Milliken Brothers *Catalogue*, 1905, p. 343)

Figure 1.22. Machine shops constructed by the Russian Government in Port Arthur (near present-day Dalian), China, *c*. 1905. Large-span structures with prefabricated trusses and fulfilling a multitude of functions were well-suited to the kinds of architectural exporting that American companies such as the Milliken Brothers engaged in during the late-nineteenth century. Here they were put to use by Russia, when that country was establishing rail and shipping links, through a weakened China, to the Pacific Ocean. (*Source*: Milliken Brothers *Catalogue*, 1905, p. 178)

Figure 1.23. Workers erecting the Cape Times Building in Capetown, South Africa. Foremen and labourers could follow with relative ease the instructions supplied to them, along with the materials, for building high-rise structures of American manufacture. (*Source*: Milliken Brothers *Catalogue*, 1905, p. 145)

Figures 1.24 and 1.25. Garlick Building, Capetown and Eckstein Building, Johannesburg, South Africa. These steel frames rising high above these two South African cities exemplified how successful the Milliken Brothers Company was in marketing its products to clients reached by seaports. (*Source*: Milliken Brothers *Catalogue*, 1905, pp. 151 and 144, respectively)

Figure 1.26. Concert Hall, South Africa. The adaptability of the steel frame to myriad uses and contexts was one of its chief selling points. (*Source*: Milliken Brothers *Catalogue*, 1905, p. 175)

the skeleton construction plan' (*Milliken Catalogue*, 1905, pp. 105, 114).

We are enabled to give our foreign customers not only a completed building, but to give them all of the 1001 ingenious American devices that are used in the construction of office buildings, stores, warehouses, etc. for which the American people are so celebrated . . . We are prepared, where customers desire, to take the land just as we find it and erect on the same a completed building . . . We are also prepared to submit drawings and specifications covering all of these different classes of work . . . making suggestions as we think desirable to meet the best American practice. A large part of our foreign business extends to tropical countries where the climatic conditions are peculiar. We have had a very large experience in constructing buildings in the tropics, and have introduced a number of novel features in some of these buildings. (*Ibid.*)

Also, as they had done in the United States, Milliken sometimes provided the tectonic means for realizing the designs of architects not employed by them. Louis Sullivan's Wainwright Building was one such example. In South Africa, it was local architects William Leck & Fred Emley who designed Johannesburg's 'first skyscraper', the ten-storey high Corner House (also known as the Rand Mines Building). Milliken thus provided the steel-framing technology to bring local architects' high-rise dreams into reality (Picton-Seymour, 1989, pp. 153–154; Greig, 1971, p. 133).

Alfred Zucker's High-Rise Skeletons for Buenos Aires

Another intriguing Milliken-related example, the Plaza Hotel, arose in Buenos Aires between 1905 and 1909 (figures 1.27 and 1.28). The architect responsible for the design of this high-rise skeleton in a South American metropolis was Alfred Zucker, an adventurous German-American architect who immigrated to Buenos Aires from New York in June 1904. Zucker, the son of a mechanical and civil engineer, was born in Freiburg, Germany in 1852 and was trained in Aix-en-Provence, Hanover and Berlin before moving to Vicksburg, Mississippi in 1874, where he practiced as an architect until 1882. He returned to Europe for a year but in early 1884 moved back to the U.S., settling in New York City where he worked for 20 years before venturing to Buenos Aires, which was experiencing a phenomenal

Figures 1.27 and 1.28. Plaza Hotel (now Marriott Plaza, as shown in figure 1.28), Buenos Aires, on Calle Florida and San Martin Park, completed 1909 and designed by Alfred Zucker a German-American architect who immigrated to Argentina in 1904. (*Sources*: *The Metal Worker, Plumber and Steam Fitter*, **83**, 12 March 1915, p. 377; photograph by the author)

Figure 1.29. Majestic Hotel (now demolished), 94th Street and Central Park West, New York, designed by Alfred Zucker, who used the steel-framing technologies marketed by the Milliken Brothers Company. (*Source*: Milliken Brothers *Catalogue*, 1899, p. 112)

building boom at the turn of the century.[8] In New York he designed several office buildings (figure 1.30), clubs and hotels, one of the most noteworthy of which was the Majestic Hotel (1894) on Central Park West (figure 1.29). At the Majestic, Zucker's design was erected using the Milliken Brothers steel-framing system. In Buenos Aires, Zucker became a major proponent of American-fashioned high-rises.

Zucker's major commission in Buenos Aires was the Plaza Hotel, 'the forerunner of the skyscraper' in that city (Johnston, 1906, p. 151). While erecting the Plaza, Zucker met the visiting editor of the *American Exporter*, with whom he conversed about the lucrative market he saw for American exporters of construction-related technologies.

While there is now a distant demand for modern equipment in every description of building, from the tenement house to the palace, South American countries are still far behind in everything pertaining to practical use, comfort, safety, sanitary appliances, and economy of space, of time and of money. The tendency has been – and in many cases still is – to continue to run in the old groove of fifty or more years ago, and it is seldom, even yet, that one meets real modern improvements as we know them in New York. The desire for the latest and best exists, however, and the money to buy is not lacking. I consider that it has been the shaping

of my career here that I have been able to show and give them something better than that to which they have been accustomed. The way for United States manufacturers to gain trade is to send salesmen here with their goods and practically demonstrate their advantage over what is now customarily used. (*Ibid.*)

That is precisely what Zucker did with his Milliken-structured hotel, and subsequently with other commissions in Buenos Aires such as the Banco Germanico (figure 1.31).

Steel-framed American Workspaces for Export

Despite the success Milliken enjoyed within certain

Figure 1.30. Union Building (in the middle of the three buildings shown), Union Square, New York. Alfred Zucker's experience designing these kind of high-rise structures in New York was crucial in his transplanting that expertise to Buenos Aires in the early 1900s. (*Photo*: David Van Zanten)

ARQUITECTURA

OBRAS DEL ARQUITECTO ALFREDO ZUCKER

Edificio del Banco Germánico (En Construcción)
Calle Reconquista

Figure 1.31. Banco Germánico, Calle Reconquista, Buenos Aires, another of Zucker's major commissions where he used American technologies to erect a tall commercial building in a growing metropolis. (*Source*: *Arquitectura* [Buenos Aires], 1913, no. 88, p. 119)

conglomerates competed with Carnegie's company,[9] an issue discussed in fuller detail in Chapter 2. Like Milliken, these companies specialized in exporting either entire steel buildings or partial building components and, like Milliken, they offered a wide variety of design choices, from arches to office blocks, and from whole factories to conveyor framing. These larger, more rationalized, corporate conglomerates either bought out companies such as Milliken or edged them out by undercutting their prices. For these steel-based conglomerates, standardized and prefabricated parts for portable structures implied profit, versatility, adaptability, constructability as well as – in an era sometimes epitomized by the word – 'progress'.

One observer perceptively noted that 'the American producer introduces economies quite outside the matters of labour and material. These

Figures 1.32, 1.33 and 1.34. Flour mills exported by the Nordyke & Marmon Company, Indianapolis, Indiana in the early twentieth century. Figure 1.32 shows a section of a typical mill building, while figures 1.33 and 1.34 show depictions of the mills in Shanghai and Japan. (*Sources*: *American Exporter*, 1898, **43**(1), p. 15; 1921, **88**(1), p. 74; and 1918, **83**(6), p. 53)

markets, the major problem the company faced was related to its economy of scale; it simply could not match the resources of larger domestic producers who also began to diversify for export markets. In 1903, for example, Andrew Carnegie capitalized on the markets for American structural steel when he established the United States Steel Products Export Company (*American Exporter*, 1903, **51**(11), p. 24; and Chandler, 1990). Between 1918 and 1929, other

economies arise from closer perception of the thing needed, the reduction of superfluous weight to a minimum, and developing to the last limit the resources of mechanical skill' (*American Exporter*, 1900, **46**(2), p. 17). That 'closer perception of the thing needed' was at the heart of the third crucial cultural product in the first phase of American architectural exporting: American-style industrial spaces. In 1876 the Nordyke-Marmon Company, for example, began to export the designs for American-style, multi-storey flour mills, and continued to do so until the early 1930s.[10]

By the early twentieth century textile manufacturers, sugar refiners and automobile makers followed suit. Standardization of building parts was matched with the standardization of labour tasks. Shifts in labour practices regarding the assembly line and the commodification of time accompanied the importing of standardized parts used to build the places where the standardization of labour was occurring.

U.S. Military Victories in 1898: Confidence, Commerce and Construction

American military victories over Spain in Cuba and the Philippines crystallized the ire of many critics who lambasted the U.S. government for engaging in imperialist activities. For example, Mark Twain's 1901 essay 'To the Person Sitting in Darkness', reflected his anti-imperialist sentiments:

Shall we? That is, shall we go on conferring our Civilization upon the peoples that sit in darkness, or shall we give those poor things a rest? Shall we bang right ahead in our old-time, loud, pious way, and commit the new century to the game; or shall we sober up and sit down and think it over first? Would it not be prudent to get our Civilization-tools together and see how much stock is left on hand in the way of Glass Beads and Theology, and Maxim Guns and Hymn Books, and Trade-Gin and Torches of Progress and Enlightenment

(patent adjustable ones, good to fire villages with, upon occasion), and balance the books, and arrive at the profit and loss, so that we may intelligently decide whether to continue the business or sell out the property and start a New Civilization Scheme on the proceeds? (Twain, 1901)

Although many scholars have researched the context and implications of these victories, which led to the U.S. acquiring spheres of influence in both the Atlantic and Pacific Oceans (LaFeber, 1963; Zwick, 1992), the effects of this social, economic and political control on the built environment of these territories has received far less attention.

In the Philippines, probably the most noteworthy example of how a significant American architect/planner became embroiled in refashioning local space was Daniel Burnham, who planned the city of Baguio in 1905 shortly before finalizing his more famous plans for San Francisco (1906), Chicago (1907–1909) and Washington, D.C. (1912). When William Taft was Secretary of War, he instructed W. Cameron Forbes, a member of the Philippine Commission, 'to engage competent advice' on the subject of city planning and Taft then convinced Burnham (and Burnham's colleague Pierce Anderson) to visit the Philippines and prepare preliminary plans for Manila and Baguio (Rebori, 1917). 'This was followed by the recommendation that an architect of suitable training and experience be appointed as consulting architect for the Government' (*Ibid.*). William Parsons became that architect. In 1905 Parsons, a graduate of the École de Beaux-Arts in Paris, was practising in New York City but in November of that year he travelled to Manila 'and served until February 1914', resigning because 'there seemed to be no further progress to be made under the scuttle policy of the present administration'. In those 9 years Parsons's mandate was to supervise the architectural design of all of the Philippines' public buildings and parks, under the supervision of Dean Worcester, the Secretary of the Interior of the Philippine Islands. He therefore was charged with interpreting the preliminary plans of Burnham and Anderson, but he also proposed plans himself (e.g., for Cebu in 1912) and urged the government to utilize Philippine hardwood over imported Oregon pine. Parsons also suggested a more widespread use of reinforced concrete 'as the standard form of construction' in the islands (*Ibid.*, p. 311). Therefore, Parsons's work in the Philippines was extensive. He designed several schools (the University of the Philippines main hall, 1913; the Normal School, 1914; Central School, 1914 and Intermediate School, 1909), as well as the Manila YMCA (Young Men's Christian Association), 1909, the Manila Club 1908, the Elks Club, 1911, the Paco Municipal Market in Manila, 1911, and the Customs House in Cebu 1911 (Doane, 1919). The U.S. Government intended that, prior to Filipinos 'developing things artistic or scientific . . . the buildings erected and the city plan improvements will stand as worthy examples, setting a high standard from which in the coming years native architects can derive abundant inspiration' (Rebori, 1917, p. 434). However, just as Burnham was the prominent tip of the Parsons iceberg, so too Parsons was only the most visible architect of a larger infrastructure of construction-related individuals and firms carried to the western Pacific Ocean because of U.S. political control there. One of the most important of these was the J.G. White Company, which won the contract to erect an American-style trolley line in Manila. The White Company decided to send

an organization of competent men as heads of departments and foremen . . . [with the] intention being to give the native laborer a trial at the work . . . The Filipinos quickly developed into very apt pupils, and soon became adept in the use of American tools. (*American Exporter*, 1905, **56**(5), p. 136)

Attacking problems 'in a bold and uncompromising manner' the White Company subcontracted with the J.G. Brill Company in Philadelphia for the adapted design of the streetcars themselves, and then erected a cement and steel power-house that was 'as thoroughly up to date as anything in the United States'. This was one of several instances at the cusp of the nineteenth and twentieth centuries when municipalities in many parts of the world hired American companies to export state-of-the-art streetcar technologies, from Australia to Argentina. At a variety of scales, then – from city plans to streetcar designs – American architects and contractors working under the aegis of a U.S. political administration (locally headed by Dean Worcester from 1901–1913) began refashioning the spatial landscape of major Philippine cities and towns (Worcester, 1914).[11] However, the Philippines served as the first, most visible example of how assiduously U.S. companies, planners, government agencies, architects, and other 'brokers' of American architectural form and space positioned themselves to work in Asia and elsewhere. Sometimes the circuit of construction activity from the U.S. to Asia passed directly through Manila. This was the case, for instance, with the engineer George Bronson Rea who, after serving a military tour of duty in the Philippines during the Spanish-American War, decided to become a journalist. He then established the *Far Eastern Review: engineering, finance, commerce* and for the next 35 years he used this professional journal to research and publicize the planning and construction-related activities occurring throughout the Asia region.

At other times, however – as with Walter Burley and Marion Griffin's planning work in Australia on the new capital plan at Canberra (1912), or Frank Lloyd Wright's design work in Japan for the Imperial Hotel (1916) – the connection bypassed the Philippines. This was true not only for noteworthy architects such as Griffins and Wright, but also for less-familiar examples such as in 1899, when a Philadelphia-based company exported the 'complete equipment for a native woollen mill plant in Tianjin (China), every piece of which was made in the United States'.[12]

Figure 1.35. Santissima Trinidad Episcopal Cathedral, Havana, Cuba, 1905 (demolished), designed by Bertram G. Goodhue. (*Source*: Bertram G. Goodhue, 1914, *A Book of Architectural and Decorative Drawings*. New York, p. 43)

Figure 1.36. Central Railway Station, Havana, Cuba, 1910–1912, designed by Kenneth Murchison. (*Source*: Narciso Menocal Collection)

On the other side of the globe, Cuba became a theatre of operations similar to the role the Philippines played for American construction-related 'brokering' in the Pacific. As American firms began to entrench themselves more firmly on that Caribbean island, they needed facilities in which to operate more effectively and, perhaps naturally, they turned to American construction experts to build them. The buildings erected for the United Fruit Company reflect this tendency (Prestamo, 1996). Architects – such as Bertram Goodhue; Kenneth Murchison; Barclay, Parsons and Klapp; or Carrere and Hastings – and engineering firms such as Purdy & Henderson also exemplified how American designers were attracted to the commercial possibilities opened

Figure 1.37. Plan of the Pan-American Exposition of 1901, Buffalo, New York. (*Source*: *American Architect and Building News*, 1901, **74**, p. 20)

up by the Cuba–U.S. political connection (Gelabert-Navia, 1996). The Pan-American Exposition (1901) in Buffalo, N.Y. likewise reflected the close associations that many Americans assumed there to be between finance, commerce and the buildings resulting from monetary investment (Rydell, 1984; Leary and Sholes, 1998; Grant, 2001).

Iron and Steel: Primary Genes comprising an Initial Exporting Code

Our exports of manufactures of iron and steel . . . go to

every country, to every section where civilization exists . . . Precisely what percentage of these shipments entered into the construction of buildings cannot be given, for the reason that their purposes are not declared on the bill of lading or ship's manifest. That a large part of them serve for building operations there is no doubt. Shipments leave the port of New York every week to equip foreign factories, foundries, rolling mills, machine shops, paper mills, forge shops, puddle mills, power and boiler houses, gas and electric light stations, car sheds and other buildings. Foreign cities are following the example of the United States in raising business temples and in securing all the conveniences which ingenuity can bestow. Iron buildings are favored for the very obvious reason that they are the best. Our shippers send many parts of these structures to places where a seven to ten story building is yet considered a marvel. (*American Mail and Export Journal*, 1893, **30**(9), p. 170)

In 1900 one of those places was Paris where, at that city's Exposition, because

the people of the Old World have never believed in the eggshell structures of the present day in America . . . the skyscraper is being sent across the ocean in the hope that Europeans may be convinced that their ideas about walls are wrong. They are to be shown that the wall, as newly constructed in America, is not a weight bearer at all; that the weight of great buildings is now supported by the steel skeletons concealed behind their fronts of terra cotta, just as the bones within a man's body maintain him in an upright attitude. (*American Exporter*, 1900, **46**(2), p. 22)

One of the ironies of this assessment was that the Eiffel Tower – an icon of steel frame construction – was only 11 years old when the 1900 Exposition was being promoted! To vivify the skyscraper, an evolving American architectural organism, the American exhibitors chose to promote the recently-erected, 18-storey Broadway Chambers Building In New York. They brought several models, one of which was 12-foot high and showed the exterior skin in plaster of Paris, and a second one ('less beautiful but far more striking, instructive, and much more troublesome to construct') showed the building's structural and mechanical entrails: its steel frame, elevators, boilers, pipes and furnace. The object lesson was complemented by an 'exact, full-size

reproduction of the engines and dynamos', along with 'a complete room . . . to expose the beams which hold up the floor, the joists which help to form the wall and the entire system of piping and fireproofing which is usually concealed behind the plaster'. Those who painstakingly assembled the more than 20,000 pieces comprising these models hoped that 'all who see this exhibit . . . will be convinced that American steel construction is the most economical and useful, if not the most artistic, method of building' (*Ibid.*). This example of skyscraper showcasing might not have been as popular as Buffalo Bill's Wild West show, which had been touring Europe for 17 years by the time the 1900 Paris Exposition was mounted (Blair, 2000), but to those viewers predisposed to building progress, the Broadway Chambers exhibit was literally riveting and electrifying. Most cities in the early twentieth century had neither the means nor the market to mount other versions of the Paris 1900 Exposition where American skyscrapers could be touted as object lessons of an emerging architectural ideal.

From Components to Systems: the American Construction Specialist

In the nearly four decades between 1876 and 1914, the exporting of American structural steel contributed to proliferating U.S. trade activities and helped create a significant platform from which later American practitioners and entrepreneurs benefited. International exhibitions, military victories, the object lessons demonstrated by high-rise construction in American cities nationwide, and sporadic but intensifying transactions between American firms and foreign clients all contributed to the creation of this platform. Architects played a role in this initial phase of American architectural exporting, but they were not the protagonists. Instead, by virtue of their scope, reflected clearly in the evidence cited above,

Figure 1.38. Masthead of the *Engineering Magazine*, with the motto 'The World is its Field'. (*Source*: *Engineering Magazine*, 1904, **27**(2))

engineers – in collaboration with manufacturers – exercised a larger role in the first phase of the exporting of American construction. Another reflection of this was how, in the early 1900s, the logo of the *Engineering Magazine* showed a globe with a banner underneath that stated 'The World is its Field'.

Although the publication was referring to its own scope, it might just as easily have been referring to engineers themselves. In October 1900 the *American Exporter* published a brief, provocative essay about the 'importance of the specialist in American engineering' (*American Exporter*, 1900, **46**(5), p. 20). The anonymous author opened by stating that

Among the industries which, because of the impetus and specialization which they have received in this country, may be classed as distinctively American is that of structural steel work . . . The cause of our supremacy is to be found in two particular brands of engineering work, in which also we have achieved distinction, namely bridge and roof work and the erection of tall buildings of composite construction. The bond between the bridge builder and the structural steel mills has been one of mutual helpfulness.

Elaborating further about the specialized skills of certain American engineers, the author quoted a London *Times* correspondent, who exclaimed (concerning the Atbara Bridge) that

the energy with which Americans 'make' business is remarkable. Steel makers are always trying to force people to use steel; they manufacture markets out of nothing. An architect says he cannot put steel in place of wood – the steel

manufacturer employs an expert to show that it can be done. He does not sit down and abuse the architect for his want of enterprise, but sets to work to force his hand.

The main article's author proceeds to praise further the efficient and inventive ingenuity of American engineers when he closes by asserting that

[Our] plan of employing experts for designing special plants, special factories and special tools is one of the secrets of our successful competition. It gives us a great advantage over other countries where the expert specialist is comparatively unknown – at least in many lines of engineering work . . . What is true of the engineers is true in a lesser degree of the contractors and manufacturers, and there seems to be lacking [in foreign countries] that common interchange of ideas and hearty cooperation which mark the relations of these three classes in this country.

The author was describing how American engineers (and others involved in construction-related entrepreneurship at the turn of the twentieth century) were creating systems out of disparate components and, in so doing, were becoming more efficient and marketable in the global marketplace. This concern for 'system' was what Frederick W. Taylor was obsessed with in his re-designing of industrial processes (Kanigel, 1997). As American industrialists standardized portable building technologies for export, and as they applied Taylor's theories of industrial production, they both enhanced and weakened design quality, depending upon geographic variation as well as the criteria applied to 'quality design.'

In the multi-national marketplace of American portable buildings, some businesses provided their clients with flexible designs using innovative standardized parts, while others sold goods off a shelf, showing less concern for the quality of the architectural spaces where those goods played a role. Prefabrication implied both proportional order and repetition, but contemporaries did not equate repetition with inferiority. Judging by what they expressed in promotional literature and trade journals, exporters of portable buildings craved profit, speed, and construction systems yielding both adaptability and universal methods. There were significant variations in where portable buildings were erected, how people reacted to them, and how well or poorly exporters fared. The specialist construction engineer 'tailored' his solution to his client's individual needs, but that same engineer 'taylored' [sic]his design and production system to maximize his own efficiency as he met his client's demands. Arguably, the virtues of specialization that the author of the above essay was extolling was an outgrowth of the 'American system of mass production' that was being refined precisely during this initial phase of American architectural exporting (Hounshell, 1984). The targeting and fine-tuning of this specialization characterized the second stage of this exporting, after the calamitous World War I which began in the Balkans in 1914.

The historian Olivier Zunz has coined the phrase 'producers, brokers, and users of knowledge' to characterize a key trend of late-nineteenth century America (Zunz, 1998), which is helpful in the understanding of what I have characterized as the foundation that buttressed the exporting of American architecture. By the end of the nineteenth century American contractors, planners, designers and building materials exporters were becoming evermore confident of their abilities. That confidence was doubtless boosted by the positive reaction they perceived from visitors and publicity regarding major exhibitions such as those in Philadelphia and Chicago, as well as from Buffalo's Pan-American Exposition in 1901. The 'flames' of American architectural expertise, therefore, began to spread in episodic, but not necessarily haphazard fashion until the turn of the twentieth century, when architects, engineers, contractors and building technology entrepreneurs began to refine and target that American expertise to a more specialized extent than they had previously. The

'brokering' of this construction-related knowledge, in a commercial sense, was also boosted by actions of the U.S. government, which already by 1898 began to provide the safe political and commercial umbrella under which the exporting of American architectural expertise occurred. Significantly, this more strategic refinement worked hand in glove with post-1898 American political and military muscle flexing on the world stage. As Emily Rosenberg has characterized it, the government 'erected a promotional state . . . and developed techniques to assist citizens who operated abroad' (Rosenberg, 1982, p. 38). Some of those citizens were involved in construction, and their activities opened the sluice gates for other American entrepreneurs to follow.

Clearly, then, as the nineteenth century turned over to the twentieth, the exporting of American steel-framed skeletons helped characterize a recognizable American version of modernity. Whether this version came in the form of a railway bridge, high-rise skyscraper or industrial workplace, it helped brand the U.S. as a purveyor of a new kind of architectural form and space. However, the skeleton alone did not possess the requisite genetic code of American architectural modernity. The flesh for the skeleton's bones came primarily in the form of concrete.

NOTES

1. For slate from Maine to Europe, see *American Mail and Export Journal*, 1879, **3**(1), p. 413; for the Eclipse Windmill Company's exporting of prefabricated windmills from Beloit, Wisconsin to several countries, see *ibid*., p. 407. By 1895 'American windmills [had] been sent to every known country on the face of the globe . . . [and] the ideas of American manufacturers have been copied by French and German makers' (*American Mail and Export Journal*, 1895, **32**(10), p. 145).

2. Edge Moor was one of the American exhibitors at the 1880 Melbourne International Exhibition. In this regard, see Proudfoot *et al.*, 2000.

3. Also see *RIBA Journal*, 1901–1902, **9**, ser. 3, p. 39; and *American Exporter*, 1902, **49**(2), p. 20.

4. The Milliken Brothers Manufacturing Company was established in 1887 as a partnership between Foster Milliken (1865–1945) and Edward Milliken (1862–1906). See 'Something about steel construction', *Architectural Record*, 1902, **11**, April, pp. 123–124; and 'Foster Milliken', *National Cyclopaedia of American Biography*, XXXIII, New York: James T. White & Co., 1947, pp. 110–111. In 1907 the company was reorganized under receivership. *Architectural Record*, 1902, **11**, April, pp. 123–124; and the *Export News*, 1919, **1**(5), p. 19.

5. A more complete enumeration of the buildings erected by the company is found in both the previously cited Catalogues and in *Architectural Record*, 1902, **11**, April, p. 124.

6. The Milliken approach was in contrast to most other companies that exported prefabricated steel parts, such as the Edwards Manufacturing Company of Cincinnati, which exported sheet metal cladding materials from 1909 to 1932. Edwards chose not to become directly involved with architectural design until 1930. *American Exporter*, 1909, **63**(1), pp. 130; 1910, **66**(4), p. 111; 1913, **72**(3), p. 112; 1914, **74**(2), p. 111; 1930, **106**(4), p. 109.

7. For the Rand Mines Building (at the corner of Commissioner and Simmonds Streets, Johannesburg), see Picton-Seymour (1989), pp. 153–154; and Greig (1971), pp. 133–134.

8. For Buenos Aires, see Scobie (1974) and Gutiérrez (2002).

9. These included the American Steel Products Co., Consolidated Steel Corp., Republic Iron and Steel Co., Vulcan Steel Products Co., Liberty Steel Products Co., R.M. Ford & Co., Pennsylvania Steel Export Co. See *American Exporter*, especially from 1919 to 1929.

10. In 1876 the company moved from Richmond to Indianapolis, Indiana. By the 1920s it was exporting entire mills to every continent. See *Nordyke & Marmon Company: An Institution*. Indianapolis: n.p., 1920, p. 18; *American Exporter*, 1898, **43**(1), p. 15; 1917, **81**(1), p. 59; 1921, **88**(1), p. 74.

11. For differences in Manila streetscapes, see Worcester, 1914, vol. 1, pp. 182, 186; for bridges, pp. 646, 650; for sewers, p. 663; and for schools, p. 338. Regarding town planning influences, also see Reade, 1928.

12. *American Exporter*, 1899, **43**(4), p. 34. M.A. Furbush & Son Machine Company sold the mill to Wu Mow Ting, a compradore [i.e., commercial go-between] of the Tianjin branch of the Hong Kong & Shanghai Banking Corporation. The mill comprised a one- to two-storey main building, a three-storey tower and a boiler house.

2 From the Steel Frame to Concrete: Foundations for a System of Contracting Abroad, 1900–c.1920

By 1905 a relatively small number of American companies were exporting steel-framed skeletons to erect high-rise buildings for clients dispersed around the globe. Frederick Esler and his syndicate might not have succeeded in erecting an American high-rise in London, but other entrepreneurs (such as those who hired Alfred Zucker in Buenos Aires) scraped the sky in other cities. Zucker was one of the first, previously U.S.-based architects to promote, design and construct high-rises derived from U.S. origins in newly industrializing metropolises outside western Europe. The Plaza Hotel in Buenos Aires stands in testimony to Zucker's ingenuity in employing the

Milliken system there. By the end of World War I Zucker was joined by other American architects, contractors and agents who similarly employed U.S. construction technologies elsewhere. Frank Lloyd Wright and William Vories were designing in Japan, Bertram Goodhue and Purdy & Henderson were operating in Cuba, Roland Curry and Henry Murphy were practising in China. Some became famous; most did not.

But steel skeletons were not enough for any of these companies or individuals. Trussed frames provided necessary, but not sufficient structural armatures. To be fully-fledged, up-to-date buildings rather than significant steel frames, other materials reflecting a fuller range of building technologies needed to complement the frame, and become integrated with it. To be a fireproof building, for instance, steel-framed buildings needed flesh as well as bones (Wermiel, 2000). What were the constituent parts, then, of that flesh? Some materials, such as hollow tile and brick, were more integrated to the frame than others, such as terra cotta, wallboard and ceiling finishes. But regardless of how integrally tied they were to any kind of structural system, in turn-of-the-century America these materials helped form a comprehensive set of constituent parts, a diversifying vocabulary of construction, which American designers, brokers and contractors not only were employing domestically, but also were exporting creatively. The steel skeleton, therefore, implied the delivery of allied technologies and materials. As one contemporary asserted:

Figure 2.1. Steel or Concrete. These two construction materials were related to the most significant building technologies marketed abroad by American architectural exporters of the early twentieth century. However, other materials and technologies also figured in the exporting picture. The N.Y.-based Federal Export Corporation, which used this graphic in its advertising, told potential customers that 'we can supply your requirements for either type of structure . . . The poured method of concrete construction has been so perfected that buildings of this material are now erected as rapidly as a steel structure. Our engineering department is prepared to assist engineers, architects and builders to apply this method to their structural work'. (*Source*: *Export American Industries*, 1917, **19**(2), p. 17)

The cheapening of steel-making and the perfection of machinery for handling great weights at great heights, the introduction of concrete and hollow tile as structural materials, the swift development of heating, ventilating and lighting methods, combined to provide the science of architecture with instruments and materials adequate to the solution of its new problems. (Kahler, 1914, p. 40)

In addition to solving the problems associated with attaching flesh to skeletal bones, designers and builders also needed to solve the challenge of how to erect the skeletal frame and its body upon a solid foundation. Increasingly in the early twentieth century, when constructors were asked how they should build that stronger foundation, they answered concrete.

However, that foundation was more than just a tangible support for a steel frame. By utilizing concrete, steel, and other innovative construction materials, American architects, engineers and builders of all kinds provided incentives for private corporations and the federal government to systematize, or make more efficient, the institutional foundations associated with those materials. As U.S. corporations expanded, merged and sometimes monopolized, exporters of American construction technologies built a foundation for a system that helped them trade, contract, design and build abroad. World War I became a crucial, if tragic catalyst for this foundation because of the way in which war changed iron and steel supply networks at a time when many regions – South America and Asia, particularly – were poised for industrial development. By the end of the war in late 1918, American architectural exporters were also poised to make new inroads in markets that previously had been thought to be exclusively European corporate domains. They faced daunting challenges along those roads, as will be shown here and in the following chapter, but ultimately, if they stayed the course with enough persistence, patience, perception and luck, they sometimes prevailed.

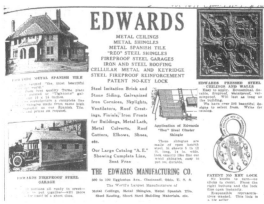

Figures 2.2 and 2.3. Palace in Kabul, Afghanistan where pressed steel ceilings manufactured by the Edwards Manufacturing Company were installed in 1911. (*Sources: American Exporter*, 1911, **68**(6), p. 101; *American Exporter*, 1915, **76**(1), p. 107)

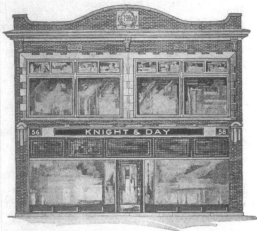

Figure 2.5. An up-to-date storefront ready for shipment abroad. (*Source: American Exporter*, 1916, **28**(5))

Figure 2.4. A Buddhist temple in Rangoon (Yangon), Burma, illuminated by gas lighting systems supplied by an American manufacturer. Examples such as this, as well as the palace in Kabul, demonstrate how distantly, and in such unusual contexts, American building technologies were being exported by World War I. (*Source*: *American Exporter*, 1911, **67**(1), p. 105)

Figure 2.6. American exporters examining a map as they discuss business. (*Source*: *Export American Industries*, 1917, **19**(5))

Concrete Components of Architectural Innovation, c. 1900–1914

Either by propping the steel frame upon concrete footings or by placing it upon a more expansive concrete raft foundation, American architectural exporters increasingly complemented steel with concrete as a problem-solving building material. By reinforcing concrete with steel rods, or by using steel machinery to form concrete blocks as prefabricated building blocks, Americans seeking a foreign market for portable buildings further diversified their architectural offerings. In so doing they provided the means for creating imaginative design solutions in places (such as East Asia, South Africa or South America) where people were experiencing the architectural spaces created by concrete materials for the first time.[1] In the early twentieth century

the most approved composition of concrete for general construction [consisted] of a mixture of broken limestone, granite or clean screened gravel . . . clean coarse sand and cement, in such proportions that the voids between the stone [were] completely filled by the sand and the voids in the sand completely filled with cement, with a slight excess of cement to insure a perfect bond with the stone. (*American Exporter*, 1907, **59**(6), p. 177)

Therefore, to create top-quality concrete, manufacturers needed equally high-grade cement. By 1900 approximately three-quarters of that material was Portland cement, named after the tiny island of Portland in the U.K. where a desirable limestone used in its manufacture was found. In 1824 Joseph Aspdin, from Leeds, was the first to produce Portland cement, but after 1872 the material was produced in the United States and its popularity spread rapidly (Collins, 1998). At the 1876 Philadelphia Exhibition, American Portland cement was exhibited as a viable building material, but production only began in earnest in 1880 and domestic cement only began to overtake European imports in 1897, by which time American machinery for crushing aggregate and

making concrete had also begun to replace European machines, even in Europe itself (*American Exporter*, 1906, **58**(3), pp. 79–87).

Table 2.1. American production of Portland cement compared with imports of foreign Portland cement (in barrels).

Year	American	Foreign
1882	85,000	370,406
1883	90,000	456,418
1884	100,000	585,768
1885	150,000	554,396
1886	150,000	915,255
1887	250,000	1,514,095
1888	250,000	1,835,504
1889	250,000	1,740,536
1890	335,500	1,940,186
1891	454,813	2,988,313
1892	547,440	2,440,654
1893	590,652	2,674,149
1894	789,757	2,638,107
1895	990,324	2,997,325
1896	1,543,023	2,989,597
1897	2,272,971	2,090,760

Source: *American Exporter*, 1899, **43**(5), p. 30.

Some of the reasons for this shift were not unlike those related to iron and steel technologies:

These results [were] perhaps partly due to the superiority of material, partly to the more perfectly systematized order of manipulation and the general intelligence of the management, but in the main to improved processes and the universal adoption of the latest types of labor-saving machinery. (*American Exporter*, 1899, **43**(5), p.30)

Technological innovations facilitated diffusion, but the demand for cement – and its more versatile complement, concrete -- was what provided the incentive for investors either to find or design the machinery that saved money in manufacturing these materials.

One of the companies that touted its creativity

most regarding concrete block was the Ideal Concrete Machinery Company, established in 1906 in South Bend, Indiana with an export office in New York. Already by 1907 the importing of American concrete block machinery 'into every land on the globe [was assuming] vast proportions' (*American Exporter*, 1907, **60**(1)). The Ideal Company was at the forefront of this activity, advertising its products of almost unlimited adaptability and artistic possibilities 'from the most massive construction to daintily beautiful styles of architecture' (*American Exporter*, 1907, **60**(4), p.3). Ideal's interchangeable products were manufactured by a face-down principle whereby a coarse mixture on the back of the block contrasted with a rich facing

Figure 2.7. The perceived advantages and appeal of the Ideal Hollow Concrete Building Block, which originated in South Bend, Indiana. The advantages are shown in the fan-like graphic above the machine. The similar graphic below shows the countries where, by 1909, the machine was enjoying some popularity. (*Source*: *American Exporter*, 1909, **63**(1), p. 3)

material. A contemporary Ideal advertisement graphically illustrates the company's rationale.

In 1907 Ideal not only sent American representatives abroad to demonstrate the company's techniques, but it also brought foreign agents to Indiana. Four were based in Asia, three in Central or South America and two in Europe.[2]

However, the company did not itself design architectural spaces using its building blocks, as Milliken was doing. Perhaps that was its downfall. By 1916, both because of competition and because it had over-extended its geographic reach, Ideal faltered.[3] By the end of World War I, cement-based firms smaller than Ideal merged into more extensive corporate entities, such as the Cement Export Company.[4] As will be shown below, this trend toward mergers and associations also occurred in other aspects of international construction enterprise. Larger, more diversified concrete-exporting firms supplanted Ideal's position, bringing not only the concrete block but also concrete slab technologies to contexts worldwide.

In the first two decades of the twentieth century the demand for cement was staggering, as manufacturers with vested interests touted the glories of reinforced concrete, and as American architects became swept along by the 'tremendous driving power' of those manufacturers.[5]

[Since 1897] so rapid has been the increase in concrete construction in every conceivable kind of building, that to

Figure 2.8. An advertisement for the Ideal concrete block shows a house in Shanghai where the material had been used. (*Source*: *American Exporter*, 1911, **68**,(5), p. 3)

Cottage at Milan, Italy. Cost Complete, $2,200.00.

Substantial Evidence
of Ideal Concrete Block
Progress in Sunny Italy

Palace of Señora Aloy de Tomba Mendoza, Argentina. Built of Ideal Hollow Concrete Blocks. Covered with Stucco.

This Beautiful Argentine Palace Was Built of
Ideal Hollow Concrete Blocks

Figures 2.9, 2.10, 2.11 and 2.12. Hollow concrete blocks from the early twentieth century still evident in Shanghai. These examples are along Yenan Road in the former French Concession although, as can be seen in figure 2.11, much of this housing stock in the early twentieth century is being progressively demolished. Figure 2.12 is near Zhapu Road in Shanghai's Hongkou district. (Photographs by the author)

Figures 2.13, 2.14 and 2.15. A 'cottage' in Milan, a 'palace' in Argentina, and a third structure in an unknown location demonstrate the geographic and ornamental range enjoyed by this humble but well-travelled, American building material in the early twentieth century. (*Sources*: *American Exporter*, 1912, **69**(4), p. 163; *American Exporter*, 1911, **68**(1), p. 3; *American Exporter*, 1912, **69**(2), n.p.)

supply the cement alone requires the united full capacity of over sixty of the largest manufacturing plants in America. In cities much of the heavy traffic is conducted through concrete tunnels. Telegraph and telephone wires are carried underground in concrete conduits. Skyscraping buildings rest on pillars of concrete built up through caissons from bed rock . . . and the structures themselves are frequently constructed almost entirely of concrete with the addition of small reinforcement bars of steel. For the building of large factories concrete is rapidly becoming one of the favorite materials. City, and especially suburban houses are extensively built of concrete blocks, while in the construction of sidewalks and street paving the use of concrete is almost universal. In railroad construction work it is rapidly superseding other materials . . . [with] shops, roundhouses, bridges and stations built of concrete. (*American Exporter*, 1907, **59**(1), p.177)

By 1900 concrete and cementitious materials in myriad forms were quickly becoming synonymous with the development of the American industrial city, and with the spatial implications derived from that expansive urbanism.

In 1905 American manufacturers began investing in machinery that could mould concrete into workable components. Just as the jigsaw in the 1870s had helped produce a multitude of wooden architectural elements, so too did concrete block machinery in the early 1900s facilitate creative uses for concrete. South Africa – where Milliken shipped some of its earliest kits for steel-framed structures – and South America – where Zucker and others promoting American architectural technologies were operating by the turn of the century – were two of the regions where exporters marketed American cement and concrete products with particular success. In 1911 the American consul in Johannesburg explained that

builders and contractors [here] must have concrete mixers if they expect to tender for foundation work, and as a result many of the local contractors have mixers . . . One firm [has] sold 25 American machines in this city . . . There is only one firm which makes a specialty of handling concrete mixers in [Transvaal] and it claims to have sold 90 percent of all the machines used here. Practically all are of American manufacture . . . I am informed that a number of mixers, all

of American manufacture, are now in use in the construction of the Union Government buildings at Pretoria and in the erection of public and private buildings in Johannesburg. (*Daily Consular and Trade Reports*, 1911, **48**(28), p. 769)

In Cuba, as American commercial and political involvement intensified after the 1898 military victory, 'Portland cement became a very important item in import trade . . . A considerable portion of the imported cement is used in constructing docks, street pavements, sidewalks, curb-stones, floor tiles and ornamental work of every description' (*Daily Consular and Trade Reports*, 1912, **240**(11), p.193). As became abundantly clear, cement and concrete were involved not just in 'ornamental work of every description', but even more pervasively in 'work' at much broader scales.

The Panama Canal as a Concrete Enterprise, 1904–1914

South America became a major sphere of American contracting influence not only because of U.S. military victories in 1898, but also because of how overtly American politicians and engineers became involved in solving the challenge of how to link the Atlantic and Pacific Oceans by creating a canal in Central America. What became known as the Panama Canal became a highly significant object lesson of American prefabrication skills, railroad engineering, contracting ingenuity, improvisation and adroitness. To excavate the Canal, engineers mobilized derricks and other iron and steel contracting machinery brought from the United States. To build the Canal, construct the locks and erect the myriad structures associated with the Canal's operations, contractors predominantly used the increasingly fashionable building material of the new century – concrete (McCullough, 1977, pp. 129, 133, 469, 471, 590). French engineers from the École Polytechnique who had excelled in Suez (1869), Panama's predecessor, greatly respected the improvisational qualities of their American counterparts, but they also disparaged the American engineers' scientific abilities. Before 1904, when stewardship for the Panama Canal's construction passed to the United States, the French relied to some extent on American 'portable' structures from New Orleans as well as largely African-American labourers, just as West Indian slave-owners had done in the 1860s. In 1905 American contractors again relied on prefabrication as the most suitable means of bringing necessary building types such as warehouses, repair shops and locomotive sheds to the Panamanian jungle (*Ibid.*, p. 471).

'The building of the Panama Canal was among other things one of the greatest of all triumphs in American railroad engineering' (*Ibid.*, p. 469). In late 1904 when John Stevens assumed control of the Canal Commission, he saw his challenge as fundamentally a railroad-related one, which is why he recruited men such as William Belding as his new chief of building construction. Belding had done the same job on the Illinois Central Railroad. In short, 'there was no building construction, no construction enterprise of any kind not associated with the railroad' (*Ibid.*, p. 470). Therefore, the Canal's construction relied upon the same sort of

Figure 2.16. U.S. President Theodore Roosevelt at the controls of a Bucyrus shovel at Pedro Miguel, Panama in 1906, showing his support for the ongoing construction of the Panama Canal by being the first President to leave the United States while in office. (*Source*: Library of Congress)

Figure 2.17. 'The Approaches to Gatun Locks', Panama Canal, sketched by Joseph Pennell in 1912, showing the scale of concrete construction that characterized some of the formidable engineering works related to the Canal's completion. (*Source*: Library of Congress)

railway bridge expertise that American iron and steel workers had shown at the Atbara Bridge – and were still showing from East Asia to South America in the decade leading up to World War I – when the Panama Canal was becoming a reality. Even though American engineers and contractors had never handled 'problems of supply, labor or overall planning on a scale even approaching what was called for' in Panama, they 'streamlined' the construction process (*Ibid.*, pp. 407, 491), much as the Pencoyd engineers had done in the Atbara case, but on a much grander scale. To facilitate that 'streamlining', John Stevens relied partially on two civilian engineers who would later figure in the exporting of American architecture in other contexts: William Barclay Parsons, who followed up his Panama experience by assisting Daniel Burnham in the Philippines; and Carl Grunsky who, a quarter of a century later, advised both Chinese and Soviet governments about city planning efforts in those countries (*Ibid.*, p. 407).

Beginning in 1909 American builders in the Canal Zone began utilizing concrete for the canal locks in new, previously unimaginable ways.

It was in the closing years of the task that the great locks took form for all to see and they were the most interesting and important construction feats of the entire effort. They were the structural triumphs at Panama. In their overall dimensions, mass, weight, in the mechanisms and ingenious control apparatus incorporated in their design, they surpassed any similar structures in the world. They were ... the mighty portals of the Panama Gateway... They were made of concrete and they were made of literally thousands of moving parts. Large essential elements were not built but were manufactured, made in Pittsburgh, Wheeling, Schenectady, and other cities. In a very real sense they were colossal machines, the largest yet conceived. (*Ibid.*, p. 590)

The effects of this prodigious engineering effort in certain U.S. regions were remarkable. In Pittsburgh, for example, there were

50 different mills, foundries, machine shops and specialty

fabricators involved in the canal, making rivets, bolts, nuts, steel girders, steel plates, steel forms for the lock walls, special collapsible steel tubes by which the main culverts were formed, steel roller bearings for the stem valves and spillway gates. The building of the gates themselves had been entrusted to McClintic-Marshall, a Pittsburgh contracting firm that specialized in heavy steel bridge construction. (*Ibid.*, p. 598)

The Panama Canal, therefore, was a prime example not only of how steel and concrete technologies worked so logically together, but also how contractors excelling in one kind of technology sometimes benefited from the growing popularity of the other.

Kahn becomes a Popular Concrete System for Export, c. 1905–1914

One of the most important of American concrete exporting companies that capitalized upon the symbiotic relationship between concrete and steel was Truscon, a firm founded by Albert and Julius Kahn, designers of some of the first U.S. automobile factories. Ford's Highland Park plant (1910) was one of the most significant (Hildebrand, 1974; Banham, 1989, p. 84), in part because of the trend it helped set domestically and also because of the impact the plant had on Europeans, such as Giacomo Matté-Trucco, Fiat's designer of the famous Lingotto factory in Turin (Banham, 1989, p. 97). The Trussed Concrete Steel Company was incorporated in 1903; in 1918 it became the Truscon Steel Company (*Moody's Manual of Investments*, 1951, p. 2878). The company's technological backbone was the steel 'Kahn Trussed Bar,' also known as the Hy-Rib, invented by Julius Kahn. The trussed bar was characterized by a horizontal main bar with flanges, combined with rigidly-connected shear members set at a 45 degree diagonal, all formed from one piece of steel. With no loose stirrups, the bars were laid in moulds into which concrete was poured to form precast elements.

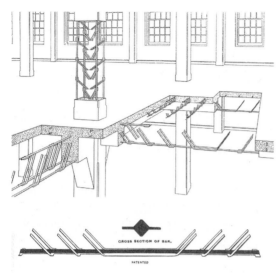

The Kahn Trussed Bar.

Figures 2.18 and 2.19. The Kahn system of concrete reinforcement, used by the Trussed Concrete Steel Corporation. In the early twentieth century the Kahn system became a major com-petitor worldwide of other concrete-reinforcing systems, particularly those from France and Germany, which in the late-nineteenth century had jumped out in front of all other countries as a source for quality reinforcing bars and other components associated with concrete. (*Source*: Trussed Concrete Steel *Catalogue, c.* 1904)

The Kahn system facilitated long span, solid-slab construction wherever shearing stresses had to be resisted.

By 1907 the Kahn system had been used not only in over 1500 U.S. and 90 U.K. structures, but also on a broader global scale. From corporate headquarters in Detroit and with a main factory in Youngstown, Ohio, Truscon was represented by four agents covering Central and South America, two in Europe and four in Asia (*American Exporter*, 1907, **60**(1), p. 85). The company diversified its prefabricated offerings, selling collapsible column reinforcements, steel joists and entire buildings. 'They are built of standardized units, yet are individually designed to meet your needs' (*The Constructor*, 1930, **12**(6), p. 71). Although some designers used other American

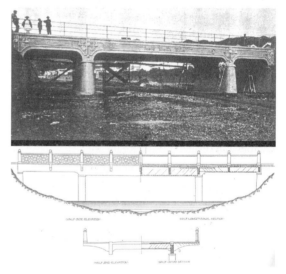

Figure 2.20. Advertisement of the Trussed Concrete Steel Company, showing its foreign distributors (lower right), as well as explaining the advantages of the Kahn system of concrete reinforcement. (*Source: American Exporter*, 1908, **61**(6), June, p. 33)

Figure 2.21. Kahn Trussed Bars adapted to highway bridges. The diagram reflects the principles of the application. The photo is of the Ponte Regina Elena in Messina, Sicily where, before 1911, this bridge was erected with the Kahn system. (*Sources:* Trussed Concrete Steel Corporation, 1904, *General Catalogue C*, figure 19; L.E. Estes, 1911, *Earthquake Proof Construction*, p. 36)

systems for concrete reinforcement (for example, Turner or Ransome), Truscon's system – because of its standardized, adaptable, durable and well-marketed components – became the pre-eminent system exported by Americans between the World Wars.

Two examples in Asia where designers employed the Kahn system in the first decade of the twentieth century – one in Guangzhou, China and the other in Melbourne, Australia – demonstrate its structural tenacity as well as the flexibility of spatial solutions derived from its use.

Concrete's introduction into China was a multifaceted endeavour that scholars are only beginning to understand. In addition to involving Chinese workers and (after 1906) some Chinese industrialists, the burgeoning concrete industry in China was promoted primarily by British, German and Japanese engineers; as well as (initially) British, Australian and American architects competing with popular, increasingly multi-national French technologies in the forms of either the Coignet, Monier or increasingly Hennebique systems of reinforcement. The last quarter of the nineteenth century witnessed the emergence of China's first company to produce the 'red-haired man's mud' (*hung mo nai cheong*), 'foreign mud' (*yang li*) or 'water mud' (*shui li*), as Portland cement was known by the Chinese.[6] The Chee Hsin Cement Company, established in 1886 at Tangshan (near Tianjin) by British engineers working for the Kailan Mining

Administration, was China's most notable cement company. However, mismanagement plagued the company during the turbulent late Qing period and it was not until 1906, when Chinese managers assumed control, that the company began to prosper, which it did until 1949 (Feuerwerker, 1967). By the early 1920s China had six cement plants, and by then concrete was also becoming increasingly popular in some Chinese cities.[7]

Three factors accounted for concrete's growing popularity and its technological transfer from more industrialized Western countries to the China coast. Foreign architects and engineers were drawn to its structural qualities, many clients appreciated its cost, and Chinese builders saw it as the wave of the future that would put them one step ahead of their competitors. In the early 1920s, for example, when foreigners began to publish China's first architectural magazines in Shanghai (for example,

Figure 2.22. The Army and Navy Club, Manila, where the Kahn system of reinforcement was used. Many kinds of buildings constructed in the Philippines after the American military victories there in 1898 used concrete as a preferred building material. The Trussed Concrete Steel Corporation which used the Kahn system, profited accordingly. (*Source*: L.E. Estes, 1911, *Earthquake Proof Construction*, p. 32)

Figures 2.23 and 2.24. Two views of the shipping yards of the Trussed Concrete Steel Corporation in Youngstown, Ohio. (*Source: Kahn System Standards*, 1913, facing title page, and p. 63)

Figure 2.25. Truscon Standardized Building Types, 1930. The Trussed Concrete Steel Corporation shortened its name to Truscon, and by the early 1930s it had developed a series of building types that could be purchased in their entirety and shipped abroad from the Youngstown yards. (*Source*: *The Constructor*, 1930, **12**(6), p. 71)

Figure 2.26. Advertisement showing how Truscon products were being marketed – through a local subsidiary – in Shanghai during the 1920s. (*Source: China Architects and Builders Compendium*, 1924, p. 108)

Figure 2.27. Shanghai Waterworks Tower. This structure was one of the earliest cases in China where reinforced concrete was used. By 1900 many Shanghai-based archtects and engineers were discussing how to use this material more extensively. American companies such as Truscon subsequently became popular suppliers of concrete materials. (Photograph courtesy of Dennis George Crow)

China Architects' and Builders' Compendium, 1924), Chinese contractors who could build in reinforced concrete proudly advertised that fact, hoping to attract new customers.

At the end of the nineteenth century in several Chinese treaty port cities – Guangzhou, Hong Kong and Shanghai, especially – certain foreign builders advocated the adoption of reinforced concrete, which was first utilized in experiments with sanitary systems: drainage pipes, sewers, pavements and a water tower. The Shanghai Waterworks Tower, erected in 1883 by the British engineer J.W. Hart, was one of the earliest examples of concrete

architecture in China (Wood, 1902–1903, pp. 8–10; MacPherson, 1987, pp. 83–122). Within a decade, in part because of these concrete examples that served as object lessons, and in part because of publicity by professional societies in Shanghai about concrete's successful use,[8] foreign engineers and architects in China extended their focus on concrete to walls and foundations (Muller, 1904–1905).

One early example of this tendency to erect walls using concrete was the five-storey tall, new headquarters of Arnhold, Karberg & Company on Shameen (Xiamian) Island in Guangzhou, designed in 1905 by a pair of adventurous architects, Arthur W. Purnell of Geelong, Australia and Charles S. Paget of Bethlehem, Pennsylvania who had formed a partnership in 1903 when they met in either Hong Kong or Guangzhou (Wright and Cartwright, 1908, pp. 788). Purnell and Paget chose the Kahn system of concrete reinforcement and employed Lam Woo, a Hong Kong contractor, to learn the technique of Kahn reinforcement and build their design. However, rather than overtly manifesting the nature of the concrete frame on the buildings exterior, Purnell and Paget obscured the material that would have such implications for twentieth-century Chinese architecture behind an embellished, eclectic, neoclassical façade. In this regard, Purnell and Paget were committing the crime [sic] that one contemporary critic asserted was prevalent among otherwise creative designers:

The architect who creates, column by column, rivet by rivet and tile by tile, a 50-story colossus for the modern city, who draws upon every tiniest ramification of modern science for the solution of his mysterious and manifold problems of technique, lapses instantly into the dusty centuries of the primitive past when he approaches the artistic phase of his labors. He discards the ancient, inadequate materials for the hidden portions of his work. He builds of steel and tile and glass and concrete where his mind sees but the practical problem, but when he takes up the task of designing the surface, he reverts to the days of Romulus and Remus. (Kahler, 1914, p. 41).

However, regardless of the nature of external stylistic treatments, the strength of the structural solution itself soon began to replace earlier, less durable

options. As the American Consul-General in Hong Kong noted in 1912,

There has been a notable change in the manner of constructing buildings in new work of this sort in Hongkong and other South China ports, particularly in the use of reenforced [sic] concrete . . . A few years ago, steel commenced to be used to an increasing extent in the better class of structures, and numerous collapses of buildings of no great age, constructed according to the old model of native materials, have given a decided impetus to the use of steel and stone and cement. In the past two years this tendency has been further marked by the increasing use of concrete and of steel reenforcement [sic] therefore. Few of the more pretentious buildings now constructed do not make use of these materials. Structural steel generally is employed more and more. For concrete reenforcement [sic] of heavier types, European metal is preferred, but the use of American reenforcement [sic] in floors, ceilings, nonbearing

Figures 2.28 and 2.29. Arnhold, Karberg Building, Xiamian Island, Guangzhou, China. This 1905 commercial structure, one of the earliest surviving reinforced concrete buildings in China, was built using the Kahn system of reinforcement. (*Sources*: above: Wright and Cartwright, 1908, p. 791; below: photo by the author)

Figure 2.31. Sniders & Abrahams Building, Melbourne, Australia, constructed 1908–09 using the Turner system of concrete slab reinforcement which, along with Truscon, were increasingly popular systems exported from the U.S. to many sites worldwide in the early 1900s. (*Source: Building*, 11 June 1910, p. 59)

Figure 2.30. A renewed fascination by some Chinese with the ideals of the United States: the Statue of Liberty as 'The New Joss'. Immediately after the 1911 Revolution, which ended the Qing Dynasty, some Chinese reformers looked to the U.S. for inspiration. Some of that inspiration was related to American building technologies and architectural design. (*Source: American Exporter*, 1912, **69**(1), p. 87, reprinted from the *St. Louis Post-Dispatch*)

walls, and for bridges, galleries, verandas and the like in first-class buildings is becoming all but universal. (*Daily Consular and Trade Reports*, 1912, **161**(10), p. 168)

In Australia, too, American reinforcement systems competed with European ones which, although established earlier, were sometimes susceptible by 1906–1907 to being replaced by one of two American systems marketed by Australian agents: a flat plate system patented by C.A.P. Turner of St. Paul, Minnesota, and Kahn's reinforced, 'Hy-rib' bar. In 1908–1909 the first building in the U.S. to use the Turner system of octagonal, spiral mushroom columns and diagonally reinforced slabs was the Lindeke-Warner Building in St. Paul. However, anticipating success in Australia, in 1906 Turner took out a patent there for his system and in 1908 he began using a local engineer, H.R. Crawford, as his agent in Melbourne (Lewis, 1988a, p. 17). In

1909 Crawford employed the Turner system in the Snider's and Abraham's Building on Drewery Lane, and subsequently in the Herald and Weekly Times Building on Flinders Street, Melbourne.

As the Snider's and Abraham's Building was being constructed with the Turner system, a larger structure nearby – what was then called the Melbourne Public Library – was demonstrating the other, even more aggressively exported American reinforcing system, that of the Kahn brothers. In 1907, 51 years after its opening, the Library's trustees decided to erect a new Reading Room to replace an antiquated wooden rotunda. After visiting major libraries worldwide for six months the Chief Librarian, E. Armstrong, decided upon a domed space reminiscent of both the British Museum and the Library of Congress (U.S.A.). The Library commissioned a local architect, Norman Peebles, to design the structure and Peebles turned to John Monash, of the Reinforced Concrete and Monier Pipe Construction Company, for help in the dome's design. This was common at the time; architects deferred to concrete specialists because they, themselves, had not been trained in the new technologies during their architectural education (Saunders, 1959, p. 43). Initially, Monash was granted

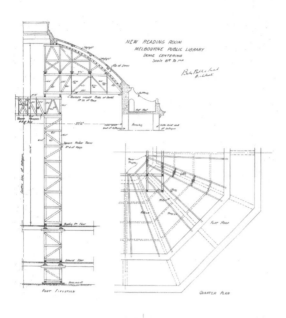

the tender, where he stipulated the use of the (French) Monier system of concrete reinforcement, but G.A. Taylor, a local editor and advocate of competing concrete interests, vehemently objected. In 1909 the Library's trustees asked for new tenders and the winner was J.W. and D.A. Swanson, who proposed using the Kahn system, supplied by Truscon (Lewis, 1988*a*, pp. 12–15 and 1988*b*, p. 3).

As one historian explained (Saunders, 1959, p. 42), one of the most logical reasons for choosing the Truscon option (administered in this case by Truscon's London office) was because it had just been proven to work so well elsewhere, such as the four-rib square dome erected in 1907 at Central Hall in Westminster, U.K. Other cases where the Kahn system was employed in contemporary Melbourne were more problematical (Lewis, 1988*a*, p. 14). When the Reading Room dome was completed in

Figures 2.32, 2.33 and 2.34. State Library of Victoria, Australia. This imposing structure in central Melbourne, erected between 1908 and 1913, utilized the Truscon system for reinforcing concrete. (*Source:* La Trobe Picture Collection, State Library of Victoria. Figure 2.34, photograph courtesy of Joe Vittorio)

1913, however, it became a significant case, in part because at 34.75 metres in diameter (and in height) it was briefly the largest reinforced concrete structure in the world.[9] Another aspect of the Reading Room's significance, though, was that it demonstrated how, before World War I, designers increasingly employed either the Kahn or Turner systems of concrete reinforcement as viable alternatives to European technologies.[10]

Irrational Warfare and Rational Corporate Systems for Construction and Trade, c. 1914–1920

Truscon's diffusion in southern China, Australia and elsewhere reflected how concrete was even more significant as part of a building system than it was solely as an innovative building material (Peters, 1996, pp. 63–78). The system of fabricating concrete blocks coalesced a transportable, and easy-to-operate machine with readily available materials. The system of constructing walls entailed imbedding steel rods in the concrete to reinforce its strength. As the Federal Export Corporation affirmed to potential clients during World War I:

We can supply your requirements for either type of structure [steel or concrete] and . . . we can aid you in altering your plans . . . The poured method of concrete construction has been so perfected that buildings of this material are now erected as rapidly as a steel structure. Our engineering department is prepared to assist engineers, architects and builders to apply this method to their structural work. (*Export American Industries*, 1917, **19**, August, p. 17)

This evidence suggests that, contrary to what some historians have earlier asserted about the 'remarkable independence of the two cultures of steel and concrete' (Banham, 1989, p. 104), these materials, technologies and cultures were viewed by exporters as very much allied in their appeal, even if their technical challenges were distinctive.

Concrete, then, was only the literal answer to the question of how to build a strong, progressive structure to complement a steel-framed one; the figurative answer was related to 'systems', or how to employ a greater integration of building processes. Historians have shown that during the later years of the nineteenth century and the first decades of the twentieth, many critical institutions within U.S. society were rationalizing, reconfiguring, and integrating vertically to become more efficient organizational hierarchies (Chandler, 1990). As some of these institutions collaborated with each other, they created what Olivier Zunz has termed an institutional matrix of inquiry:

This matrix . . . gained in strength throughout the first half of the twentieth century as Americans explored new markets and mobilized the nation's resources for two world wars. As a knowledge organization, the matrix enabled investigators from separate fields of inquiry and institutions to come together and collaborate. The American matrix . . . was flexible, allowing industrialists, managers, scientists, engineers, self-taught inventors, and other entrepreneurs to move among institutions. (Zunz, 1998, p. 4)

Certain segments of American contracting industries similarly coalesced, seeking more efficient means of adapting to the challenges of building, either domestically or (increasingly) abroad as well.

Such was the case when, by the turn of the century, American manufacturers established an Association of Portland Cement Manufacturers. In 1905 at its convention in New York this Association discussed plans for the development of the American export trade in Portland cement. The group urged the employment of 'special agents who will be sent to investigate the large export trade which may be obtained in South Africa and South America', and it created a committee to petition Congress 'to make reciprocity treaties which would aid in the development of the export end of this industry' (*American Exporter*, 55, January 1905). Thus, cement manufacturers were attempting to create their own institutional matrix for the propagation abroad of building materials that were becoming directly linked to American manufacturing progress and high-rise urbanism. Those manufacturers were also building upon the important precedents of the National Association of Manufacturers (1895) and the Cabinet-level U.S. Department of Commerce (1903), refining the general concept of association to the particular case of the cement industry.

An even more well-developed cluster of construction-related organizations were associated with the steel industry. The first, and probably the most controversial of these because of its monopolistic tendencies, was the U.S. Steel Export Company. Other steel exporters followed U.S. Steel's lead. In 1899 Milliken was among the first U.S. companies to see the potential of global markets for the exported American skyscraper, but the U.S. Steel Products Export Company quickly overshadowed the 'scale and scope' (Chandler, 1990) of exporting ventures such as the Milliken Company. Like Milliken, U.S. Steel was deeply committed to convincing customers of 'the economy of American methods and standards' as well as 'their safety and practicability', but the conglomerate, with a greater economic force behind its global reach, further geared its efforts to local

conditions (*Far Eastern Review*, 1911, **8**(2), p. 51). By 1911, at 'leading foreign points' such as Buenos Aires and Shanghai, U.S. Steel maintained an engineering organization that could make what the firm called a 'straight bid', whereby its client would know 'the actual cost to him of the erected structure, terms of payment being arranged locally in the funds of the country, all the correspondence being conducted in the language of the customer' (*Ibid.*, p. 52). European competitors were prone to make a low price-per-pound bid, but then submitted designs 'cumbersome in character' so the actual tonnage was greater and the final cost to the customer higher.

Just before World War I some American trade experts believed there were serious handicaps facing American exporters that needed to be addressed more systematically if those exporters wanted a larger share of an ever-globalizing marketplace. One of those was Paul Reinsch, an eminent U.S. diplomat in China, who in mid-1914 summarized what he saw as 'the [five] greatest deficiencies which prevent the development of American commerce and enterprise in China', but Reinsch also thought they held true more generally for 'the organization of American trade and investment abroad'. These deficiencies were:

1. the absence of financial institutions for handling foreign loans;

2. the lack of an investment company which would subject proposed improvements to scrutiny and gather up the means for promoting sound enterprises;

3. the lack of American commission houses;

4. the lack of an organization of exporters with representation in important foreign markets . . .; and

5. the lack of commercial attaches who could assist the diplomatic missions and consular offices in coordinating and rendering more efficient the work now performed by those agencies. (Reinsch, 1914, p. 984)

Figure 2.35. Foreign branch offices and warehouses of the U.S. Steel Products Company, 1920. This conglomerate, which amalgamated several firms listed here, also established a constellation of foreign offices to market its products after World War I, in response to a global thirst for American steel. (*Source: Iron Age Catalogue of American Exports*, 1920, vol. 1, p. 114)

Reinsch was lamenting the lack of an efficient series of organizations and institutions to buttress the interests of American traders. He was implying that despite some helpful federal initiatives – such as the establishment of the National Association of Manufacturers and the Department of Commerce – the U.S. government needed to take more strategic and focused action on behalf of American exporters.

In 1914 the government did take action concerning Reinsch's number 1 deficiency (the absence of financial institutions empowered to handle foreign loans) when Congress passed, and the President signed, the Federal Reserve Act into law. This allowed American banks to establish offices abroad. One of the first to take advantage of this latitude was the National City Bank of New York, which acquired the International Banking Corporation in 1915 and during the next 6 years established 85 foreign branches: 56 in Latin America, 12 in Europe and 17 in Asia (Mayer, 1973; Phelps, 1927). Other major banks, such as Chase Manhattan and the First National Bank of Boston, soon followed suit. As will be demonstrated in further detail below, these banks became symbols of a sea change in international commerce that occurred in conjunction with World War I and then proceeded apace through the 1920s until Wall Street's crash in October 1929. Part of that change came in the form of 'direct exchange', whereby dollars were not only quoted in foreign markets, but also payments from those markets to U.S. banks were made in dollars.

That great instrument of credit, the acceptance, prior to 1914 was practically a neglected factor in American banking. We consequently did not possess the means for making dollar exchange an important international factor. Since the inauguration of the new banking system of the U.S., however, the growth in volume of bank acceptances has been rapid [from only $93,000 in February 1915 to $750,000,000 in August 1918]. (*Export American Industries*, 1919, **23**(2), p. 49)

The sanctioning of American banks to operate abroad was but one step in the direction that Reinsch had urged. Another was the creation in late 1915 – almost simultaneously with U.S. banks establishing offices abroad – of the American International Corporation, a consortium of major American interests 'to develop enterprises abroad with American capital' (*American Exporter*, 1916, **78**(1), p. 73). Before World War I, it was largely Europeans who controlled surplus capital to invest in industrial development projects worldwide, but due to the war much of that capital had shifted into American hands. As one analyst expressed it,

[The surplus capital] will be used to develop new railways and other enterprises in South America, China, and other markets dependent upon foreign capital for much of their transportation and industrial progress. The only distinction will be that this capital will be subscribed by American investors, instead of European, and employed under American management. (*Ibid.*)

And many of the twenty-four executives who managed this Corporation were either bankers, railway developers, steel exporters or engineers geared toward international construction efforts: Frank Vanderlip of National City Bank, Chairman of the Board; Charles A. Stone of the engineering firm Stone & Webster, President; Willard D. Straight, formerly of J. P. Morgan & Company and experienced with Chinese trade, Vice-President. Taking its cue from this Corporation, 'other financiers and large contracting companies [began to work] along similar lines. Thus the J. G. White Engineering Company has formed a new corporation and is investigating the possibilities of taking on some of the railways in Brazil' (*Ibid.*). The American International Corporation, therefore, addressed Reinsch's number 2 deficiency: the lack of an investment company to target sensible projects worldwide.

However, despite the globalizing expansion implied by the Federal Reserve Act and the American International Corporation, World War I intensified even further the five deficiencies Reinsch had outlined in 1914. As it did in so many ways – and as it did with respect to exporting and international construction activities – World War I challenged the assumptions of those who had grown complacent with the *status quo*. Because of World War I Britain, Germany and Belgium lost their supremacy in exporting steel worldwide. Because of the ravages of the war, reconstruction activities shifted demand within Europe for American products. Because of intensifying demand from customers worldwide, American companies specializing in marketing steel building components followed U.S. Steel's lead. Some of these enterprises had flourished domestically due to railroad and urban expansion; they then moved into the export market, and often merged with one or two firms of similar scope, when they noted swelling demand not only from war-torn Europe but also from industrializing Central and South America, American-controlled territories in the Pacific, and East Asian coastal cities from Japan to Malaysia.

During World War I, when iron and steel in Europe were significantly diverted from industrial to military uses, American suppliers continued to export steel rails, engines and building components to European allies. But the effects of the war upon international trade in iron and steel reached well beyond Europe and the United States. Any country 'dependent on an imported supply found their industrial development severely handicapped' (Howell, 1920, p. 4). Argentina, which before the war depended upon the U.K., Germany, Belgium and the U.S. for its iron and steel, was a case in point. From 1909 to 1913 Britain exported 1.8 million tons to Argentina, but from 1914 to 1918 that amount plummeted to 530,000 tons. Because of the blockade of Germany and the occupation of Belgium, those two sources dried up completely. Meanwhile, American products were shifted largely to the European war effort, thus starving Argentinean capitalists of products they urgently wanted to purchase for industrial development. The United States suppliers therefore tried to step into the breach of low supply created by the war, but they faced a daunting challenge, both from a supply standpoint, because of equally surging domestic U.S. demand, and from

a competitive corporate standpoint, because of the aggressive activity by the U.S. Steel Products Export Corporation that preceded individual companies' efforts during the war (*Export American Industries*, 1920, **24**(3), p. 52).

Despite these challenges, in order to meet the starved demand for steel products, machinery and building components worldwide as a result of the war, several American iron and steel companies began to export their commodities globally (*Export*, 1922, **29**(1), p. 22). These conglomerates, whose operations abroad were naturally assisted by the financial infrastructure of globalizing American banks, competed from headquarters that centred most often in either New York City or Philadelphia. For example, Spartan Products Company, in New York ('not merely as a company but as an institution equipped for the most exacting service') aimed to 'eliminate the non-productive moment' by reaching out to clients abroad (*Export American Industries*, 1918, **20**(1), p. 12). So, too, did Lucey Manufacturing Company, also operating from Manhattan, where it sought to acquire an edge by virtue of

years of experience in export shipping and international transactions. [We have a] worldwide organization of offices, stores and factories with unlimited resources and experienced salesmen and engineers in all parts of the world, caring for details and rendering valuable assistance . . . We will undertake to furnish our foreign customers with anything that is within the jurisdiction of the Government regulations. (*Export American Industries*, 1918, **20**(1), p. 4; and Landau, 1918, p. 73)

In early 1917 entrepreneurs combined forces to create the New York-based Vulcan Steel Products Company, reputed to be 'one of the important factors in the development of the great international commerce of the United States', with particular focus on South America and Europe (*American Exporter*, 82, March 1918). A year later Vulcan launched an advertising campaign designed to reach all parts of the world. Unsettled conditions of the mails have necessitated the conducting of the greater part of the Vulcan business through cables . . . and hundreds of photographs are made daily of the [products] sold by the engineering machinery division. These are used by the salesmen where it is not possible to show actual samples. (*Ibid.*)

Similarly, in New York – the Peerless International Corporation, R.M. Ford & Company, the Hedden Iron Construction Company, the Blaw Steel Products Company, Berlin Construction Company and Liberty Steel Products Company – in Philadelphia, the Pennsylvania Steel Export Company, Smythfield Export Company and Belmont Iron Works – and in Birmingham, Alabama the Ingalls Iron Works – were created to handle the upsurge in contracting business abroad.[11] All these companies were responding to U.S. government avowed intentions to

maintain and foster the pleasant relations which have been built up with foreign consumers of steel during the last few years, and there is no doubt that with the exercise of a little patience, and mutual forbearance, the ties which unite us will become ever closer. (Landau, 1918, p. 74)

The ties uniting the building supply companies themselves also became stronger, thus creating competing collusions of construction-related

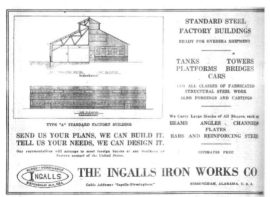

Figure 2.36. Advertisement of the Ingalls Iron Works, Birmingham, Alabama, 1919. By the end of World War I many U.S. steel manufacturers were engaging actively in foreign trade. (*Source: American Exporter*, 1919, **84**(4), p. 64)

interests. Although the U.S. Steel Products Company had leapt out in front of its exporting competitors before the war, two other conglomerates soon began going head-to-head with U.S. Steel for the growing market. In 1917 entrepreneurs in New York established the Federal Export Corporation, 'an organization sufficient within itself to conduct every detail of producing, delivering and financing orders in any volume' (*Export American Industries*, 1917, **19**(1), p. 3). The Corporation was created to meet the need of 'Allied Governments' which found that 'the old method of placing separate orders was inadequate to their needs of prompt production and delivery' (*Ibid.*). Federal Export not only had a manufacturing division to produce an array of goods, but also a shipping division to deliver those goods and a banking division to help finance them.

The second attempt at coalescing steel (and related) interests to compete with U.S. Steel Products was the Consolidated Steel Company, created in December 1918 by eleven of the leading independent steel manufacturers. Consolidated's organizers expected that 'other steel producing interests will join later . . . to represent in export trade substantially all important steel producing companies of the country outside of the United States Steel Corporation' (*American Exporter*, 84, February 1919). Operating from headquarters in New York, Consolidated created a constellation of branch offices and foreign representatives worldwide. In spring 1920, for instance, Consolidated opened an office in Shanghai, which marked 'the beginning of an aggressive campaign for steel business in China by Consolidated' (*Export News*, 1920, **2**(1), p. 61). Ventures such as this established

intimate contact between customers and Consolidated manufacturers. The customer [was] thus assured that the manufacturer [would] understand his exact requirements and that every shipment [would] contain exactly the articles ordered, correct in every detail. (Bregenzer, 1920, p. 108)

This rosy picture of a contented customer and

satisfied manufacturer was far from universal in the exporting of American architecture, but it reflected a contemporary, American industrialist ideal soon after World War I that trade expansion was almost limitless. For example, the Ingalls Iron Company boasted: 'Send us your plans, we can build it. Tell us your needs, we can design it' (*American Exporter*, 1919, **84**(4), p. 54; 1919, **84**(6), p. 76). Many exporters reflected this boundless confidence after the debacle of World War I, fuelled by domestic surpluses of steel, competitive concrete technologies, a resurgence of industrial development, an American government that had begun to respond to calls for export-related

action, and increasingly efficiency-driven tendencies within many building material exporters. And as will be shown in the following chapter, during the 1920s confidence and efficiency were pervasive qualities in other U.S. construction-related organizations as well. By the end of World War I, there were in place the foundations for a system of contracting abroad. Now what became necessary was the nurturing of a system – the humanizing and transformation of it in different cultural contexts – so that what was becoming trademark American efficiency, standardization and confidence in construction did not become rigidity, formula and arrogance when taken abroad.

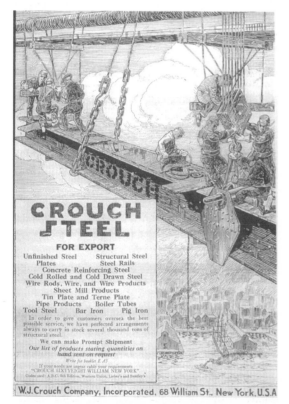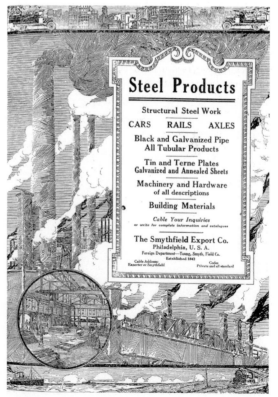

Figures 2.37 and 2.38. Advertisements of Crouch Steel and Smythfield, two of the myriad steel companies exporting their wares at the end of World War I. The graphics in these advertisements, which highlight the I-beam as well as the variety of industrial uses to which this versatile structural member could be put, capture some of the hubris related to contemporary American steel exporting. (*Sources: Export American Industries*, 1918, **20**(4), p. 31; *Export American Industries*, 1918, **20**(1), p. 113.)

NOTES

1. This situation was not as prevalent in regions under French colonial control because either Coignet, Monier, or increasingly at the turn of the century Hennebique's patented concrete systems were more often employed there. I thank Dr. Chris Luebkeman, Ove Arup Associates, for bringing this trend to my attention. See also Delhumeau, 1999.

2. Quotation from advertisements in the *American Exporter*, 1907, **60**(2), p. 6; 1907, **60**(4), p. 3. In late 1907 agents were in Kobe, Sydney, Calcutta, Penang, Havana, Mexico City, Buenos Aires, Glasgow and Budapest.

3. Between 1907 and 1918 competition for the export market of concrete blocks came from the Century Cement Machinery Co. (Rochester, N.Y.); Ransome Concrete Machinery Co. (Dunellen, N.J.); Cement Machinery Co. (Jackson, Michigan); Waterloo Cement Machinery Co. (Waterloo, Iowa); and Concrete Machinery Sales Co. (Wichita, Kansas).

4. The Cement Export Company was incorporated in 1919 and conducted business from N.Y. acting as the sole exporter of eleven cement companies and handling orders 'such as no individual company could possibly maintain'. See *Export News*, 1920, **1**(10), p. 79; and *American Exporter*, 1919, **85**(2), p. 176.

5. Quotation from Ericsson, Henry (1942) *Sixty Years a Builder*. N.Y.: Arno Press (reprinted 1972), p. 282; cited in Wermiel, 2000, p. 183.

6. Clements, J. Morgan (1922) The cement industry of China. *Millards Weekly Review*, **20**(12), pp. 454–458.

7. See, for example, 'Cement Works', *Rea's Far Eastern Manual*, 2nd ed. Shanghai published by *Far Eastern Review*, 1924, pp. 242–245; and 'Chinas Tribute to Cement'. *Far Eastern Review*, 1925, **21**(5), p. 203.

8. One of the examples that engineers discussed in Shanghai soon after it was completed in 1903 was the Ingall's Building in Cincinnati, Ohio. The implications of this reinforced concrete example, which served commercial functions in a central business district, resonated with Shanghai's foreign builders, whose clients were often wanting to erect buildings serving similar functions in central Shanghai.

9. The Melbourne Library's Reading Room was surpassed by Max Berg's Jahrhunderthalle dome in Breslau, Germany, which was 64.55 metres in diameter, completed later in 1913.

10. I thank Sue Balderstone, of Heritage Victoria, for calling my attention to the Reading Room and supplying me with relevant references about its construction. I also appreciate Kent Ball, Librarian at the State Library, providing me with copies of scholarly articles about the Library, which is undergoing a major redevelopment project that will last until at least 2004.

11. All these companies advertised intermittently in the *American Exporter* during 1918 and 1919.

3 American Builders Abroad at a Fork in the Road: Adjust or Go Home, 1918–1930

Many American designers, builders and entrepreneurs became increasingly confident in their abilities to export their construction expertise because of global macroeconomic shifts associated with World War I. Markets thirsty for American steel, concrete, timber, plasterboard and other desirable building materials provided incentives for entrepreneurs to try their hand at foreign trade. Other lures stemmed from easier banking transactions, domestic material surpluses, more well-developed shipping and, as will be shown below, assistance from professional associations or federations. But as most Americans who responded to these enticing incentives found

out, exporting architecture from the U.S. as a set of constituent building parts or technologies was only the first step in trying to graft either novel methods of construction or new building forms onto dynamic, indigenous building practices. Building abroad implied not simply transplanting a seed, but also genetically modifying a series of culture-specific construction operations.

Between the end of the so-called 'Great War' and the onset of the Great Depression, as U.S. architectural exporters increasingly became aware of the cultural and eco-political challenges they faced in trading overseas, they stared at a fork in the road. The longer, more circuitous route to success required them to adjust. As they worked within pre-existing matrices of construction, those American architectural exporters taking this fork in the road familiarized themselves with local practices, nurtured their markets abroad and tried to dovetail their products, technologies or exported building forms as seamlessly as possible with what was already present at the receiving end of their transactions. As one anonymous exporter exclaimed,

The only thing that I can lay to our success in entering new markets is that we always make a very close investigation before going ahead. There is not a country that we have sent a representative to that we were not first positive that that country was going to be a fertile field for our building material. (Wyman, 1914, p. 48)

However, if exporters took the shorter branch in the road – one where they delivered architectural materials but remained on the fringe of local architectural culture – then they didn't adjust successfully. Instead, often after losing both patience and money, they returned home. These American exporters, more cavalier in their attitudes toward customers, opened themselves up to importers' charges of 'dumping' and lack of concern about the nature and implications of what they were shipping. In 1912, Cuba was one place where some exporters could be seen opting for this shorter road.

During periods of commercial depression in the U.S., certain American manufacturers have worked up good trade relations and patronage in Cuba in order to keep their factories going, and then after normal business conditions at home rebounded, they have quoted prohibitive prices and even refused orders from their Cuban and Latin American customers. When home prices were again unremunerative and they endeavored to regain their export trade they found to their surprise that their former agents and customers were no longer interested in their product. (*Daily Consular and Trade Reports*, 1912, **240**, October 11, p. 195)

Data are more scant concerning many of those who took that shorter road. Flashes in the pan, these exporters' activities have left fewer traces in either the journals or the organizations' publications that monitored them. For example, did the Edwards Manufacturing Company, which supplied pressed metal ceilings for the palace in Kabul (see above, Chapter 2) follow up this venture with more extensive exporting throughout the region? Probably not, although precise sources are silent (Simpson, 1995). One contemporary author, B. Olney Hough, who wrote several primers on export practices for American traders, cautioned against becoming either casually or superficially engaged in foreign commerce. In 1909 he warned that 'export trade ought never to be attempted by the firm that is not thoroughly in earnest about it, that does not mean to follow it shrewdly and patiently, through thick and thin, in fair weather and foul, to the goal of success . . . But few American manufacturers have any adequate or realizing appreciation of the great battle for the world's markets that is so surely impending' (Hough, 1909, p. xv). Hough also cautioned against exporters' complacency once initial sales were made abroad. 'Trade once established, no matter how, will

THE MAN WHO SELLS ABROAD

Figure 3.1. 'The Man Who Sells Abroad'. Ocean-going vessels, wharfs and tropical settings were part and parcel of the mystique associated with American exporting prior to World War I. The cost- and system-conscious trader next to a wooden crate and hand truck helped complete an archetypical image of a contemporary American export merchant. (*Source*: *System*, 1914, **26**(5), p. 483)

not continue forever to take care of itself', Hough asserted, 'it must be nursed and cultivated if it is to be developed adequately' (Hough, 1921, p. 163).

Between these two extremes of those exporters who chose the shorter branch and those who selected the more circuitous route were many cases where sometimes exporters acted with flexibility and care as they began to build stronger foundations for exporting American architecture. But then they altered their course. Some steel exporters were a case in point. During World War I there were several attempts to export steel for structural uses as efficiently as possible to the broadest spectrum of clients. The American Steel Export Company was a case in point. In 1917 it published *Export Engineering and Contracting*

edited solely for the overseas builder, telling you exactly what we can do for you [in English, Spanish or French] if you have to erect a Power House, a Rolling Mill, a Factory Building, Loading and Unloading Equipments, Sugar Central, Textile Installation, Ice Making Plants, Abattoir, etc. (*American Exporter*, 1917, **81**(3), p. 11)

However during the 1920s the nature of American steel exporting changed, with more rough material exported and more finished material imported, as European steel-exporting countries such as England and Belgium rebounded from the war's disastrous effects (*Iron Age*, 1928, **121**(11), p. 741). By the late-1920s, American steel export practices notably differed from those of their European competitors. American companies were generally willing to furnish ample trial shipments without charge. They provided agents with illustrated booklets (sometimes in the local language) featuring their products and they backed up their goods with reliably standardized quality. However, despite U.S. Steel's attempts to provide sales literature in the languages of their target markets, many other American companies still only used English. Their prices were also usually higher and they quoted their estimates in dollars per ton, whereas Europeans

Engineering and Contracting

This book was edited solely for the overseas builder—telling you exactly what we can do for you, if you have to erect a Power House, a Rolling Mill, a Factory Building, Loading and Unloading Equipments, Sugar Central, Textile Installation, Ice Making Plants, Abattoir, etc., etc.

Our Engineering Department working from submitted plans or our plans drawn up from information supplied can concentrate their energies and the entire equipment at times is shipped under one bill of lading and mark, effecting considerable saving in ocean freight, insurance, and insuring prompt delivery, etc.

This is only one of the many advantages afforded builders abroad, and we solicit inquiries from you stating your requirements now or in the near future that we may save you expense on your next construction.

Figure 3.2. Advertisement for *Export Engineering and Contracting*, a 1917 publication of the American Steel Export Company, headquartered in New York City. This short booklet, 20 pages of text with some additional data, reflected attempts by some American architectural exporters to accommodate foreign builders by anticipating their needs. The advertisement boasted that the company's Engineering Department could work efficiently from submitted plans, and then could ship completed equipment under one bill of lading. (Source: *American Exporter*, 1917, **81**(3), p. 11.)

more often communicated in the local language, marketed cheaper goods, geared their quotations to local currencies and used variable weight calculation systems (*Iron Age*, 1930,**125**(8), p. 584).

Therefore, between 1918 and 1930, as the volume and complexity of American exporting activity increased, a spectrum of possible outcomes emerged for those associated with architecture in all its aspects who set out on the export road. Several cases below reflect the twists and turns of that road, as well as the dimensions and character of the spectrum.

'New Spirit of Construction?': Federations of Contractors and their Challenges to Rationalize

Near the end of World War I, 'many thoughtful observers among [American] contractors [began to realize] the instability, lack of harmony, and generally uncertain conditions that beset their industry' (*Constructor*, 1929, **11**(2), p. 38). These included:

(a) inefficient methods of financing;

(b) confusing relations with engineers, architects and property owners;

(c) vague, contradictory and non-uniform standards of construction;

(d) turbulent labour relations;

(e) conflicting government policies regarding construction; and

(f) frequently short-sighted and conservative con-struction company owners (*Ibid.*)

Until 1918, American construction companies lacked a coherent forum for mutual discussion of these challenges, which threatened to rent their industry even further asunder. However, in response to the malaise felt by many in the construction industry, and because of the 'stress and demands of the war', several visionary contractors 'saw no good reason why they should not enter into national organization, like every other major industry in the

country' (*Ibid.*, p. 40). They therefore 'broadcast an appeal to solidify the scattered power and resources of their industry and to endow construction with its position as the keystone to prosperity' (*Ibid.*, p. 38). Partially because of these initiatives, in July 1918 at Atlantic City, New Jersey the U.S. Chamber of Commerce organized the National Federation of Construction Industries (hereafter NFCI) as a 'War Services Committee'.[1] In his remarks at the opening of the conference – attended by 280 from twenty-two states – Harry Wheeler, the President of the Chamber of Commerce, explained that his office had been investigating the relations between several U.S. industries and the war effort, and 'we have found no single industry so far-reaching [and yet] so much disintegrated as the building trades' (Wheeler, 1918, p. 6). Although Wheeler and others hoped that the Federation would help end petty squabbling and have 'the united cooperation of every industry in the building trades', this did not occur (*Ibid.*, p. 7). The initial nine-member Executive Board included representatives of the Universal Portland Cement Association, the National Lumber Manufacturers' Association, the National Association of Builders' Exchanges and the Engineering Council, but some constituencies felt themselves under-represented.

These included general contractors and architects. The creation of the NFCI thus prompted several prominent contractors to create an Association of General Contractors because 'they felt they could not be properly represented in the Federation' (*Constructor*, 1929, **11**(2), p. 40). This Association worked in tandem with, but parallel to the NFCI and it, too, worked throughout the 1920s not only for greater standardization of American building practices – what the Association saw as an offshoot of how 'construction has been so rationally developed' – but also for 'wider foreign fields' (*Ibid.*, p. 38). Despite the differences between them, both the NFCI and the Association of General Contractors still shared the dual concerns for greater 'rationalization' (i.e., efficiency and standardization) as well as for more abundant activities by contractors in non-U.S. settings.

During its first year the NFCI was mostly concerned with war-related matters (NFCI, 1919, Bulletins 5–10) but a year after the November 1918 Armistice the Federation settled into a more strategic position to address not only the gnawing issues listed above, but also matters concerning the exporting of American construction goods and services. In October 1919, 43 years after Philadelphia's Centennial Exposition, the Federation organized, from its headquarters in that same city, a Foreign Trade Committee 'with a staff devoted to studying and developing foreign trade in construction materials' (NFCI, 1919, Members Service Letters, Letter 13).

In that same month, October 1919 – 'to serve representatives of American construction interests' – members of the Committee attended the convention of the American Manufacturers' Export Association (Ibid.). The Foreign Trade Committee – 'so far as is known, the only Foreign Trade Service operating exclusively for the construction interests of the United States' (Ibid.) – began collecting information both from disparate secondary sources and from Federation members themselves, whom staff urged to send them answers to the following questions:

1. Have you a surplus which you would like to sell in foreign markets? If so, of what does the surplus consist?

2. Is this surplus temporary or are you producing a permanent supply for export?

3. Have you a foreign business now? If so, are you satisfied with the present methods for handling this business?

4. What seem to you to be the chief obstacles in the way of foreign trade development and what suggestions can you give for overcoming those obstacles?

5. What suggestions can you give to aid in guiding the Foreign Trade Committee in its work? (Ibid.)

Although the specific results of this canvassing have not survived, clearly many 'American construction interests [were] realizing and grasping

as never before the opportunities for branching out into world trade'. 'Are you', the NCFI provocatively asked its members, 'taking advantage of them?' (NFCI, 1920, Members Service Letters, Letter 18). By early 1920, in addition to cooperating actively with the U.S. Chamber of Commerce and the American Manufacturers' Export Association, the NFCI was 'working closely' with the Bureau of Foreign and Domestic Commerce, Chambers of Commerce worldwide, the National Foreign Trade Council, several banks, shipping interests and 'the great agencies of the world's trade' (American Exporter, 1920, **87**(4), p. 152). In less than a year NFCI's Foreign Trade Committee, in addition to its surveying activities, had disbursed to NFCI members over 800 trade opportunities for construction products, issued several reports on conditions related to construction abroad, and 'succeeded in interesting American manufacturers who had not previously done business abroad in export trade' (Ibid.).

Among the more important projects on which [NFCI] has worked are:

1. the collection of figures to show the desirability of erecting American office buildings in London, to be transmitted to large British interests in England, to aid in overcoming the lack of proper office space in the British Isles;

2. the equipment of a slaughterhouse and sausage factory in Norway;

3. the introduction of modern office buildings in Rio de Janeiro, Brazil;

4. the equipment of a streetcar system, the sale of American roadmaking and brickmaking machinery, the building of a tunnel, and the sale of rails and steel products in Colombia;

5. the erection of an engine works in France;

6. the display of an American model concrete house and equipment in an exposition in Buenos Aires; and . . . one of the best pieces of work it has accomplished was when it stepped into the breach . . . and enabled the Government of Uruguay to obtain a large amount of construction materials urgently needed on some large public works. (Ibid.)

Curiously, both South America and Europe figure prominently as foci for the Committee's initiatives.

Asia, Africa and the Middle East were notably absent in this regard, a fact that takes on greater significance in the light of future endeavours, as will be seen below. It is also noteworthy that the Committee was involving itself in operations of different scales, from sausage factories in Norway to public works projects in Colombia and Uruguay. And in light of previous instances where American builders and entrepreneurs were actively promoting high-rise commercial towers, the dissemination of the 'modern office building' in both London and Rio de Janeiro is also compelling.

At its first Annual Meeting in Chicago in March 1920, the NFCI highlighted the prominent roles played by 'Foreign Trade' and 'Americanization' in the construction industry by devoting two of its six 'subjects of vital interest' to these topics (*Ibid*.). The Foreign Trade Committee broadcast the range of its interests, solicited wider assistance in its mandate, and shared with members both NFCI's and the Committee's widening vision associated with import-export.

NFCI proposes to have investigators and representatives in the commercial centers of the world. These representatives will maintain relations with the ministers of public works and transportation and with large financial and business interests of the countries in which they may be stationed. They will keep these ministers and business men informed of conditions affecting the construction industry in the U.S. They will advise members of the NFCI of contemplated public and private construction enterprises contemplated in their territories and will endeavor to make it possible for member firms and corporations in the U.S. to submit bids on these enterprises and to compete on equal terms with interests from other countries. Through using the NFCI's foreign trade service, the manufacturers of the U.S. will secure constant representation in all branches of the industry and distribute the burden of the expense. (*Ibid*.)

This kind of globalizing attempt to create a level playing field regarding tendering was remarkable, but largely idealistic.

Equally remarkable was how, by the early 1920s, the motion picture was beginning to be used as a means of propagating the efforts of the NFCI, with the cooperation of organizations, such as the Young Men's Christian Association (YMCA), similarly venturing abroad at that time. In 1905 the YMCA had established an International Committee that began seeking suitable foreign locations for its activities.

In 1921 the NFCI urged its members to rent films about U.S. construction distributed by the Motion Picture Bureau of the YMCA's International Committee. 'Motion picture films showing the manufacture and use of building and construction product or material should be used to their utmost during the winter months when plans and specifications are being prepared,' the NFCI advised. It further proclaimed that

[there has been] a direct-to-consumer distribution . . . reaching four million, with 13,000 exhibitions in 45 states, showing at schools, churches, clubs, plants, factories and YMCAs . . . [with] salesmen tie-ups and report system. . . Educate the people concerning your product, increase your sales through returns on your film investment by keeping your prints busy. (NFCI, 1921, **3**(28), n.p.)

This cinematic approach to advertising the glories of American construction methods and materials was also sometimes used in foreign contexts, although precise details about which films were shown, and in what locations are largely unknown. But during the 1920s export officials began noting the 'imponderable but undeniably tremendous influence' that American motion pictures were beginning to exert on consumers around the world, many of whom began imagining themselves occupying the impressive spaces depicted on celluloid.

A business man of Buenos Aires or Helsinki, strolling into a movie theater and witnessing on the 'silver sheet' a scene of high-pressure activity in an American office is apt to be seized with a passionate yearning to see himself surrounded with similar impressive appurtenances, which symbolize in his mind efficiency and success. (Klein, 1929*b*, p. 90)

One curious instance of American film glorifying American skyscrapers occurred during the summer

Figure 3.3. Motion picture films being used to disseminate information about American products. Although this particular case dates from 1944, as early as the 1920s, American contracting exporters understood how compelling American-made movies could be for foreign audiences. (*Source*: *American Exporter*, 1944, **135**(4), p. 66.)

of 1930 when John Harris, of the contracting firm Hegeman-Harris (New York), showed delegates at two building conferences, first in London and then in Paris, a 'talking film' featuring the construction of Chicago's Tribune Tower, Board of Trade Building and Daily News Building as well as New York's Daily News Building, American Radiator Company Building and Panhellenic House. Those who saw the film, which focused on technical aspects of construction, considered it 'extremely clear and impeccably produced' (Fédération Internationale, 1930, no. 10, p. 4). It was 'widely appreciated' by the European delegates not only because of its entertainment value, but also because of timeliness, when 'attempts at constructing these buildings are being undertaken throughout Europe' (*Ibid*.).

The London gathering was the Fifth Congress of the International Federation of Building and Public Works, an organization established in 1905 by François Van Ophem, a Belgian architect-engineer who sought to promote, on an even more expansive scale than the NFCI, international cooperation in

the building trades (*Fédération Internationale*, 1932, no. 18, p. 1). The International Federation had four goals: to establish ongoing relations with members; centralize commercial, industrial, scientific and social information for members' use; encourage the creation of associations of building trade employers in member countries; and highlight the international importance of construction trades in the context of international business. As the *Herald Tribune* (N.Y.) reported: 'in a word, to stimulate, coordinate and assemble information from diverse areas of national and international construction activities' (*Fédération Internationale*, 1930, no. 10, p. 7). Between 1905 and the outbreak of World War I the Federation had organized three smaller Congresses (Liege in 1905, Paris in 1908 and Rome in 1912) but in 1925, after a series of post-war meetings convened by Van Ophem throughout recovering Europe, he assembled a much larger group for a Fourth Congress in Paris. Not surprisingly, at this conference several executives from prominent U.S. construction-related companies represented American interests.

One of the most important U.S. delegates was Truman Morgan, an editor and publisher of several catalogues and journals related to the American construction industry (including *Architectural Record*), who was appointed by U.S. President Calvin Coolidge to be one of nine American delegates at the Congress. In Paris, Morgan was chosen to be Vice-President of the Building Section and he worked actively with the Federation until the early 1930s, when its operations waned because of the desultory effects of the global Depression and François Van Ophem's death in 1932.[2] In the first quarter of the century Morgan had witnessed what he called the 'complete revolution in the architectural and mechanical treatment of structural detail due to the adaptation of steel to modern demands of U.S. congested areas' and he was anxious to share information about this 'revolution' with interested activists from other countries (almost all of whom were European). He was also anxious to hear from them about the construction and city planning-related lessons they had learned in their own countries, such as how to construct better dock facilities for industrializing cities, plan more efficient water or sewer systems, and construct electric power stations that might be better integrated with city-wide and regional needs (*Fédération Internationale*, 1930, no. 7, n.p.). American planners, engineers, architects and contractors were certainly familiar with the challenges posed by these kinds of projects, but Morgan and the other American delegates, in what some contractors called a 'new spirit of construction' (*Constructor*, 1929, **11**(2), p. 38) were trying to address the American building industry's deficiencies not only by venturing abroad as exporters of new American methods, but also by being better listeners, friendlier colleagues and wiser planners.

At the Fifth Congress, held in London, thirty-five nations were represented by 550 delegates, 300 of whom were British, 50 'British colonial' and 200 from (primarily) Europe and the United States (Greensfelder, 1930, p. 34). Except for 'British colonials', there were no representatives from Asia, only one from Africa (Tanganyika), one from the Middle East (Turkey), and one from Latin American (Uruguay). A decade earlier in the U.S., the NFCI's 'international' initiatives largely meant Europe (as a primary focus), with some attention paid particularly to both South America and Asia. Africa and the Middle East were *terrae incognitae*. In 1930 in London, 'international' for this Europe-based Federation implied collaboration within the broad sweep of Europe – from Yugoslavia to the Baltic and from western Russia to the Atlantic – with increasing eyes on the United States, 'British colonials' and a sprinkling of deference to other contexts. Eleven delegates from the U.S. attended the Congress,[3] which featured sessions on housing, research reports from individual countries, and rationalization – 'a subject', one of the American delegates prophetically predicted would 'receive

Figure 3.4. Delegates at the Fifth International Congress of Building and Public Works, in London's Central Hall, May, 1930. Meetings between contracting professionals such as this were helpful to American construction company executives because they could share information with peers, as well as learn some of their strategies. Upon returning to the U.S., American delegates tried, with varying results, to convince their colleagues at home to invest more time and money in foreign markets. (*Source*: Greensfelder, 1930, p. 34)

much attention in the construction industry in the coming years' (*Ibid.*, p. 35).

Both the NFCI and the International Federation demonstrated that in the early twentieth century (and as is still the case in the early twenty-first), engineers and architects often needed to work with contractors, other commercial agents and governments to achieve sometimes elusive construction goals. This was the case in 1899 with the Atbara Bridge; it proved to be critical shortly thereafter at the Panama Canal; and it persisted beyond World War I because of American capitalist enterprise and foreign clients who, as will be shown below, sought to learn how American builders were erecting 'monuments to the gods of business of trade' (Cody, 1996*a*). The increasing 'rationalization' of American contracting, both within U.S. borders and beyond, suggested that it would be wiser for export-oriented builders to adopt a comprehensive outlook toward possible ventures overseas, rather than move on an *ad hoc* basis. Implicitly, NFCI was suggesting that those in the building trades ready for adventures abroad should be daring and inventive, but careful and efficient; innovative and streamlined, but flexible and engaged for the long haul.

'Acquiring Mental Angles of Approach': the AIA's Foreign Relations Committee, 1920–1930

Between World War I and the Depression, many American architects seemed generally less well-prepared for practicing abroad than many of their counterparts in civil engineering, building contracting, or material exporting. There were certainly some notable exceptions (such as Frank Lloyd Wright in Japan, and others introduced below) but American architects often rode abroad cautiously on the coat tails of others in the building industries. In this regard, design and construction were dynamically interrelated activities (Strike, 1991). Architects such as Alfred Zucker in Buenos Aires brought his favoured steel framing technology with him from New York when, independent of direct corporate affiliation but still affected by his intimate familiarity with Milliken's practices, he ventured south. And at the NFCI's inception in 1918, some architects were rubbing elbows with contractors, even if the latter greatly outnumbered the former. As one architect noted,

there are four elements making up the personnel of this convention: the manufacturing, contracting, selling and professional . . . [and] seven-eighths of the members represent the [three first elements]. We [professionals] are in the great minority, but as [everyone] is aware, we architects are united in the one purpose of doing whatever we can in the winning of the war. (NFCI, 1918, Proceedings of First Conference, p. 20)

Laudable as that was, American architects found themselves moving more slowly than the other three 'elements' where international practice was concerned. The American Institute of Architects (AIA), U.S. architects' pre-eminent professional organization, established in 1867, was to some

extent sensitive to foreign contexts. After all, Richard Morris Hunt, the first American architect at the École des Beaux-Arts in Paris, was one of the founding members of the AIA. Furthermore, since so much of American architectural education was based upon European ideals and practices, it was only natural that Americans aspiring to be first-rate architects needed to be cognizant of non-American precedents, styles and forms. However, it was not until 1920 that the AIA formed a 'Foreign Building Cooperation Standing Committee', and that only lasted until the dawning of the deep Depression.

Judging by the AIA's membership lists at the beginning of World War I, there seemed to be few American architects practicing outside U.S. borders. In the 1914 *Annuary*, for example, only four members were listed as living at addresses beyond the continental U.S.: J. Edward Campbell, Mexico City; William Cresson, Quito; Antonio Nechodoma, San Juan, Puerto Rico; and Clinton Ripley, Honolulu. However, addresses could be deceptive. Some members, such as Henry K. Murphy, were practicing multi-nationally. Murphy received his AIA materials at his New York City office, but in 1914 he was visiting building sites for several months in China, Japan and Korea. Throughout much of his largely China-focused practice, in fact, he maintained his U.S. address and was listed in the AIA membership rolls as a New York-based architect. There were undoubtedly others like him, who began working abroad more actively after World War I but who did not want to cause problems with either their AIA membership status or their receipt of mail by changing their addresses to more exotic foreign cities. Also, some American-born architects practicing abroad decided not to join the AIA. This was apparently the case regarding Louis N. Thomas (introduced below) who practiced in Buenos Aires, as well as William Vories in Japan, Rowland Curry in China and probably others. However, data from the AIA's 'Honorary Corresponding members' list suggest that by 1914 'foreign' involvement related to the organization was wider than the full-fledged members' list suggests.

Table 3.1 AIA's Honorary Corresponding Members, 1914.

England	11
USA	7
France	6
Spain	3
Germany	3
Japan	3
Italy	2
Canada	1
Scotland	1
Holland	1
Russia	1
Mexico	1
TOTAL	40

(*Source:* AIA 1914 *Annuary*, p. 31)

By the end of the war, the AIA began to turn its attention more proactively to the myriad issues associated with practicing architecture abroad. In 1920 the Institute's twelve-member Foreign Building Cooperation Standing Commitee's actions reflect increasingly diverse challenges.[4] In 1921, for example, the Committee 'gathered together and shipped to France for exhibition a collection of drawings and photographs of American architecture' (AIA Proceedings, 1921, p. 156) but by 1923 there emerged a clear AIA focus on 'foreign' being equated primarily with architectural developments in Latin America, a tendency that persisted until about 1930. In 1923, at the Second Pan-American Congress of Architects in Santiago, Chile two AIA delegates (William Plack and Frank Watson) were among the sixty-five who attended from throughout the hemisphere. Their report to William Faville, AIA's President, about what they had learned there was both illuminating and prophetic:

No doubt the question will arise – what are the opportunities in South America for architects from the U.S.? The answer is a most difficult one, and would involve a much longer discussion than the space allotted will permit. However . . .

1. The ethical code under which the practice of architecture is conducted in South America are [*sic*] totally different from ours. In most cases the architect and builder are the same individual . . .

2. The ethics of competition are as yet unsettled. We found a keen interest in our methods.

3. Our conceptions are so absolutely different that it is impossible for the North American architect to have anything like the proper understanding of South American problems, until he takes up residence there, not of a week or month, but sufficiently long to acquire the languages and the mental angles of approach. Here again looms up the argument of the interchange of students. There is no doubt that there is a rapidly increasing open-mindedness towards North American ideas in architecture as well as other things, which is creating a demand and adding to this we have the ever-growing North American population living in South America.

We believe that *in time* [emphasis added] many agreeable and profitable associations may be affected by North American architects in South America, and by South American architects in North America. We consider this a matter of great interest to our young men. (AIA Foreign Relations Committee, folder 8, undated report)

Plack and Watson were sensitive to the need for American architects who wanted to practice successfully in South America to take the longer, more culturally rich road south of the border. They would have to develop 'mental angles of approach' which were at least as difficult to learn as Spanish or Portuguese. North Americans would face ethical challenges and unclarified competition logistics, Watson and Plack warned, but they would also find a receptive clientele and a rising demand for American materials and architectural know-how, as well as the potential for many 'agreeable and profitable associations'. The two North American delegates were witnessing first hand what many other trading experts were observing with increasing intensity, that 'New York's skyscrapers and the marvelous facilities for speeding up the life of that "magical city" have become, to many minds, a legend and a goal' (Klein, 1929b, p. 90; Cohen, 1995).

In 1925 Frank Watson became the Vice-Chairman of the AIA's Foreign Building Cooperation Committee, and in that position he again urged the AIA to nurture 'rapprochements' with Latin American visiting delegations, 'a contact which otherwise has not been developed at all' (AIA Proceedings, 1925, p. 49). A year later Watson continued the 'cordial relations with Latin American societies [that had been] so successfully established in recent years', in part by sending copies of AIA journals to the Presidents of four (unnamed) Latin American societies (AIA Proceedings, 1926, p. 119). In 1926 the Committee observed that because 'our foreign relations are becoming of increasing importance in our daily life, we need [AIA members'] assistance in carrying on our job' (Ibid.). And in 1927, when William Emerson chaired the Committee, he observed that 'we have to stretch ourselves considerably to meet the various types of demands made upon this Committee's time', which included hosting foreign visitors, organizing delegations of American architects to attend Pan American architectural congresses, and mounting exhibitions featuring American architecture for shipment to South America, Europe, Australia and New Zealand (AIA Proceedings, 1927, pp. 87, 164; 1928, p. 134). Watson and Emerson were feeling the effects of the

countless visits of delegations from foreign countries to our shores since the termination of the war. Some of these were motivated mainly by the desire to 'find out how we do it', so they might go home and introduce like methods in their factories. But many other delegations came on errands not intimately related to manufacturing processes, and their studies and observations have unquestionably rebounded to the benefit of our exporting industries. (Klein, 1929b, p. 90)

Throughout the 1920s, then, the activities of the AIA's Foreign Relations Committee proliferated. By 1927–28 more American architects had decided to practice abroad, especially in South America and East Asia. Two of the most notable Americans who settled in Latin America were both graduates of the University of Pennsylvania, William P. Preston (class of 1900) and John P. Curtis (class of 1909), who moved to Rio de Janeiro in 1927 to establish an office after receiving a U.S. government commission to design the U.S. Consulate there. A year earlier, in response to U.S. businessmen's complaints about the sad state of U.S. diplomatic missions abroad, Congress had passed the Porter Act, which created the Foreign Service Building Committee. This then directed a major, federally-financed building programme of U.S. embassies and consulates, which not only provided prestigious commissions for American architects, but also provided them with an alluring incentive to consider foreign settings where they might practice architecture (Loeffler, 1998, pp. 13–36). Therefore, beginning in the late-1920s one can find examples worldwide of the embassy as a building type being designed by many U.S. architects, some of whom (like Preston and Curtis) remained afterward to practice in the country where they had designed a building serving U.S. diplomatic missions.

In East Asia, American architects included not only Murphy, Vories and Curry but also several Americans working for these architects' practices, such as Elliott Hazzard and Edward Phillips who worked for Murphy in Shanghai. By the 1920s several other Americans were either working, or had worked as missionary architects in Asia. These included Paul Wiant in Fuzhou, China who helped create Mission Architects' Bureaus throughout the country. American architects likewise found work abroad because of the expansion of educational, charitable or philanthropic organizations, such as Yale-in-China, the YMCA and the Rockefeller Foundation's sponsorship of Peking Union Medical College. As U.S. cultural and religious influence became more pervasive throughout Asia in the 1920s, so too did the presence of American architects and builders who followed the lead of these clients.

Warren Laird, Dean of the University of Pennsylvania's School of Fine Arts, took great pride not only in Penn's American alumni such as Preston and Curtis, but also in the increasing numbers of foreign students, particularly from South America, who after attending Penn had returned to their native countries: Francisco Squirrú (class of 1915) and Renato Thierry (class of 1919) from Argentina; and Christiano das Neves (class of 1911) and Edgar Vianna (class of 1919) from Brazil, for example (Laird, 1928). Although Laird's emphasis here was on South America, he might have also mentioned the growing numbers of Americans practicing in Asia (Cody, 2001) as well as the significant contributions Penn was making during the 1910s and 1920s regarding the education of Chinese architects. Liang Sicheng (class of 1923) was probably the most famous of these students, because of his subsequent work in China as an architectural educator and historian, as well as his publications in English about China's historic architecture (Liang and Fairbank, 1987; Fairbank, 1994). However, besides Liang, there were several other noted Chinese architects who attended the University of Pennsylvania over the period 1911 to 1930. These included Yang Tingbao, Chen Zhi, Zhao Shen, and Lin Huiyin. They all were funded with scholarships from the Boxer Indemnity Fund, created with reparation money from the Chinese government after the 1900 Boxer Rebellion, and in Penn they found not only a high-quality curriculum, but also sensitive and caring professors, notably Paul Cret, one of the initial members of the AIA's Foreign Relations Committee. Chinese, South American and other foreign students attended other U.S. architectural schools – M.I.T., Cornell, the University of Illinois, Armour Institute of Technology (Chicago), the University of Minnesota – and they were instrumental in bringing American practices, standards and other influences back to their homelands as they acquired their own novel

'mental angles of approach' from their experience in U.S. programmes.[5]

Julius Klein's Four Key Questions

In 1929 – that fateful year which brought global economic calamities, just a few months before the Fifth Congress of the International Federation in London, and as the AIA's Foreign Relations Committee was reaching the peak of its activities – Julius Klein, a noted American exporting expert who had just served 9 years as the director of the Bureau of Foreign and Domestic Commerce,[6] confidently wrote that 'American industrial growth is in the main a matter of steadily advancing machine technique, of super-organization and of management engineering and equipment efficiency, all of which are factors of continued rapid advancement and change' (Klein, 1929a, p. 24). Klein believed that foreign trade was

an indicator of the general trend of our commercial and industrial growth . . . The nation's business men are becoming 'foreign trade minded', not through any emotionalism or flamboyant patrioteering, but simply because they have seen . . .the necessity of appraising and being guided by the practical dollar-and-cents value of this steadily strengthening contributor to our entire commercial well-being. (Ibid., pp. 141–142)

Shortly after writing these words, Klein witnessed Wall Street's stock market crash, which altered his prediction that 'it is no longer likely that [our commercial growth] will suffer hectic gyrations' (Ibid.).

During what Klein termed 'the dramatic decade' of 1919–1929, if American exporters wanted to succeed, they faced the challenge of how to adjust their businesses, products, finances and operating systems to new contexts. The challenge was equally daunting to clients abroad, who often needed to adapt to American standards as well. This challenge was clear to the NFCI, to the International Federation of Building and Public Works, and to the AIA's

Foreign Relations Committee. In Klein's words: 'Foreign markets . . . adaptability: the juxtaposition of these two words brings us to a consideration of certain important questions in connection with "world success" of our merchandise' (Klein, 1929*b*, p. 89). If architectural and building components represented some of that 'merchandise', then American exporters of architecture clearly needed to address the four main questions Klein posed for exporters a few months before the Depression:

1. To what extent are typical American commodities suited to the needs of remote regions of the earth?

2. What are some of the varying reactions toward them?

3. What influence on trade is exerted by deeply rooted customs, traditions, superstitions, physical peculiarities, distinctive environment, ingrained preferences and prejudices? [and]

4. Is it essential . . . to alter American merchandise to conform to those conditions – or else be compelled to abstain from participation in the market? (*Ibid.*)

Essentially, in this last question Klein was asking whether exporters wanted to take the shorter road to frustration or the longer road to reconciliation with local contexts. The two examples below illustrate at a more detailed level how American architectural exporters addressed Klein's compelling questions. These cases – building banks in commercial centres and exporting reinforced concrete technology – also exemplify the longer or shorter roads travelled by a diversifying cast of American characters who became enmeshed in architectural exporting before the Depression.

Taking the Longer Road: Building Banks in Argentina and China, 1917–1924

Klein's first question asked – long before American fast food franchises were established – how well-suited were 'typical American commodities' to non-Americans' diverse needs. One 'typical

American architectural commodity' was an up-to-date banking structure which, as a result of the Federal Reserve Act in 1913 and new investment possibilities, some U.S. banks began erecting in many financial centres worldwide by World War I.[7] Two examples of this trend, the First National Bank of Boston's headquarters in Buenos Aires and the International Banking Corporation's branch in Shanghai, illustrate how two major U.S. financial institutions exported 'citadels of commerce'[8] abroad during the 'dramatic decade' between the end of the war and the crashing of the stock market. They also suggest how American architecture was exported both as a set of technological systems and as cultural icons of economic power during this period.

In 1914 during an exploratory trip to Latin American cities after the passage of the Federal Reserve Act, Abbot Goodhue, one of the directors of the First National Bank of Boston targeted Buenos Aires because of the city's booming growth at the end of the nineteenth, and first two decades of the twentieth centuries (Gutiérrez and Tartarini, 1996, p. 20). Rich pasture and arable land fostered cattle-raising, wool production and grain growing. Railway expansion throughout the country as well as remarkable investments in urban infrastructure led several American companies to market their services and products there. In the late-1880s U.S. firms were exporting primarily timber and kerosene, but by the 1890s American contractors and engineers began to engage more actively in several Argentinian cities, where they competed with British, French and Italian interests (*Export and Finance*, 1889, **1**(6), p. 86). In 1898, for example, in a case curiously reminiscent of the Atbara Bridge, the Argentinian city of Córdoba hired American engineers and agents to build a hydroelectric dam and related structures along the Río Primero. 'The Córdoba Light and Power Company is the first purely North American company started in Argentina', one pro-U.S. journalist noted, 'and this fact makes us hope for its success, since nothing would assist the development of this country more than the addition of American pluck and energy to the perseverance and tenacity of British enterprise' (*American Exporter*, 1898, **41**(6), p. 30). A year later several American bridge and steel export companies were working in Buenos Aires, where they were installing electrical equipment and buildings for the Capital Tramway Company (*American Exporter*, 1899, **43**(5), p. 18). At the turn of the new century, as planners in Buenos Aires cut wide, Haussmannian-derived boulevards such as the Avenida de Mayo through the city centre, as streetcar networks proliferated and wharf structures rose at the Puerto Madero, Buenos Aires seemed poised for untrammelled growth.

In many ways Argentina was a 'ready market overseas' for American commercial agents, but some residents had also grown cynical of those North American businessmen who had used Argentina 'as a convenient place to dump goods when their domestic trade falls away rather than as a place in which to establish themselves firmly' (Joseph, 1918, p. 70). In other words, American exporters were too often taking the seemingly easier road to short-term gain instead of the deceptively harder road to long-term commitment. However, in 1917 this situation apparently began to improve, as 'the American exporter has commenced to make greater and more intelligent efforts to gain the confidence of the Latin American customer' (*Ibid.*, p. 78).

This was precisely when the First National Bank of Boston began its operations in Buenos Aires. In spring 1917 three directors of the Bank arrived in the city to formalize procedures for opening a branch office, which occurred in July 1917. But by 1920, with business mushrooming, the Bank realized that this branch was too small and it therefore purchased, only a block away from its earlier location, a larger lot on the Diagonal Norte at the corner of Calles Mitré and Flórida (Gutiérrez and Tartarini, 1996, p. 35). The Bank hired two architects who had cemented

a partnership after 1905: Paul Bell Chambers, born and trained in Britain, who had emigrated to Buenos Aires in 1896, and Louis Newbery Thomas, a U.S. native who had been raised in Argentina but received his architectural education at Brooklyn's Pratt Institute (class of 1897). Chambers and Thomas had a thriving practice when they were hired by the First National Bank of Boston and they were well qualified to handle many of the design challenges inherent in the commission, but the client also decided to employ a U.S.-based firm that specialized in banks. Edward York & Philip Sawyer, those partners who had worked with McKim, Mead & White in the 1890s before starting their own partnership in 1898, had just been hired by the Bank to design a new headquarters in central Boston.[9] For construction and engineering work related to the Buenos Aires structure, the Bank hired Stone & Webster, another prestigious American firm engaged on the Boston project (Keller, 1989, p. 155). Therefore three firms collaborated on the bank's design and construction.

Stylistically, the architects opted for a re-interpretation of Spanish 'Plateresque' architectural traditions, a contemporary trend toward articulating a 'national style' that had been prevalent in territories culturally tied to Spain since the beginning of the century. In the first years of the century Gaudi, Domenech y Montaner and other Catalan architects struggled with this challenge, and several U.S. architects (e.g., Bertram Goodhue, Julia Morgan, and Shepley, Rutan & Coolidge) likewise experimented with 'mission style' adaptations of Spanish traditions. In Buenos Aires, Chambers and Thomas were similarly experimenting with how to be respectful of Spanish traditions and yet distinctively up-to-date. Structurally, the Bank desired a steel-framed, well-functioning series of spaces that would meet North American standards. For 2 years the Bank, its architects and the municipality struggled with a series of possible solutions at the pivotal, but irregularly configured site.

Buenos Aires - Banco de Boston

Figure 3.5. Banco de Boston, Buenos Aires, 1921–1924, This branch of the First National Bank of Boston represented how hopeful contemporary U.S. bankers were about foreign trade with Latin America after World War I. The design and construction of this steel-frame edifice epitomized how consciously American architects and engineers tried to set a high standard for office construction in this booming metropolis. (*Source*: undated postcard)

Figures 3.6 and 3.7. Site plan and aerial view (*c.* 1950) of the Banco de Boston, showing its pivotal location at the corner of Calle Florida and Diagonal Norte, a prime intersection that attracted many commercial clients. (*Source*: Gutiérrez and Tartarini, 1996, pp. 36 and 103)

The banking structure began to rise in June 1921 and it was completed in October 1924. For the frame, Bethlehem steel was imported from the U.S., and the building was faced with Indiana limestone. Although local Portland cement was used, the Bank's bronze grilles, ceramic tiles, metal windows and all electrical equipment were brought from the U.S. (Gutiérrez and Tartarini, 1996, pp. 90–95). Journalists from New York and Boston, as well as from Buenos Aires itself, hailed the finished bank as a 'triumph of art and utility' and 'one of the best examples of North American bank architecture, that never before has been erected outside the United States' (*Ibid.*, p. 100). During succeeding decades, the Bank

Figure 3.8. Steel frame of the Banco de Boston being erected in 1921. The construction of this major commercial enterprise began 5 years after the death of Alfred Zucker (see Chapter 1), who would have been overjoyed to see an American high-rise being built in central Buenos Aires. (*Source*: Gutiérrez and Tartarini, 1996, p. 89)

Figure 3.10. The Banco de Boston as it appeared in 2000. (Photograph by the author)

of Boston became a safe financial haven for scores of American companies that operated in Argentina throughout both stability and turmoil.

An ocean away to the west, another North American bank was finding similar (and yet also distinctive) architectural, political and social challenges in establishing a long-term presence in Shanghai. Originally erected in 1906 between the Russo-Chinese Bank and Alfred Dent & Company, by 1908 the five-storey, former International Banking Corporation Building, 50 m behind Shanghai's Bund, was known as the 'International Bank' (Wright and Cartwright, 1908, p. 628). The building's eclectic massing, fenestration, and main façade details demonstrated its clients' and architects' late-nineteenth-century picturesque sensibilities.[10] In 1920 the building underwent architectural plastic surgery, as its main façade was classicized when the bank became part of a multi-national constellation of banking branch offices for the International Banking Corporation (hereafter IBC). Henry Murphy and architects in his Shanghai architectural office were the 'surgeons' who masterminded this transformation.

Figure 3.9. Main banking hall of the Banco de Boston, as seen in an undated contemporary photograph. York & Sawyer, an American architectural firm with an expertise in bank design, advised the Bank of Boston to use high-quality marble and brass to adorn the principal space for clients. (*Source:* Gutiérrez and Tartarini, 1996, p. 101)

Murphy began his China work in 1914 with Yale-in-China in Changsha (Hunan), Fudan University in Shanghai and Qinghua University in Beijing, and for 4 years he continued to elaborate these designs exclusively from his 'Oriental Department' in New

Figures 3.11 and 3.12. The International Banking Corporation (IBC) branch office in Shanghai, showing how it appeared before, *c.* 1908, and after its transformation by the architectural firm of Murphy & Dana in 1920. (*Source*: left: Wright and Cartwright, 1908, p. 628; right: photograph by the author, 1988)

York City. It was in this department that several young Chinese architects, such as Lu Yanzhi and Robert Fan, worked after graduation from American architectural programmes. In the 1920s, with help from these and other architects, Murphy designed several other significant campus plans in China, most notably Yenching University (today's Beijing University) and Ginling College for Girls (today's Shifan Daxue in Nanjing) that Murphy considered was part of an 'adaptive Chinese renaissance' which he was helping to foster (Cody, 2001). However, these glories were still well ahead of Murphy in Spring 1917 when he began to consider opening a Shanghai branch of his New York practice, which he shared with Richard Henry Dana. The partners, seeking a variety of new

commissions, were fortunate to find the favour of H.T. Green, President of the International Banking Corporation, who was responsible for deciding upon the nature of the Bank's expansion into China (*Number Eight*, 1926, **26**(10–11), p. 3; Lin, 1990; Starr, 2002). Between 1915 and 1921 the IBC established eighty-five foreign branches: fifty-six in Latin America, twelve in Europe and seventeen in Asia (Mayer, 1973; Phelps, 1927). During this period, when there was 'a flurry of American interest in China from Wall Street', President Woodrow Wilson, the U.S. Minister to China, Paul Reinsch, and several major U.S business executives negotiated assiduously with Chinese counterparts to broker a deal whereby U.S. commercial interests could be better promoted in

China, in part by virtue of the IBC (Pugach, 1997, pp. 19–23). It was in the context of this expansion that H.T. Green and his cohorts hired Murphy & Dana to design six IBC branches in China, all of them called Hua Qi Yinhang and all constructed between 1917 and 1923: Hankou and Beijing, 1917–18; Tianjin, 1918–21; Shanghai, 1920–22; Guangzhou, 1920–23 and Shenyang, 1923 (Mazuzan, 1974; Dayer, 1981; Israel, 1971; Cleveland and Huertas, 1985).

IBC executives entered the Chinese banking field at an opportune but challenging period of indigenous Chinese bank restructuring. The first Chinese republic was founded in 1912 after the toppling of the Qing empire, and China's first president, Yuan Shikai, began borrowing heavily. After 1914 two of China's principal banks (*yinhang*), Zhongguo Yinhang (est. 1913) and Jiaotong Yinhang (est. 1907) engaged in a rivalry to disburse loans to the government, which suffered a setback in 1916 when Yuan Shikai died. These important yinhang were not the only 'banks' that functioned in cities such as Shanghai; there were also several kinds of *qianbu* and *qianzhuang*, smaller operations than *yinhang* that held deposits and dispensed loans (McElderry, 1976, pp. 10–17). By 1916 in Shanghai wealthy Chinese found foreign banks a safe place for their funds. IBC joined several other foreign concerns, such as the Hong Kong & Shanghai Bank, the Banque de l'Indochine and Yokohama Specie Bank, trying to capitalize on their perceived shift in confidence from smaller local banks to nascent multinational ones. After World War I, when Shanghai was particularly well-situated for foreign investment, foreign banks profited handsomely (Bergère, 1986).

When IBC expanded to China, therefore, it was one of many players in a growing field of commerce, where it needed to distinguish itself architecturally. It did that by invoking on the façades of its China branches one of the bank's New York trademarks, colossal columns *in antis*. With so many variations of banking in Chinese cities, Western bankers assumed

Figure 3.13. The headquarters of the International Banking Corporation at 55 Wall Street, New York City. The architects used this imposing structure as an inspirational prototype, which was then whittled down when its key characteristics became trademark features of many of the firm's overseas branches. (Photograph courtesy of Rosetta Kwong)

they should emphatically convey in their branches cultural messages associated with stability and order. Each of IBC's China branches was a derivative of the IBC's headquarters at 55 Wall Street in New York, originally constructed in 1842 as the Merchants' Exchange and then re-designed in 1908 by McKim, Mead & White.[11]

Therefore, the redesigning of the Shanghai branch in 1920 was in keeping with the reworking of the bank's central offices 12 years earlier. One of the main exterior changes McKim, Mead & White made on Wall Street was to place two, superimposed rows of twelve colossal columns *in antis* on the bank's principal façade. In keeping with contemporary American tastes for monumental urban structures that boasted Classical Revival-style architectural vocabularies, they placed Corinthian columns above the Ionic, thus creating temple-like peristyles.

In China, the National City Bank clients and their architects both retained and deviated from the prototype on Wall Street. Each IBC in China was built of reinforced concrete, a technology that McKim, Mead & White had used in their renovation, but Murphy's firm then faced the branches in China with locally quarried granite and finished them with a cementicious stucco. The architects retained the idea of organizing the street façade with a row of columns *in antis* but budgetary constraints limited how many columns were used. The trade-off was that, once erected, they imparted an 'air of dignity and strength' to the structure.[12] The architects suggested that IBC buy its reinforcing steel from the U.S. Steel Products Export Company and employ the Fu Shing Engineering & Construction Company, one of the earliest contractors in the Chinese capital to adapt to this technology.

The *in antis* configuration of Western classical elements became an architectural trademark of the IBC in many of its Asian branches, part of the company's 'plan of uniformity' (*Number Eight*, 1924, **19**(11), p. 5). Murphy and those architects working for him in China also followed McKim, Mead & White's lead on Wall Street by placing attic stories above full entablatures on each branch office's principal façade. Another architectural advertisement for the bank derived from its logo. In New York, the bank had a flagpole for its standard that surmounted the two screens of columns on the main façade. In China, eyes were drawn to the initials 'IBC' that were scrolled in either stone or cement within a crest centred above the attic and angled down to the street. The IBC signature was also seen in iron as part of the exterior window grilles. In Hankou, the first IBC branch in

Figure 3.14. The Hankou branch of the International Banking Corporation. This building, on the waterfront of Hankou, China, was surmounted by a large globe (representing the global reach of the IBC in the 1920s), on top of which was an eagle, symbolizing the United States. (*Source*: Citicorp in China, 1988, p. 39)

China, the bank was located adjacent to the Hong Kong & Shanghai Bank, and perhaps because of that premium address, IBC dedicated more money for overt symbolic gestures, such as a sculpture of an American eagle resting atop two globes and centred on the main façade's parapet facing the Yangzi from the Hankou Bund (now demolished).

The Beijing IBC, constructed contemporaneously with the Hankou branch, also boasted a prominent address, 36 Dongjiaomingxiang, between the Russo-Asiatic Bank and Banque de l'Indochine in the fashionable Legation Quarter. The architects purchased reinforcing and stuccoing materials locally and used a local construction firm to build in conformity with New York City building codes, but some sub-contracting was managed by the Andersen & Meyer Company in Shanghai (Ferguson, 1931, pp. 73–83). In these first three designs for the IBC, the architects and client sought to reflect on the buildings' exteriors what they termed the monumentality, dignity and strength of the central offices in Manhattan (*Number Eight*, 1924, **19**(11), p. 5).

In Shanghai, where the bank's officers commissioned Murphy & Dana in 1920 to remodel their existing property on Jiujianglu, they had in mind a balance between warmth and power that could not be easily struck with the existing building's complexion, which was not in keeping with the more Beaux Arts-influenced, classical stance that IBC was trying to create. Because it was too expensive to demolish the existing building, the architects and client decided to gut the structure's ground floor and insert a series of free-standing colossal columns to articulate more clearly the kinds of Western banking spaces they desired. Outside, they attached a new, two-storey classical portico to the pre-existing façade. In the early-twentieth century, appropriating a temple front for a bank façade was conventional in North America or Europe and many bankers took for granted that since they were marketing banks' employees to be both counsellors and friends, the bank itself should adopt a classical style because then it would appear both familiar and authoritative (Hopkins, 1922). When the Hankou branch opened in March 1921 Western journalists remarked that it was 'modern, handsome, commodious, imposing and indicative of flourishing American commercial transactions in Hankou' (*Journal of the Association of Chinese and American Engineers*, 1920, **1**(2), p. 53).

Those transactions occurred within the Shanghai IBC building, too, where Murphy and his architects used Ionic or Corinthian pilasters and columns to emphasize the banks' solidity. These same Western elements divided the main building hall spatially while also imparting a sense of grandeur. Murphy's firm also inserted large skylights to illuminate the interior and highlight its richly-textured surfaces. The designers were trying to strike a balance between majesty and ostentation, to avoid conveying the wrong message that the bank was wasting its lenders' money. The operative tendency in the design of the IBC branches, then, was not only to recall the bank's Manhattan headquarters by virtue of stylistic elements (a reference doubtlessly lost upon some observers who missed the aesthetic connection),

but also to impart the main bank's steadfast virtues through architectural elements derived largely from Greece and Rome (Booker, 1990; Gibbs, 1984).

If these banks were to be didactically 'read' as symbols of U.S. dignity and poise, then how well or how appropriately did Chinese contemporaries read them? Some Chinese contemporaries were pleased with Western-style architectural façades that provided a background that they deemed appropriate for social or commercial interactions between Chinese entrepreneurs and Western investors. Other Chinese sometimes interpreted Greek, Roman or Renaissance Revival-style architecture as objects that reflected comparatively positive values of Western versus Chinese ideologies (Fruehauf, 1993). Most Chinese contemporaries remained mute in their opinions about the foreign-style icons (Cody, 2000). The Chinese who experienced the banks most directly were primarily those engaging in commercial activities. However, the Chinese would have probably 'read' the building according to their own familiarity with, or ignorance of the foreigners' intentions to create a 'dignified or strong' structure. *Maiban*, Chinese commercial go-betweens who functioned within some of the building's spaces, would have read the IBC buildings differently than those who simply glimpsed the bank's façades from the exterior. This was similar to the situation a generation earlier in North American contexts when skyscrapers first appeared (Domosh, 1996; Moudry, 1995).

Another way to convey stability and order for both Chinese and Western users of the bank was not only through the ornamental qualities of spaces, but also through the careful division of functions within the architectural envelope. How, then, were these functions clarified? The answer, primarily seen in the buildings' plans, is that they functioned as separate and unequal corporate entities. The main banking floor was reserved primarily for foreign clients who entered the bank through its central door on the principal façade, passed through a vestibule, and transacted their business by talking to banking officials in the open, where they could be seen by fellow business associates. On the other hand, Chinese clients (*maiban* and others) entered the building via a side alley and conducted their business behind the main banking spectacle in less generous spaces, so they were not so easily seen by Western patrons.

The architectural plans, then, indicate that the banks' architecture ratified not only social stratification but also at least partial commercial segregation. Many Western bankers took for granted the desirability of this separation, even if they sometimes tried to ignore social stratification and, in theory, treat everyone as being equal. The separation was further indicated by how residential quarters were allocated. In some of the branches, for example at the Beijing IBC, the bank manager and his foreign staff lived in apartments located in the bank's upper storeys, a practice found in other contemporary banks in China (Hietkamp, 1998). The apartments had verandahs, 'modern sanitation' and were 'fitted up in accordance with the best American practice'. However, Chinese servants lived in detached, simpler, 'special buildings' behind the main banking structure (*Far Eastern Review*, 1919, **15**(7), p. 514). *Maiban* lived even further removed from the bank, often in Western-style villas or apartments.

The IBC's presence in Shanghai was potent and yet restrained, an echo of Wall Street and yet absent from Shanghai's prime commercial Bund, a palace of commercial security for American businessmen and yet a house divided when it came to Chinese patrons. In a climate where U.S. commercial interests were adopting a strategy of greater involvement with China, the bank's managers decided to transplant a Western classical vocabulary into a foreign concession area where that vocabulary was already being spoken. In that way the bank could be both consistent with its home-based architectural

programme and yet surreptitious in its new guise as one of Shanghai's power-sharing and power-wielding commercial anchors.

The IBC strove for a middle ground off the Bund in four ways. First, it was located in both an older building but also one that, thanks to a capable series of architects, had a new classical cachet that belied the building's turn-of-the-century eclecticism. Second, that classicism was tied to the world that many Westerners called 'Old' – Greece and Rome – but there were also elements of the so-called 'New' world that fit convincingly in the bank's spaces – eagles, flags and dollars. Third, this was a U.S.

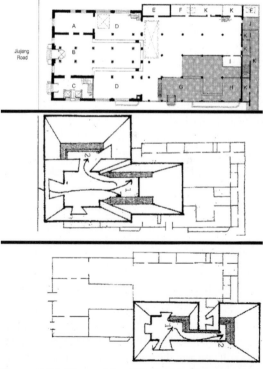

Figure 3.15. Plans of the IBC Shanghai branch, which show how Chinese clients used side entrances and dealt with officers at the rear of the main hall, while non-Chinese customers used the main entrance. This racial segregation, confirmed in the bank's layout, reflects one of the ways that the original prototype was altered in the process of being transplanted abroad. (*Source*: Cody, 1999a, p. 342)

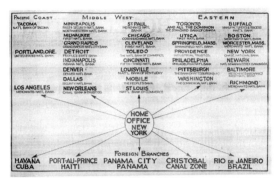

Figure 3.16. Graphic showing 'World Wide Foreign Trade Service'. This diagram of the American Foreign Banking Corporation demonstrates how its home office served as a fulcrum between geographically dispersed domestic U.S. banks and a small constellation of foreign branches in Central and South America. (*Source*: American Foreign Banking Corporation, 1919, *American Exporter*, **84**(3), p. 181)

bank and yet it was spatially linked to the Bund, a place usually associated with Europe. Shanghai was the Paris (not the New York) of the Orient. Finally, it invited foreign clients through its central portal, but also welcomed Chinese patrons through a side door into less grandiose spaces. The former bank is one of myriad artefacts of globalizing economic power that characterized pre-1949 Shanghai, foreshadowing more recent trends.

These two examples of American banking expansion abroad during the 1920s suggest how architecture often ratified American commercial power. These 'citadels of commerce' were steel-framed towers that symbolized the growing ascendancy of the dollar as a major global currency. Structurally, they embodied the literal rise of steel. Semiotically, they imparted the palpable strength of money. If one uses these banks to answer Klein's four questions, a summary might be:

1. To what extent were the banks, as typical American commodities, suited to the needs of Argentina and Shanghai? Answering this depends upon how one defines 'needs'. As capitalist investors in these cities were searching for safe havens in which to place

capital, the banks served their needs well. The shell of the architecture complemented the substance of the functions performed within. However, as the IBC was being completed, the Chinese Communist Party was being founded a few hundred metres away. The bank as an icon of foreign domination served other needs in that case. This, then, helps answer Klein's second question:

2. What were some of the varying reactions toward the 'typical American commodities'?

3. What influence on trade is exerted by deeply rooted customs, traditions, superstitions, physical peculiarities, distinctive environment, ingrained preferences and prejudices? As the IBC case showed, racial prejudices were to some extent confirmed by the bank's plan, and local contractors were trained to build an up-to-date structure according to New York City building codes. However, these effects were more long lasting in a construction sense than they were regarding trade *per se*. Contractors learned new skills and added them to their repertoire. The banks, then, helped set significant precedents.

4. Was it essential to alter American merchandise to conform to the conditions in question 3? To some extent, yes, because not all parts of the new structures could be imported from the U.S., and it was often more economical to employ locally-based contractors instead of paying the considerable expenses of bringing teams of American-based workers.

Taking the Shorter Road: the Fuller Construction Company of the Orient, 1920–1926

The Bank of Boston and IBC's longevity in their respective cities is a measure of their tenacity in the face of dramatic political and social changes in the past 80 years. The long road of each bank continues to this day. However, in the case of the

Fuller Construction of the Orient, the road taken was much shorter – six remarkable years – which nonetheless had far-reaching implications for Japan, the country where (simultaneously with the IBC and Bank of Boston cases) Fuller tried to export its version of American architecture.

The first American builders began teaching and practicing in Japan after the creation of the Ministry of Technology in 1870. They were three in number: William Wheeler, a professor of civil engineering at Sapporo College; Horace Capron, who opened an architectural practice in Hokkaido; and N.W. Holt, Capron's partner and a specialist in American balloon frame construction (Koshino, 1979, pp. 124–126). As early as 1885 some Japanese clients expressed a preference for American steel bridge design, and by the late-1890s American civil engineers were building examples of these bridges using American steel products (Calhoun, 1973, p. 299; Finn, 1995, p. 146; Wadell, 1897). In 1897 the Japanese Weather Bureau hired the American architect W.J. Bond to design a steel-framed edifice patterned after the St. Paul Building in New York, 'the first structure over three stories high ever yet erected in the Orient' (*American Exporter*, 1897, **40**, September, p. 24; Finn, 1995, p. 191). In 1908 the American missionary architect William Merrell Vories founded the Omi Brotherhood in Omi Hachiman, where he practiced architecture until 1943, constructing hundreds of buildings throughout Japan (Vories, 1931; Thomas, 1937). In 1911, when many Japanese contractors were intrigued by the construction in Yokohama of a reinforced concrete building by the Mitsubishi Company, they 'anticipated that important further development in this kind of building will follow' (*American Exporter*, 1912, **69**, March, n.p.). This proved to be accurate. Certainly one of the most famous of all such buildings was the Imperial Hotel, constructed between 1916 and 1922 by Frank Lloyd Wright.

However, with respect to building technology transfer, American construction companies were as important as university teachers or practicing architects. After World War I one of the most important of these firms, which taught Japanese builders on site how to erect reinforced concrete and steel-framed structures, was the George A. Fuller Construction Company of the Orient, Ltd. The company was a branch of the main Fuller Company which, in the early twentieth century, many contemporaries believed to be the most prominent American construction company. Founded in Chicago in 1882 and incorporated in New Jersey in 1901 early noteworthy examples of the firm's work in New York City were the Flatiron Building, Pennsylvania Station, Wall Street Exchange, the National City Bank and the Plaza Hotel (Daly, 1957). In Chicago the company erected the Tacoma Building and the Monadnock Building. Other major North American cities also featured Fuller Company buildings (*Fireproof Building Construction*, 1910). The Fuller Company was one of the first U.S. construction companies to rationalize its operations by creating in-house departments (e.g., bricklaying, carpentry or painting), rather than following the standard American practice of hiring sub-contractors from other companies once it had secured a bid. One result of this streamlining was that Fuller could complete a building in much less time, and for significantly less money than other builders. Furthermore, tradesmen enjoyed working for the company because Fuller provided steady employment, paid wages promptly, remedied grievances effectively and took on-site safety measures more seriously than other companies (Commons, 1903–04). By 1920 the company claimed it was the world's largest construction company, with executive offices in New York, Boston, Chicago, Philadelphia, Washington, Miami and Montreal. It later boasted that it had helped meet 'the problems of American expansion' and that that expansion occurred as 'the drive of the people gained more scientific guidance by the turn of the century and especially after World War I' (George A. Fuller Co., 1952).

An unexpected aspect of 'American expansion' after World War I became evident to Fuller Company executives such as Paul Starrett and William S. Black when, in 1919, they were contacted by a small delegation of Japanese businessmen. The group included Baron Shibusawa, a member of the government who had already demonstrated a keen interest in promoting projects exemplifying municipal progress (*Engineering-News Record*, 1922, **89**, September 21, p. 476), and executives from the Nippon Oil Company, the Nippon Yusen Kaisha (Japan Mail Steamship Company), and the Mitsubishi Banking Company.

This delegation crossed the threshold of the Fuller Company offices because of Japan's increasing prominence in trade, as a result of World War I. Japan had emerged from the war with 'a vast amount of world trade at her door [but with] an acute shortage of buildings to house her increased business' (*Far Eastern Review*, 1922, **18**, October, p. 638). Some of that business was generated as a result of the city planning initiatives of the influential Viscount Shimpei Goto, who had visited the United States at the end the war to examine the means by which American municipal experts were seeking to improve American cities using city planning methods associated with 'science' and/or 'efficiency'. When Goto visited the New York Bureau of Municipal Research he became close friends with Charles Austin Beard, the noted political economist. On his return to Japan he advocated that his government invest heavily in the construction of roads, railways and other municipal infrastructure (Zunz, 1998, p. 41). In the U.S. Goto had also seen first hand some of the high-rise office towers that were beginning to capture the world's attention. When he measured his own country's commercial architecture against that of American cities, he judged Japanese office buildings to be both stylistically and technically insufficient. Goto therefore proposed that Japan send a team of statesmen and businessmen to America, not only to see for themselves what dramatic changes

were occurring in American cities, but also to find an American construction company that would transfer some of its technical expertise to willing Japanese workers. The Fuller Company was the delegation's choice. The Japanese clients asked Paul Starrett and William Black if the Fuller Company would be interested in sending a team of engineers and builders to Japan to erect two, and possibly more office buildings on the American model.

They had chosen two Tokyo sites where Fuller could erect seven-storey buildings to serve as object lessons. One was to be a structure of 200,000 square feet on a 160-foot square site for the Nippon Oil Company and the other of 300,000 square feet on a 160 foot by 190 foot site for the Mail Steamship Company.

This latter site was to be in the Marunouchi district, a particularly significant location near the central railroad station and in front of the Imperial Palace and Diet. It was here that in 1886 the German architect Wilhelm Boeckmann had been asked by the Japanese government to plan a grand, axial entry to the Palace, and although Boeckmann's scheme was never realized, the question of how the Marunouchi area might help set the character of a modernizing Japan remained paramount in the minds of many Japanese businessmen (Finn, 1995, p. 93). Shortly after the Mail Steamship Company hired Fuller, so too did the Mitsubishi Company, which had acquired a 350 foot by 300 foot site adjacent to that of the Mail Steamship Company. The Mitsubishi Company's eight-storey building, known as the Marubiru, became Asia's largest office building in 1921 with a rentable floor area of 632,000 square feet (*Far Eastern Review*, 1921, **17**, p. 819).

By hiring the Fuller Company to build three such imposing structures in the Marunouchi district, these corporate clients were demonstrating that it was in this district that the heart of a trade and business-oriented Japan should be located. Soon thereafter, a fourth commission was added when Brunner, Mond

& Company asked Fuller to construct the Crescent Building in Kobe; it was to be a reinforced concrete frame structure with long-span floor tile arches. The Japanese team had determined that because 'American business buildings are superior to all others', it was necessary to find 'the best brains in the business of erecting monuments of steel, concrete and granite dedicated to the god of business and trade' (*Far Eastern Review*, 1922, **18**, p. 638). Four monuments to that god were conceptually on the drawing boards; now the task was to mobilize the 'best brains in the business' to erect them.

One of those who became most influential in the construction of the four buildings was William A. Starrett, an architect, engineer and member of a dynasty of American construction experts in the early twentieth century. William's third brother, Paul, became president of the Fuller Company in 1903. Between 1901 and 1919 William Starrett proved himself to be an accomplished engineer, a military commander in World War I, and a capable construction manager of projects in several cities of Canada and the United States. In March 1919, when

Figure 3.17. Nippon Oil Company, Tokyo. This commission, one of the three that lured the Fuller Construction Company to begin working in Japan in the early 1920s, became an object lesson for Japanese contractors keen to understand how to erect up-to-date American high-rises in East Asia. (*Source: Far Eastern Review*, 1922, **18**(10), p. 640)

he was released from the U.S. Army, Paul Starrett and William S. Black, agreed that William Starrett should be Fuller's chief emissary to Japan.[13]

When William Starrett ventured to Japan for three weeks in the summer of 1919 he was surprised by what he saw.

[One can see] the same stodgy European types [of business buildings] of fifty years ago – stolid stone, iron-shuttered warehouses, with beams projecting from above loft openings, after the manner of our merchant ancestors who traded from old India House . . . [There are] sometimes a few modern jimcracks, the offering of enterprising American commercial agents, but essentially [they are] the same types introduced into Japan nearly a century ago. (Starrett, 1923)

Starrett was struck by a seeming stagnancy in the contemporary architecture of Japan, even though after the Meiji Restoration of 1868 many Japanese became more interested in adapting foreign technology to Japanese needs. The 1870s was a particularly fertile period of cross-cultural transfer of engineering knowledge between Victorian Britain and Meiji Japan. In 1870 a Ministry of Technology was created, and from 1876 to 1888, for example, Josiah Conder from Britain became the first instructor of architecture at Japan's Imperial College and in the 1880s Japanese architectural students began to travel to Europe and North America. However,

Figure 3.18. When the Marunouchi Building (also known as the Marubiru) was completed in 1923 – just before the Great Kanto Earthquake which devastated Tokyo – it was the largest building in Asia. The Fuller Construction Company shepherded the project to completion, but subsequently decided to leave Japan and return to more secure turf in North America. (*Source: Far Eastern Review*, 1921, **17**(12), p. 819)

after these young architects returned to Japan, they seemed unable to move beyond what William Starrett characterized as a kind of 'banal' architecture that generated 'thick exterior walls ... [and] cumbersome interior cross walls, all in a country of soft and soggy bottoms, where lightness of construction and scientific engineering should have been the first consideration' (Brock, 1981). Starrett theorized that one reason the Japanese architects had not managed to overcome banality was that, upon their return from foreign schools, they had been unable to collaborate with structural engineers, as American architects had done when they returned from European stints:

to gain and apply that structural skill which was then fast being whipped into a science – a science which might literally be said to have been developed almost in a decade by contemporary American constructors leading the world in the art of building. (Starrett, 1923)

One of those leaders was William Starrett's brother, the Fuller Company President Paul Starrett. In New York he was enticed by these design opportunities, but he was also perplexed by how to set up an efficient subsidiary venture of his company in distant Tokyo. To handle initial administrative details, he turned to James Lee Kauffman, a partner in the law firm of Melvor, Kauffman, Smith & Yamamoto. Kauffman and Starrett set up a separate corporate entity to operate in Japan: the Fuller Construction Company of the Orient, Ltd. This subsidiary became yet another department of the company, similar to those Paul Starrett and other Fuller executives had created less than 20 years earlier when the company had so successfully crafted a conglomerate corporate structure based upon departments organized by construction trades.

In addition to his brother William, who had returned to New York by October 1919, Paul Starrett selected a team of nine other Fuller employees to serve as the core of the new venture. H.A. Harris, who had already logged 15 years with Fuller, was named Vice President and Managing Director of the new, wholly-owned subsidiary company. G.H. Norris was appointed as outside superintendent of construction, J.H. Morgan as chief architect, Paul Wunderlich as mechanical engineer, Robert Trimble as assistant manager of construction, Samuel C. Bartlett, Jr as interpreter and traffic manager, and three others as clerical staff. In January 1920 this team sailed from San Francisco to Japan to focus on the logistical details associated with erecting the first four 'monuments to the god of business and trade'. William Starrett remained in New York, becoming the chief liaison with Harris and the other Americans employed by him.

Meanwhile, in Japan the corporate clients of those four buildings had begun hiring architects to create detailed design documents for the Fuller team. The Tokyo-based architectural firm of Sone-Chujo was selected to design both the Nippon Oil Company building and the one for the Nippon Yusen Kaisha. Sone-Chujo was chosen in part because of highly-praised work the firm had done for the Tokyo-Taisho Exhibition at Ueno, Tokyo in 1914. The clients specified to Sone-Chujo that the materials for both structures should be 'skeleton-type structural steel, with reinforced concrete floors, and main façades treated with native granite and stone, and architectural terra cotta' (*Japan Advertiser*, 1920, 14 May, p. 2). The Marunouchi Office Building (Marubiru) for the Mitsubishi Goshi Kaisha was designed by the Mitsubishi Corporation's own architects in its Real Estate Section (Stewart, 1987, p. 114). Fuller's architect, J.H. Morgan, designed Brunner, Mond & Company's Crescent Building in Kobe.

In the early phase of the Fuller venture in Japan, from late 1919 through 1921, some of the commercial aspects of the construction work were resolved with relative ease. Kauffman handled the bilateral legal details and Fuller's construction experts began to collaborate with their Japanese clients and architects. However, more daunting problems of a technical

Figures 3.19 and 3-20. In the early 1920s, Japanese indigenous construction practices – with 'native pile driving rigs' and 'native women pile drivers' – were baffling to Fuller Company foremen who were teaching crews of workers as well as supervising the erection of a high-rise that met U.S. construction standards. (*Source: Scribner's Magazine*, 1923, **74**(3))

nature arose almost immediately. The four main construction challenges were: (1) how to build a proper foundation; (2) how to transport materials to the sites; (3) how to organize and train the workers at those sites; and (4) how to erect suitable scaffolding. William Starrett explained some of the logistical realities by saying that

[although] it is easy to stand in a Japanese city and visualize a Woolworth Building or a Boston Public Library on any corner, it is a very different matter to construct out there a modern structure, to marshal the leadership and instruct the native labor, to organize where no organization exists, to translate drawings from shaku and meters to feet and inches, and accurate notations from Japanese to English. These are only a few of the problems. (Starrett, 1923, p. 275)

The Fuller team set out to resolve them.

One of the first site investigations the Fuller engineers conducted was to determine the geological profile by specifying the depth of the soft silt that characterized much of Tokyo's soil. The structural steel and reinforced concrete had to rest on a suitable foundation. The Japanese delegation had been impressed by Fuller's use of pneumatic caissons in erecting foundations. In contemporary Tokyo, foundations were commonly constructed by sinking thin, short, wooden piles using large hammers handled exclusively by women labourers.

William Starrett thought it was picturesque but inefficient to see 'gangs of women, each pulling on a separate rope that leads to the main line used to raise the weight. They chant, heaving in unison, and at a signal let go together, releasing the hammer' (*Ibid.*, p. 280). Before changing this method to American caissons, the Fuller engineers sank borings; however, they forlornly discovered that they hit 'hard-pan' a deep 60 feet below surface. They therefore attempted an open-caisson method, although this solution also proved elusive.

One of the features of the scheme was the use of a diving outfit, to be worn by the workman who would dig at the bottom of the caisson. Unfortunately, when the caisson 'dropped,' the workman in his diving suit was apt to be catapulted up and out of the caisson, paraphernalia and all. A workman was found who could actually stand this ordeal, but the hazard was very great, however commendable his willingness; and since the operation in hand would require some hundreds of caissons, it was deemed advisable to adopt some speedier and surer method than one depending on the genial willingness of this aquatic virtuoso. (*Ibid.*, p. 276)

The answer proved to be importing 13,000 wooden piles from Oregon, capping them with concrete, and then sinking them with steam pile-drivers (not using the gangs of chanting Japanese women), an operation which Starrett exclaimed 'rent the calm of Tokyo for three months'.

Transporting the 13,000 piles and other building materials to the four sites was a second technical hurdle. In keeping with the Fuller Company's rationalized approach to construction, Starrett believed that 'building [was the] accumulation in an orderly sequence of a variety of things of great and small weight' (*Ibid.*, p. 279). He affirmed that carriers and traffic were fundamental to the task, and that in the U.S. recently-invented construction machinery had rendered more manageable the formidable tasks associated with transporting heavy materials to a building site. These conveniences included motorized trucks that rolled on wide macadamized roads, as well as derricks, cranes and steam shovels.

To erect the four buildings, Fuller transported to Tokyo 11,000 tons of structural steel for columns, girders and boilers; twenty-five elevators; 1,300 tons of ornamental terra cotta and 82 miles of plumbing pipe. This material was unloaded at Shibaura, in Tokyo Bay, and then stored in a common yard before being dispatched to the sites.

Since Japan was still labouring, Starrett said, with a 'one-man-power unit' on narrow streets, with light bridges and shallow waterways, the transporting of heavy building materials posed a problem of great magnitude. The solution to that problem was to use 'bullock carts' in conjunction with motorized trucks. However, the Japanese police force was nervous because of what damage those trucks and their cargo might inflict on recently constructed roads, not to mention the traffic problems that the laden, slow-moving vehicles posed. Starrett observed that

the landing of a ten-ton column made in Pittsburgh, at the job site in Japan, after all the interminable tribulations that these difficuties induce, is a triumph that savors of victory; and even the picturesqueness of the bullock-carts, pressed into service for the unusual task, is not lost on these practical Americans who have planned and worried, and finally succeeded in this adventure. (*Ibid.*, p. 280)

Figures 3.21 and 3.22. The transporting by truck of massive steel structural members through Tokyo's streets was an awe-inspiring sight for many onlookers. Japanese who got closer to the construction process, such as these riveters, came to understand the logic behind the surprises and eventually mastered the initially alien ways of the American builders. (*Source: Scribner's Magazine*, 1923, **74**(3))

A third problem concerned how to envelope the building site and how to gain proper access to the rising building during construction. Traditionally, a Japanese tall building would have been erected with the aid of pole scaffolding encased in reed matting. The Japanese expressed four rationales for using this cage-like structure: (1) it was cheap and effective; (2) it prevented the architect from seeing his designs until completion; (3) it shielded the Emperor from being offended by seeing an unfinished structure; and (4) it protected passers-by from being harmed by falling building materials. The Fuller builders were not convinced by these reasons. They insisted on using metal 'patent scaffolding' in the accustomed American fashion, which required them to convince the police that this imported method of accessing the structure would be safe. Onlookers stared in amazement as the steel skeletons of the monuments to the god of business and trade rose skyward without the characteristic reed matting. After some initial scepticism, the workers became content with the stability of the hanging scaffolds, and even the police relented, after 'twigging the wire cables and tapping them with their swords' (*Ibid.*, p. 284).

Finally, a fourth problem concerned how to resolve the two labour-related problems simultaneously. The first one related to the imparting of new construction skills, such as the mastery of power-driven riveting guns, taking measurements accurately, and the application of plaster finishes.

The other problem related to the inculcating of new labour concepts, such as the idea that 'each man does only a part and a group must work to a predetermined plan'. Traditionally, Japanese workers were organized into guilds and directed by bosses who Starrett characterized as 'childish, stubborn, crafty, cunning, but generally industrious and responsive to intelligent leadership' (*Ibid.*, p. 280). Foreign builders of the Fuller Construction Company of the Orient came to respect the work of the 'nimble' Japanese carpenters working with

'curious tools' to produce 'the world's most exquisite woodwork'. They marvelled at the quality of the lithic ornamental details carved by Japanese stone masons. As Starrett saw it, the main problem was that despite their group nature, guilds perpetuated what he called the 'one-man-power standard', or in the case of the pile-drivers, a one-woman standard. In other words, although a builder might be skilled in many tasks so that he might complete a structure from start to finish, that same builder had not been trained in systematized construction work that was the hallmark of the American approach. The transplanting of construction skills from the American builders to their Japanese counterparts was, therefore, not as straightforward as it had appeared from the outset. 'Constant vigilance by a corps of engineers' was needed, as virtually the entire indigenous labouring process was transformed into a Western-driven 'system', along the lines of factory production rationalized by American theorists such as Frederick Taylor (*Ibid.*, p. 283).

The vigilance required by the foreign supervisors was both satisfying and stressful. Between Spring 1920 and Fall 1922 the Fuller Construction Company of the Orient met these four challenges simultaneously at their work-sites, each of which became 'schools for native Japanese engineers and architects throughout the empire' (*Far Eastern Review*, 1922, **18**, p. 638). All four buildings were completed by mid-1923. One result of these 'schools' was that Japanese companies themselves began to market their abilities to construct steel-frame and reinforced concrete buildings on the Western model, in so doing ultimately becoming competitors of Fuller. Two of Japan's oldest contracting firms, Shimuzu Gumi and Obayashi Gumi, were the first to tout their newly-acquired skills. As the Fuller builders were directing the two projects in the Marunouchi district, Shimuzu Gumi acquired the contract for a steel-framed structure for the Bank of Chosen and another for the Katakura Raw Silk Spinning

Company. Obayashi Gumi followed suit by raising a similar, American-style, steel-framed structure for the Nippon Kogyo Bank (*Far Eastern Review*, 1922, **18**, pp. 685–687). Fuller also began to make successful bids on future commissions, which caused further consternation among the Japanese builders, who feared that Fuller might be getting too prosperous (*Far Eastern Review*, 1924, **20**, p. 28).

The largest of these new jobs was the Mantetsu General Hospital at Dairen (Dalian), China, designed by the Japanese architect T. Onogi for the Southern Manchurian Railway Company. To ease logistical concerns, in December 1922 Fuller sent Wilbur S. Sample from New York to head a team of eight architects and engineers who lived near the site during construction. Grading work and excavation commenced on April 10, 1923, two weeks after a Shinto ritual consecrated the ground before construction. The first concrete for the foundation was laid in early May and by November 1923 approximately one-half of the building was completed, although it was not until 1926 that it was finally complete, 2 years behind schedule (*Far Eastern Review*, 1922, **18**, p. 608).

Construction conditions in a Chinese region under intensifying Japanese influence were different from those in metropolitan Japan. Nine hundred Chinese carpenters, blacksmiths, masons and concrete mixers were employed to work with Japanese foremen. A new railway line had to be constructed to transport building materials, most of which came from Japan, but timber was brought from the Chinese city of Changchun. Reinforcing bars, boilers and hardware were imported from the U.S. The Fuller Company's shift to China and the delays that resulted there, as well as some grumbling from Japanese contracting executives, suggested that by 1923 commercial and social difficulties were equalling the technical problems the company had first faced when it began working in Tokyo and Kobe.

There were three additional complications. First,

Figure 3.23. Mantetsu General Hospital, Dairen (today's Dalian), China, erected from 1923 to 1926. This project was also supervised by the Fuller Construction of the Orient, but it became the last commission undertaken by the firm before its dissolution, leaving behind this imposing structure. (*Source: Far Eastern Review*, 1923, **19**(4), p. 249)

Fuller managers in 1923 reported that 'the outlook for new business in Japan is not very bright . . . [because most new business] prospects have either been abandoned or postponed' (George A. Fuller Company, 1923, pp. 7–8). The god of business and trade seemed to be dormant. Furthermore, those future buildings to be erected would be competitively bid with those same Japanese contractors who were irked that Fuller had been awarded the Mantetsu project.

The second complication was that Fuller's first managing director in Japan, H.A. Harris, a man of great 'energy, experience and ability', decided to retire once the first four buildings were completed. Harris's retirement coincided with the departure from Fuller of Paul Starrett, who had served as President of the company for 19 years, and who left to create a new construction company with his brother William and Andrew Eken – Starrett Brothers & Eken Company – the company that won the construction contract in 1929 for the Empire State Building (Starrett, 1928).

In New York, after Paul and William Starrett resigned from the Fuller Company, William Oehrle became the new liaison manager for the firm's Japanese work. In Japan, Harris was replaced by James Lee Kauffman, the lawyer who had helped Paul and William Starrett establish the Fuller

Construction Company of the Orient in 1919. In the 3 years of Harris's tenure as Managing Director, the number of Fuller Company personnel in Tokyo increased from an initial nine to as many as twenty-eight in early 1922. However, during 1922 that number dropped to seventeen, a sign of Fuller's downsizing and wavering commitment towards remaining in Japan.

And then came the third and most unpredictable complication: the Great Kanto Earthquake on 1 September, 1923. Understandably, many looked carefully at how the four Fuller Company buildings had withstood the quake. Although they had suffered 'considerable surface damage, which gave rise to some criticism of [the company]', the buildings' structure had endured the earthquake in relatively good condition (George A. Fuller Company, 1924, p. 5). However, in the aftermath of the quake, business prospects in Japan continued to be uncertain. The main office of the Fuller Company in New York began to experience fiscal difficulties subsequent to Paul Starrett's departure as President, leading to a decision by the company's new executives in New York to close down the subsidiary in Japan. They moved a smaller contingent of builders to Manchuria, and then left East Asia entirely once the Mantetsu Hospital job was completed in 1926.

By 1926 it was clear the Fuller Company venture in Japan and China had made an impact. First, as Viscount Shimpei Goto had hoped would happen, Japanese companies had learned from Fuller's object lessons and were well on their way to adapting steel-frame and reinforced concrete technologies to the building market of contemporary Japan (*New York Times*, 1924, 13 January, IX, p. 2; Dan, 1932). As a result of the 1923 earthquake and concomitant changes in Tokyo's building laws, engineers invented ways to resist earthquake damage, including steel latticed columns with supplementary corner angles, double girders and diagonal braces between floors (Pickworth and Weiskopf, 1927). Tokyo's

built environment after the 1923 earthquake was qualitatively different from what it had been before. The reinforced concrete die was cast and the steel frame was increasingly popular, due in no small measure to the construction lessons that Japanese engineers, architects and contractors had learned from the Fuller Company foreigners (Siedensticker, 1990).

Second, new markets had been created for American building materials associated with those technologies, such as iron, steel and terra cotta. These boosted American exports to East Asia before the Stock Market crash of 1929, before the Sino-Japanese Wars of the 1930s, and before President Franklin Roosevelt's suspension of steel exports to Japan in Spring 1941.

Third, at least five other American construction companies almost immediately moved to fill the void created by Fuller's departure. The most significant of these was the Trussed Concrete Steel Company (Truscon), of Youngstown, Ohio. Others were the H.K. Ferguson Company, of Cleveland, Ohio; and three New York based construction companies: the Stauart Company, the Foundation Company, and the James Stewart Company (*Far Eastern Review*, 1924, **20**, p. 475).

These initiatives by American construction companies in Japan should be seen in the context of the NFCI, being created just as Fuller was getting started in Japan, and the International Federation of Building and Public Works, which persisted after Fuller departed. In 1920, at the first meeting of the International Chamber of Commerce in Paris, American contractors argued that the time had come for an international survey of construction. Noble F. Hoggson was the most vociferous proponent of this endeavour. A year later in London, at the First Congress of the International Chamber of Commerce, Hoggson was again at the forefront of organizing such a survey. He was joined by the American John R. Wiggins, both of whom convinced the International

Chamber to support conducting such a survey. They affirmed that

those interested in the Orient, Russia, China, India, Africa and South America will have a chance to learn definitely the needs of the construction industry in those countries; how they can pay for whatever materials can be furnished them; what native materials, labor and transportation will be available; and in general how to do business with them. (Wiggins, 1921; Hoggson, 1920)

Although the Fuller Company was not directly involved in this survey, the results of which were never widely disseminated, Fuller's work in Japan exemplified what Hoggson, Wiggins and others were hoping would occur in the future, as American contractors used their rationalized, scientific and organizational abilities to expand into wider foreign fields. The intensity of this expansion was seen in the mid-1920s not only in Japan, but also on a global scale.

Some of the Americans who had worked for Fuller in Japan, in fact, were intrigued enough with the construction opportunities that they decided to remain in Asia after Fuller left. J.H. Morgan, Fuller's chief architect in Japan, who had designed the Crescent Building in Kobe, was one such individual. In 1922 Morgan opened his own office in Yokohama where he practiced until 1937. Robert Trimble, also in the original Fuller team of 1920 as the assistant manager of construction, was another. In 1929 Trimble was working in China where, benefiting from the work of the Foreign Service Building Commission, he designed the American Consulate in Shanghai (*Far Eastern Review*, 1929, **25**, p. 460; Loeffler, 1998, p. 23).

The Fuller Company pulled up stakes early in Asia. The company took the shorter road. It showed no indication of transferring what it had learned back to America to solve contracting challenges at American work sites. It did not collaborate effectively with Japanese firms. Although it shifted focus in 1922 to work briefly in China, it missed a chance to

expand regionally within east Asia. After the collapse of good will between the U.S. and Japan at the onset of the Sino-Japanese War in the 1930s, it was decades before American construction experts again began to exchange ideas with Japanese counterparts. When that occurred, Americans all too rarely paid attention to existing Japanese building practices. Construction arrogance, contracting ignorance and/or cultural naïveté, thwarted their efforts to penetrate the Japanese construction market effectively until relatively recently. The Fuller Construction Company of the Orient unwittingly set an illuminating, but still obscure precedent in these cross-national contracting challenges.

Although they differ in many respects, the three case studies presented above share the common denominator of scale. The Bank of Boston, the IBC in Shanghai, and the Fuller buildings in Japan are examples of initiatives at the scale of individual structures. Each building imparts its own series of meanings where the exporting of American architecture is concerned, but the buildings are (or in cases were) individual icons of American power and knowledge. However, by the 1920s – building upon experiences from the Panama Canal to the

Figure 3.24. An American trader working for the Federal Export Corporation which, during World War I, invited inquiries from 'railroad directors, manufacturers, mine operators, builders, contractors and government departments who wish to obtain American products promptly made and delivered'. This kind of comprehensive treatment prepared the groundwork for city-scale architectural exporting after the War. (*Source: Export American Industries*, 1917, **19**(1), p. 3.)

Philippines – many American builders, architects, engineers and city planners increasingly responded to possibilities of designing and constructing larger-scale projects, from port facilities, tunnels and power stations to whole cities. Skyscrapers, steel framing and reinforced concrete helped create both incentives and an armature of exporting for those in the construction trades who were increasingly being either drawn or led abroad during what Klein dubbed the 'dramatic decade' of 1919–1929. Rationalized processes of construction and trade, the creation of several professional federations and committees, and the increasingly strategic actions of the U.S. government combined to prop up that armature even more firmly. Exporters of American architecture were thus able to move beyond the scale of a site-specific individual building or object. In some curious cases they were exporters of more broadly-conceived dimensions of American urban landscape, from infrastructure and industry to cities and suburbs.

NOTES

1. As explained by Wheeler, 1918, p. 6, after the U.S. entered World War I, President Woodrow Wilson's National Defense Council asked the U.S. Chamber of Commerce 'to organize the industries of the country to see that [they] had acceptable and representative War Services Committees, [so the Council could] deal with these committees rather than with the units of the industry. [The Council] foresaw the necessity of dealing with an industry, instead of with a unit of the industry, because of the tremendous task that would fall to the governmental authority if it had to pick out A, B, C and D and deal separately with each unit.'

2. Truman S. Morgan (1868–1940) became involved in both publishing and construction as early as 1894, when he edited the *Journal of Building* in Pittsburgh, which was purchased by the F.W. Dodge Company in 1902. Morgan continued with the Dodge Company in Pittsburgh until 1920, when he moved to New York and became President of the organization, which became one of the pre-eminent publishers of news and data about construction in the U.S. See *National Cyclopaedia of American Biography*. N.Y.:

James T. White & Co., 1951, vol. 37, p. 297; and Morgan's obituary in the *New York Times*, 1940, 22 December, p. 30.

3. In addition to Truman Morgan and John Harris the delegates were John Gries, U.S. Department of Commerce; William Starrett, Louis Comstock and Edward Simmons, N.Y.; Gerhardt Meyne, Chicago; A.P. Greensfelder, St. Louis; David Riffle and Edward Lang, Pittsburgh; and William Doyle, Philadelphia.

4. The Committee was chaired by Charles Butler. Other members were Walter Blair, Paul Cret, William Emerson, Charles Ewing, Charles Favrot, George Gray, L.C. Holden, Robert D. Kohn, Julian C. Levi, William Stanley Parker and Charles H. Whitaker. (*AIA Annuary*, 1920–21, p. 9).

5. Unfortunately, there has been no comprehensive scholarly study of the details related to this important trend. However, for China, see Cody, 2001.

6. From 1915 to 1919 Julius Klein (1886–1961) taught at Harvard University, where he specialized in Latin American economic history. In 1919–1920 he was commercial attaché, in Buenos Aires and in 1921 he began directing the Bureau of Foreign and Domestic Commerce, which had been established in 1913. During the 9 years he directed the Bureau, the number of countries where it opened offices increased from twenty-one to fifty-one, which was yet another measure of American trade activity during this period. See *National Cyclopaedia of American Biography*. N.Y.: James T. White & Co., 1930, Vol. 100, p. 23; and Klein's obituary in the *New York Times*, 1961, 16 June, p. 33.

7. However, even before 1913 some American architectural firms were designing banks beyond the U.S. borders. McKim, Mead & White, for example, designed the annex of the Bank of Montreal in 1901–05, which 'opened the way to prestigious commissions for former employees of the firm' in Montreal. See Gournay, 1998, p. 130.

8. This phrase derives from *System: The Magazine of Business*, 1910, **18**(3), p. 251.

9. This structure, at 67 Milk Street, opened in September 1924 but has since been demolished. See Gutierrez and Tartarini, 1996, p. 39. York & Sawyer were among the most respected of American architects concerning bank design. In 1924 they also designed the Federal Reserve Bank in New York, and in 1928 their design for the Royal Bank of Canada in Montreal was completed.

10. The British architects who designed the building in 1906 at 41 Jiujianglu, where IBC's former branch is located, were Smedley, Denham and Rose. Shanghai Chengjian Dananguan [City Construction Archive], File #A 3728.

11. The Merchants' Exchange was designed by Isaiah Rogers and became the U.S. Custom House in 1863. See Smith, 1908; Stein and Levine, 1990, pp. 73–74.

12. See *Shanghai Gazette*, 1920, October 21, p. 4; and *Far Eastern Review*, 1919, **11,** p. 514.

13. For William Starrett (1877–1932), see Malone, D. (ed.) (1977) *Dictionary of American Biography*. N.Y.: Charles Scribner's Sons, vol. 9, pp. 536–537; *National Cyclopaedia of American Biography*. N.Y.: James T. White & Co., 1935, pp. 24, 42–43; Marquis, A. N. (ed.) (1930)*Who's Who in America*. Chicago: A.N. Marquis Co., Vol. 16, p. 2087; and *Architectural Record*, 1932, **57**, April, p. 275.

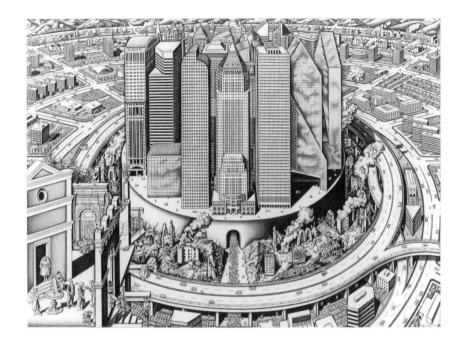

4 Exporting the American City as a Paradigm for Progress, 1920–1945

In the 1920s, as American investors increasingly traded internationally and as the market for American architectural products and processes continued to expand, the range of American construction-related exporting increased to the scale of the city. During this period – as will be shown below – some American architects, engineers and contractors began operating overseas as city planners, just as some American city planners began finding in contexts abroad a market for their services. In 1900 the American skyscraper began to symbolize for some observers the vanguard of an architectural form; by 1920 American commercial and industrial landscapes

began to represent for others the future of working spaces (Cohen, 1995, pp. 63–83). It was during the first third of the twentieth century that some U.S. city planners, architects and landscape architects began to influence more substantially – through either published theories or built projects – others in their professions who by the 1920s were practicing not only in Europe, but worldwide. Some of the most notable of those who exerted such a compelling influence on their American peers practicing abroad were Daniel Burnham, Charles Mulford Robinson, Frank Lloyd Wright and Frederick Law Olmsted. However, precise indications of their influence, or indeed of others' influence, over American expatriate architects and planners are difficult to pinpoint because so little empirical research has been done on those expatriates (Cody, 2001). By the end of World War II, when the U.S. government began to play a more proactive role in facilitating the exporting of American architecture, much of the fundamental foundation for this role had been laid by a host of American entrepreneurs, professionals and adventure-seekers.

One such figure was Joseph Ehlers, who exemplified a hybrid combination of the latter two kinds of expatriate American builders. Trained as a civil engineer at Cornell University, in 1919 Ehlers 'decided to break away for a while from the strenuous life of smoky Pittsburgh and the hard work of running around all the steel mills and bridge shops' (Ehlers, 1966, p. 9). 'Greenest of the green', Ehlers first ventured to western Canada and Alaska, but in April 1920 one of his former engineering professors, J.A. Waddell, who was then working in China, invited Ehlers to join him there to teach engineering. This assignment propelled Ehlers onto an unpredictable road of construction-related adventures throughout Asia for the next decade, exposing him (as he put it) to 'geography à la carte' (Ibid., p. 47). Unbeknownst to him, Ehlers fits within a pattern of American architects with wanderlust – from Alfred Zucker in Argentina, discussed above in Chapter 1, to Rowland Curry in China, introduced below – who found non-U.S. environments to be more stimulating places to practice than the familiar ones where they had previously worked.

In clarifying the warp and weft of that pattern, the American city will come into clearer focus as a paradigm for progress, which, between the two World Wars, many urbanists and politicians across the globe, regardless of their ideology, adopted as an ideal to emulate. That emulation helped fuel the exporting of American architecture. In addition to the commercial architectural components – such as banks and office buildings in central business

districts – that many believed to be fundamental to an up-to-date urban landscape in the 1920s and 1930s, American architectural exporters were also simultaneously planning sanitation systems, transportation networks, power stations, industrial developments, and housing projects, all of which comprised city-wide shifts in work, residence and leisure. As they exported the spaces and places that were meant to evoke urban novelty and municipal progress, Americans involved in construction who ventured abroad were altering the socio-dynamics of production and consumption. They were proffering a new urban paradigm, a modernizing matrix of construction and city planning, that disparate politicians and other kinds of clients abroad bought into as a ticket to the future. In the interwar period these clients could be found as close to American shores as Cuba or Venezuela and as distant from them as Russia or China. Accordingly, this chapter will largely, although not exclusively, focus on trends associated with city building in South America, the Soviet Union and republican China.

AFTER ALL, IT IS BY OBSERVING OTHER MEN IN ACTION, BY STUDYING MEN APPLYING MOTION TO MATERIALS, MEN DRIV-ING NAILS, SHEARING STEEL PLATES APART, SWINGING STEEL BEAMS INTO PLACE, FILLING OUT ORDER FORMS, DISPLAYING GOODS AT COUNTERS, THAT WE CAN MEASURE AND VERIFY THE EFFICIENCY OF OUR OWN METHODS AND PERFORMANCES, AND DISCOVER THE REACTION OF OUR OWN THOUGHTS AND ACTIVITIES UPON THOSE WE WOULD HAVE ALWAYS FOR OUR CUSTOMERS, ASSOCIATES, FRIENDS

Figure 4.1. An image taken from a painting by Fred Dana Marsh, showing (in the foreground) construction workers and (in the background) a cityscape of high-rises in the midst of construction. The gender-biased prose below the image is related to the journal *System*, in which this image appeared, but the words also capture a contemporary passion that many in the U.S. contracting trades held for action, motion and 'swinging steel beams into place'. (*Source*: *System*, 1914, **26**(5), n.p.)

From U.S. 'Metropole' to Latin American 'Peripheries'

Some of the most overt examples characterizing the exportation of the American city were directly related to the aftermath of American military victories over Spain in 1898. In both the Philippines and Cuba, American military engineers significantly altered the morphology of cities throughout those dominions. As outlined in Chapter 1, Manila, Baguio and other cities in the Philippines became the focus of American city planners and architects such as Daniel Burnham and William Parsons. In Cuba, too, the American government's intentions to create new markets for U.S. products, to 'stabilize' unrest and to extract natural resources more cheaply for U.S. industrial appetites (Jacobson, 2000, p. 40) were given form by American engineers, architects, planners, and their clients. Some of these were transplanted foreign nationals while others were indigenous elites.

In the first 20 years of the twentieth century, several other countries south of the U.S. border began to experience significantly more intense urban and industrial development based upon American priorities.   For example, Venezuela, Colombia, Ecuador, Peru, and (even more overtly) Puerto Rico came increasingly under the sway of American political, economic and cultural influence. Some historians have characterized this evolving relationship as one between the metropole (U.S.) and the peripheral regions of Central and South America (McCormick, 1990; Wehler, 1974). Others have seen the set of relationships between financial centre and dependent margins as an example of 'social imperialism', whereby 'the preservation of well-being and security in the metropole rested on its ability to ameliorate domestic social woes through its ties to the periphery' (Schoonover, 1991, p. 3). Politically, one can see this shift by (either vice or) virtue of the fact that U.S. Marines were sent to intervene in Caribbean disputes and 'establish

"stability" on American terms' twenty times between 1900 and 1920 (Jacobson, 2000, p.40).

Many historians have examined the South American continent's increasing industrial attachments to the United States in the late-nineteenth and early-twentieth century (Cardoso and Faletto, 1979; Frank, 1967). Quantitative data show exports from the U.S. skyrocketing in the first two decades of the century. For example, in 1901 Cuba bought $26 million of U.S. goods, but that had reached $165 million by 1916.

Puerto Rico, meanwhile went from being the 27th largest market for American products as Congress debated the island's political fate in 1900, to the 11th by 1910, after ten years of U.S. 'tutelage' in the wake of Spain's defeat. Elsewhere in Latin America, a country like Colombia would by 1919 import over 70 percent of its commodities from the United States. (*Ibid.*, p. 41)

In Puerto Rico during the first decade of the century one British journalist effusively described its principal city San Juan as being

suddenly beset and overwhelmed by the lusty, virile Yankees, roused out of its somnolent state and fired with cosmic urge, the spirit of the times, the desire for advancement, for emulation, for a closer kinship with the outside world of thought and action. (Macmillan, 1911, p. 153)

There was no mistaking the United States as the target of that emulation and, often more specifically, New York as the States' commercial capital.

Greater San Juan . . . will be given over entirely to business places in the same way as the 'down-town' section of New York is now wholly a vast, throbbing, commercial arena peopled by myriads of hurrying humanity by day and deserted and lonely by night. Points of similarity in each city's problems readily suggest themselves; each is built on an island, long and narrow, entirely inadequate in area for the housing of the people it supports, whose homes are in the suburbs, and the transportation of whom presents identical features; Catano is the Brooklyn, and Santurce and Rio Pedras the Harlem and Westchester of San Juan. (*Ibid.*, p. 154)

By the end of 1917 San Juan was experiencing the most explosive building boom in its history, with over $1 million in investments being focused on the construction of schools, hospitals, office buildings, warehouses and newly-paved roads. Most building materials for these projects – 'principally cement, reinforcing steel, lumber, hardware, plumbing and electrical supplies and roofing' – were imported from the United States (*Building Age*, January, 1918). Changes in the design of upmarket residences were also evident in Puerto Rico during the 1910s, in part because of a local architect Antonin Nechodoma who, enamoured of the U.S. bungalow, designed local variants built with concrete for himself and several clients. Anthony King (1995) has documented how trans-national the building type of the bungalow had become by the early twentieth century. In dominions that came under the control of the U.S. because of the Spanish-American War, such as Puerto Rico and Hawaii, the U.S. variant of the bungalow was being actively promoted and constructed in increasing numbers by the end of World War I (*Building Age*, August 1918; Stoddard, 1924).

American trans-national firms involved in 'culture industries' became 'agents of production of new institutional models' (Mattelart, 1983, p. 13), particularly in the diverse field of communications. By the late-1920s, for instance, the large U.S. advertising company J. Walter Thompson had branch offices in Latin America and India. Throughout the 1920s trade journals such as the *American Exporter* were engaged in their own version of a marketing blitz, trumpeting in print the latest recreation and retailing crazes in the United States. As a Chilean diplomat wrote in 1928, 'the remarkable development of U.S. trade with Latin America is due . . . to a cycle of growth originating from the powerful expansion of American production and merchandising' (*American Machinist*, 1928).

Whether one measures publishing tastes (for example, reading comics in American-influenced

MILLIONS are playing

MILLIONS are paying

TOM THUMB GOLF

PATENTS PENDING IN ALL COUNTRIES

Figure 4.2. Tom Thumb Golf, a popular recreational activity in the U.S. *c.* 1930, just as the country was experiencing the Depression. Some American entrepreneurs began exporting this recreation which, although not as popular as going to the cinema, enjoyed certain popularity in some contexts (e.g., Italy). (*Source*: *American Exporter*, 1930, **107**(4), p. 24)

newspapers), recreation (for example, playing 'mini golf' and watching Hollywood movies), or eating habits (for example, purchasing U.S. products in U.S. packages from retail stores reminiscent of U.S. prototypes), what was becoming evident during the first quarter of the century was that American influence abroad, particularly in urban settings, was pervasive, overarching and tenacious. What is equally evident in the early twenty-first century is that the precise dynamics of that influence are only beginning to be properly researched.

American initiatives related to the built environment were also seen in places where European influence persisted in either formal or informal colonies. During the late-nineteenth century many European colonizing powers had embarked upon a variety of city planning initiatives in those former colonial places that had acquired sovereignty (Rabinow, 1990; MacPherson, 1987; Home, 1997). It was hardly surprising, then, that in the later nineteenth century, soon after American politicians began re-engineering the American city for the sake of better public hygiene (Melosi, 1999; Schultz, 1989), other American municipal politicians abroad sought to 'improve' urban conditions in places they either began to administer directly (such as Puerto Rico), or where they were invited by local politicians to advise about urban development (such as Costa Rica and Ecuador). In 1912 the Costa Rican government

asked the U.S. to lend it the services of a number of U.S. Army engineers to make a preliminary survey and estimate for the building of a new Pacific Coast port at Puntarenas. Even Ecuador, which has for so many years stood upon her dignity and has declined (sometimes in unpleasant terms) offers of the U.S. to supply sanitary engineers, has at last consented to the sanitation of the city of Guayaquil. Ecuador . . . has requested the loan of Colonel Gorgas, who has won a worldwide reputation in the sanitation of the Panama Canal Zone. (*American Exporter*, 1912, **70**, September, p. 287)

The 'improvement' of 'uncivilized countries', which Theodore Roosevelt termed 'waste spaces', was bound up with assumptions that many Americans made about bringing the virtues of 'civilization' – and all which that entailed in terms of production and consumption – to wayward territories (Jacobson, 2000, pp. 49–51)

One of the most significant of those places was Cuba, an island whose architectural landscape at the turn of the twentieth century was based

on two urban models of the industrialized world: the multistory urban building and the suburban residence set on its own plot in an uncontaminated landscape . . . The transformation of the city was achieved by adapting solutions developed in Europe and the United States to local traditions but never by reproducing them exactly. (Venegas Fortias, 1996, p. 16)

This selective transplantation in Cuba of both European and North American metropolitan planning solutions occurred in roughly three stages:

1. from initial U.S. military victories in 1898 to the creation of the Republic in 1902;

2. over the course of the next 23 years, when many architects, engineers and planners took significant but largely uncoordinated actions; and

3. from 1925 until 1933, a period of heightened planning activity associated with the presidency of Gerardo Machado y Morales, which ended in a military coup that ousted Machado and ultimately led to Bautista's dictatorship.

Regarding Havana's metamorphosis from a peripheral colonial outpost to a metropolitan centre of commerce, there were four main measures of U.S. architectural influence. Laced together in a hybrid patchwork were: (1) individual buildings (often strikingly monumental) designed by American architects and firms; (2) industrialized workplaces sponsored by American companies, where labour practices in factories provided object lessons about American-style capitalism that was increasingly employing ideas from Frederick Winslow Taylor's principles of 'scientific management'; (3) urban infrastructure that was often, but not exclusively, based upon U.S. standards or patterns, and designed by U.S. engineers; and (4) indirect influences from increasingly significant U.S. planners and urban designers whose ideas were being applied to challenging Cuban problems either by Cuban or other non-American urbanists. The pervasively important extent of U.S. influence can be more clearly understood by unravelling that patchwork without destroying its dynamic pattern.

In 1898, during what I above call 'stage 1' of selective transplantation, U.S. President William McKinley commissioned Colonel George Waring, a prominent American sanitation engineer, to investigate Havana's sanitary conditions. As early as 1878 Waring had specialized in upgrading drainage systems in southern U.S. cities, such as Memphis and New Orleans, which were susceptible to virulent outbreaks of yellow fever, cholera and other water-born diseases. 'All these experiences eminently fitted [Waring] to draw up the sanitary plan of a campaign for a final assault on the great stronghold of the yellow fever scourge – Havana itself' (*American*

Exporter, 1898, **43**, December, p. 18). Waring sought to 'improve the city . . . [through] tram service, expansion of the electric and telephone systems, and the modernization of the sewage systems' (*Ibid.*). As he sought to sanitize a city that many Americans perceived to be unhealthy and chaotic, Waring altered Havana's, and more broadly Cuba's approaches to municipal hygiene.

These transportation, communication and public health initiatives fit within a broader context of land reclamation by American engineers along the Malecón seafront district of Havana. Their threefold objective was 'to improve the sanitary conditions along a chaotic coastline, establish a major artery able to handle future traffic, and embellish the city' (Lejeune, 1996, p. 173). The Malecón project brought glory to some American engineers. Unfortunately for him personally, however, Waring's luck ran out in Cuba; in October 1898 he was attacked by yellow fever and died soon after returning to New York. Despite his untimely death, the findings of his report commanded

great deference in Washington. The drainage improvements recommended by Colonel Waring for the port of Havana will cost several millions of dollars, and will be worth in the course of the next few decades several hundred millions in the protection they will afford to the United States, not to mention the protection of Cuba itself. (*American Exporter*, 1898, **43**, December)

During what I call 'stage 2' of selective transplantation, from about 1902 to 1925, the T.L. Huston Contracting Company and United Engineering and Contracting Company were two of the U.S.-based enterprises that benefited from Waring's recommendations. By 1910 Huston was erecting 'memorable buildings catering to every kind of social, public or administrative need' (Montalvo, 2000, p. 190) and United was installing sewage systems not only in the capital Havana, but also in less-populated cities such as Cigarros (*Bulletin of the General Contractors Association*, June,

1910, p. 56). In so doing, Huston and United joined other U.S. contractors after the establishment of the Republic in 1902 who organized building activities more efficiently (i.e., in line with North American tendencies toward Taylorism, as shown above, in Chapter 3) and who helped create

an ideology of progress [that] led builders to turn their backs on history and look for new directions in the international repertory and to [introduce] new techniques of construction, such as reinforced concrete . . . Architects found that these novel materials and building techniques allowed them possibilities for satisfying their clients' increasingly demanding decorative and functional expectations. (Venegas Fortias, 1996, p. 23)

As has been shown in previous chapters, however, the selection of a progressive structural solution was not limited to reinforced concrete. Steel was the other dominant option. In 1900, for instance, when the North American Trust Company applied for its construction permit, it described its office building as 'a five-story edifice of American construction', meaning that it would have a steel frame and stone, brick and concrete partitions (Llanes, 1985, p. 232, quoted in Galmiche, 2001, p. 25). However, when Havana's first School of Engineering and Architecture was established in 1900, its professors also advocated reinforced concrete as a preferred building material for 'modern' structures (Galmiche, 2001, p. 25). In the first years of the century, then, some popular architects were indigenous Cubans who either were graduating from Havana's School of Engineering and Architecture, or were receiving their training abroad, such as Francisco Ramírez Ovando, the first Cuban architect to graduate from the École des Beaux-Arts in Paris. There was also a cohort of prominent foreign architects who secured commissions from a burgeoning bourgeois clientele attracted to modes of living derived increasingly from the United States. Between 1916 and 1933 popular periodicals such as *Social* attested to this taste for American-focused consumerism by featuring financial and shopping opportunities for prosperous Cubans in the United States (*Ibid.*, p. 24; Gelabert-Navia, 1996, p. 133).

Among this latter group of foreign architects, beginning in 1905 and thriving until the worldwide economic Depression in the early 1930s, were several Americans: Bertram Grosvenor Goodhue (1869–1924), Kenneth McKenzie Murchison (1872–1939) and partnerships such as McKim, Mead & White; Barclay, Parsons & Klapp; Carrère & Hastings; Schultze & Weaver; and Walker & Gillette. These and other architects helped design what has sometimes been called

Havana's Wall Street, an American-style financial district [among the narrow streets in La Habana Vieja] reflecting the U.S.'s political and economic impact on the island. Up until the 1930s, American commercial and banking concerns opened offices at a rapid rate on either side of a well-defined line. This axis ran from the harbor, the Lonja del Comercio (commercial exchange) . . . and the maritime customs' complex . . . and it crossed La Habana Vieja from east to west along traditional shopping streets. It encompassed banks, office buildings, warehouses . . . insurance companies, architects' offices, real estate businesses and hotels. (Galmiche 2001, p. 20)

Another historian has described this fertile territory for American architects as follows:

Figure 4.3. Hotel Nacional, Havana, 1930, designed by the eminent U.S. architects McKim, Mead & White, along with Purdy & Henderson, who were consulting engineers. This structure, built to U.S. standards, helped advertise American up-to-date construction in Havana. (*Source*: Purdy & Henderson papers)

In the space of twenty-five years, the work of North American architects in Cuba would move from the profoundly 'regional' design of Bertram Goodhue's Santísima Trinidad Episcopal Cathedral (1905) to the universal classical style of McKim, Mead & White's Hotel Nacional (1930). The profusion of detail of Goodhue's façade gradually gave way to the Spanish colonial quotations present in Kenneth Murchison's Central Railway Station (1912) and Barclay, Parsons and Klapp's Customs House (1914). By the 1920s Schultze and Weaver all but reduced the regional interpretation to a series of refined decorative details. The programmatic charge was clearly to move away from the reserved Cuban Baroque prevalent during the period of the Spanish colony and into the fashionable Beaux-Arts style that was flourishing in the United States . . . (Gelabert-Navia, 1996, p. 133)

From 1905 to 1930 these architects' stylistic evocation of prevalent U.S. architectural fashion was matched by more functional overhauling from American engineers, planners and contractors who continued redesigning large portions of Cuba's urban infrastructure. For example, more up-to-date sewers below Cuba's city streets implied more securely paved highways on the ground that covered them. By 1912 several Americans were planning, building and asphalting those roads. In that year Clarence D. Pollock, a Secretary of the (U.S.) Association of Municipal Engineers, decided to relinquish his post as Acting Chief Engineer of Highways in Manhattan so he could become Chief Engineer in charge of both sewer and paving work in Havana (*Bulletin of the General Contractors Association*, March, 1912, p. 80). The merging of the two functions was clearly not coincidental. Pollock only stayed in Havana for a year and a half, however, before taking similar employment in San Antonio, Texas (*Ibid.*, November, 1913, p. 353). Another contractor famous in Cuba for his road building was C. Hempel, whom one journalist dubbed an 'ingeneer' [*sic*] because of his 'ingenuity' not only in building 120 km of Cuban roads, but also in erecting bridges, supplying machinery and operating 'in many directions . . . Briefly, there is no branch of engineering or general contracting in which he does not operate' (Macmillan, 1911, p. 106). One of those directions or branches concerned the water works Hempel erected at Palatina, and another was related to electric power plant construction for Havana's Presidio and Arsenal, as well as for the towns of Guanbacón, Cárdenas and Matanzas. A similar kind of diversification characterized the firm of Champion & Pascual, known primarily in Cuba as importers of furniture and Underwood typewriters from the U.S., but also renowned as 'one of Cuba's leading houses contracting for machinery and engineering . . . They built the bridge over the Almendares River, the slaughterhouse at Cienfuegos, and supplied thirty-two of Cuba's icemaking plants. They [also] own the Cárdenas Water Works (*Ibid.*, p. 86). Pollock, Hempel and the firm of Champion & Pascual exemplified how, by the 1910s, American municipal 'ingeneers' [*sic*] and ingenious entrepreneurs were beginning to alter the spatial landscapes of Cuban cities.

A more institutional measure of how pervasively American city-focused professionals were shifting those Cuban landscapes was reflected in the formation in 1919 of the Association of Members of American National Engineering Societies. As its tongue-twisting name implied, to join this Association one had to be a member of one of several professional engineering bodies in the United States. The list suggests the broad range in which American engineers were by then operating in Cuba: the American Societies of Mechanical Engineers, Civil Engineers, Electrical Engineers, Chemical Engineers, Agricultural Engineers, Refrigerating Engineers, Mining and Metallurgical Engineers; the American Institute of Architects, American Iron and Steel Institute, or the American Chemical Society (*American Exporter*, 1919, **85**, July, p. 142). Curiously, in that same year on the other side of the globe, the Association of American and Chinese Engineers was also established, although no evidence suggests a direct connection between

these two organizations. Instead, the creation of these professional societies should be seen within the context of proliferating amalgamations of institutions (as discussed concerning American contractors in Chapter 3), that 'sought to develop the capacity to interact with the gigantic firms of the world economy on an approximately equal level of organization' (Schoonover, 1991, p. 11; Amin, Arrighi, Frank and Wallerstein, 1990).

An even more significant sea change occurred in 1925, when Cuba's new President Gerardo Machado y Morales assumed office. From then until the 1933 coup, during what I have characterized as 'stage 3' of the process of selective transplantation in Cuba, U.S. engineers, architects and municipal planning experts benefited even more directly from Cuban government contracts. In 1925 Machado embarked on 'an ambitious public works program [that] included building a central highway connecting the whole island, constructing a capitol that sought to rival its United States counterpart, and launching numerous other engineering and construction projects largely concentrated in Havana' (Gelabert-Navia, 1996, p. 141). Part of the impetus for Machado's plans stemmed from the provocative writings of several architects and urbanists who published critiques of Havana's contemporary architecture and planning in the *Revista de la Sociedad Cubana de Ingenieros*, established in 1909, and *Arquitectura*, established in 1917 (Lejeune, 1996, p. 164). Two of the most influential of these critics were Pedro de Chacón, an engineer who became chief of urban beautification in President Machado's Public Works Secretariat, and Pedro Martínez Inclán, who wrote a passionately persuasive analysis of Havana's urban disarray, *La Habana Actual*, between 1919 and 1922, which was published three years later. In that book, Martínez Inclán reflected how fervently he had adopted ideas about civic beauty and coordinated urban planning from the American Charles Mulford Robinson (1869–1917), who had published two major works that enjoyed sustained popularity in the United States: *The Improvement of Towns and Cities* (1901) and *Modern Civic Art* (1918). Machado was strongly influenced by Martínez Inclán's work and used his political power to coordinate Havana's urban planning in a more scientific manner (Montalvo, 2000, p. 192).

The most significant urbanist associated with Machado's programme was the French planner Jean Claude Nicolas Forestier, who visited Cuba three times at Machado's invitation between 1925 and 1930, when he died before his urban designs were entirely realized. Trained as a civil servant in Paris, where he was made caretaker of walkways in that city's western districts in 1898, Forestier won acclaim for his redesign of the Parc Bagatelle in Paris between 1905 and 1908, 'based on the comprehension of history and the rejection of pastiche' (Le Dantec, 1994, p. 244). By this time Forestier was being influenced by the park and planning-related theories of the noted American landscape architect, Frederick Law Olmsted. As Forestier wrote in 1906,

[American cities] have realized that a city plan is insufficient if it does not include a coordinated plan that contains interior and exterior open spaces for the present and the future – one with a system of parks and parkways. (Forestier, 1906, p. 14)

Forestier implicitly lauded Olmsted's park designs for a multitude of American cities which, by the first decade of the new century, were influencing many landscape designers abroad, Forestier among them, who then began to apply these principles in other contexts. In 1911, for example, as he joined other French compatriots in establishing the Société française des urbanistes (S.F.U.), Forestier was hired by the Spanish city of Seville to design the new Parque de María Luisa (completed 1914) along the Guadalquivir River, where he melded Arabic geometric patterns with indigenous Andalusian landscapes. Forestier then followed this success with another in Barcelona in 1915, when he redesigned Montjuic Hill in anticipation of the 1929 Exposicíon

Internacional, the event that prompted the erection of Mies van der Rohe's famous pavilion.

In the next decade Forestier worked not only in Europe, but also began applying his principles related to the civic art of gardens in contexts as dispersed as Morocco, Buenos Aires and Havana. In Buenos Aires in 1924, Forestier planned a series of Olmsted-derived parks and parkways, as well as the unrealized Avenida Costanera, 'inspired by Burnham's plans for Lake Michigan in Chicago (1894–1909)' (Lejeune, 1996, p. 156), which would have created a Lake Shore Drive along the Río de la Plata. Forestier was unwittingly a star in a virtual constellation of French urban planners and landscape architects who worked in South America from the 1910s to the 1950s. As one historian has noted, '[Ernest] Hébrard worked in Guayaquil (1910s), Norbert Maillart in Montevideo (1920s), Donat-Alfred Agache in Rio de Janeiro (1930s and onward) and Maurice Rotival in Caracas, from 1938 to the 1950s' (Lejeune, 1996, p. 155; Underwood, 1991). These European planners were sometimes overtly and at other times inadvertently competing with their American counterparts for the attention and commissions of Central and South American clients. In so doing they were engaging in what one historian has termed 'metropole rivalry' (Schoonover, 1988), a situation that had historical roots in the nineteenth century when North Atlantic powers from both sides of the Ocean tried gaining commercial footholds in what one historian has called 'the American Mediterranean' (Langley, 1976).

In Havana, Forestier worked with a team of Cuban engineers, architects and artists to 'transform the colonial image of the city into a metropolitan vision in tune with [President Machado's] ambitions of the Republic' (Lejeune, 1996, p. 151). Forestier and Machado's Secretary of Public Works, Carlos Miguel de Céspedes, either reconfigured or planned anew a series of plazas, boulevards and parks in conjunction with major monuments that would fuse nature and architecture with that broader metropolitan vision. In this way Forestier was applying 'Hausmannian [ideals of civic] rationality with [his] knowledge of American regional and landscape theories of Daniel Burnham and of the City Beautiful Movement' (*Ibid.*, p. 155). These places included the Parque Central, the Paseo del Prado and, most notably, the Plaza de la Fraternidad Americana, which became a major civic space accented by the Capitolio (see figure 4.6).

One of the most prominent of the American engineering firms that profited from many of these architectural, engineering and planning ventures in Cuba – and one that bridged all three stages of selective transplantation – was Purdy & Henderson. The partnership of Corydon T. Purdy and Lightener Henderson began in the early 1890s in Chicago, became more firmly established 1896 with headquarters in Manhattan, and then expanded shortly thereafter to Havana.[1] In New York the firm became renowned for helping to erect the Flatiron Building, the National City Bank, the Plaza Hotel, and Pennsylvania Station. Corydon Purdy (1859–1944) was educated as a civil engineer at the University of Wisconsin at Madison, where he specialized in bridge design, and he began working in Chicago in 1889 at a time when that city's steel-framed, high-rise office buildings were beginning to command international attention. It was in 1900 that Purdy first ventured to Cuba, where

the subsequent rapid development of Cuba brought a large volume of business to [the]office. Although originally the Havana office was to be an engineering office similar to those in the U.S., it soon became evident that this idea was not adaptable to general business practice in Cuba. To continue the office, it was found necessary to enter the construction field. In turn, a subsidiary company [Purdy & Henderson Trading Company] had to be organized for the importation and distribution of building materials and equipment. One of the firm's Cuban activities and interests was the construction of branch banks for the Royal Bank of Canada in all parts of Cuba and on some of the other islands in the Caribbean. (*Ibid.*)

Some of Purdy & Henderson's construction work in

Cuba, then, fits squarely within the scope of concern outlined in the preceding chapter concerning the expansion of North American banks (in this case Canadian ones) to cities outside the northern hemisphere in the first decades of the twentieth century. Their diversification, from a strict engineering/ contracting firm to one that imported materials and equipment, was similarly evocative of the flexibility shown by other contracting companies seeking to expand abroad during this period. Furthermore, Purdy & Henderson's persistent staying power within Cuba – lasting until approximately 1956 – suggests how the company was taking the longer, more deliberate road to commercial success rather than the seemingly shorter, faster but ultimately less cautious path to quick profiteering.

Besides bank branches, the company built (and sometimes designed) sugar mills and office buildings for sugar companies; churches, private clubs and residences; telephone company offices; the National Theatre (El Centro Gallego) designed by the Cuban architect José Toraya in 1911; as well as retail stores and hotels, including the National Hotel in Havana, designed by the prominent U.S. architectural firm of McKim, Mead & White. A partial list of the company's projects from *c.* 1956 reflects the wide range of construction-related endeavours in Cuba which sustained Purdy & Henderson there for over half a century.

Of all these projects, the Capitolio (also known as the Palacio del Congreso, or National Capitol Building) was probably the most significant from the standpoint of its political and monumental importance within Havana. This structure, designed and erected between 1925 and 1928, was not only stylistically based upon the U.S. Capitol in Washington, but it was also structurally tied in large measure to U.S. standards of construction. For example, drawings from the project indicate that

details in general shall be according to the American Institute of Steel Construction's specifications, but rivet

Table 4.1. Partial list of projects outside the U.S. completed by Purdy & Henderson Company, *c.* 1955.

Project	Location	Cost ($)
U.S. Naval Operating Base	Bermuda	30,000,000
Palacio del Congreso (Cuban Capitol)	Havana	15,000,000
Sugar mills and related buildings	Cuba	8,000,000
Hotels (4)	Havana and Bahamas	7,300,000
Miscellaneous construction	Canada	5,000,000
Residences and other structures	Cuba	3,134,000
'Edificios' (11 office buildings)	Cuba	2,158,000
Banco Nacional de Cuba	Havana	2,000,000
Palacio del Centro Asturiano	Havana	2,000,000
Camp Las Casas (U.S. Army)	San Juan, Puerto Rico	2,000,000
Palacio del Centro Gallego	Havana	1,500,000
Royal Bank of Canada (18 branches)	Cuba	1,060,000
Royal Bank of Canada	Havana	1,000,000
Edificio Lonja del Comercio	Havana	1,000,000
Edificio La Metropolitana	Havana	1,000,000
Edificio Barraque	Havana	900,000
Banco Nacional de Cuba (12 branches)	Cuba	485,000
YMCA	San Juan, Puerto Rico	200,000
F.W. Woolworth	Havana	140,000
TOTAL		83,877,000

Source: Condensed Brochure, Purdy & Henderson Company, no date, pp. 4–5.

values shall be reduced to 90% of [those] values. Where beam reactions are not shown, beam connections shall develop beam capacity under uniform load, but shall in no case be less than the American Institute of Steel Construction standard connections or their equivalents.[2]

Therefore, from the most micro-level scale of the individual components to the more macro-level scale of urban monuments and infrastructure, American firms such as Purdy & Henderson were transforming urban spaces (as shown in several figures above), setting new standards of construction (as indicated by the Capitol's drawings), proliferating U.S.-derived retail establishments (such as F.W. Woolworth) and, in an aggregate sense over more than 50 years, altering the forms, norms and spaces of Cuban cities. From World War I to the Depression of 1929, other American companies were similarly active in other

cities throughout Central and South America. Their construction activities were largely diversified among four kinds of architectural and planning venture: (1) transportation improvements associated with rail, but increasingly road works; (2) harbour upgrading in certain coastal cities; (3) the planning of company towns for the exploitation and trans-shipment of key natural resources; and (4) sporadic construction for influential urban clients. These categories were not mutually exclusive. Rather, the reverse was more characteristic. Harbour improvements facilitated shipments out (increasingly to the U.S.) of unprocessed resources, and eased shipments in of processed goods (increasingly from the U.S.) for consumption in cities and hinterlands. The paving of roads facilitated the introduction of U.S.-produced automobiles, often driven by local elites who wanted

Figures 4.4 and 4.5. Centro Asturiano, central Havana, constructed by Purdy & Henderson in the early 1920s. (*Source*: Purdy & Henderson papers)

Figure 4.6 and 4.7. National Capitol of Cuba, patterned on the U.S. Capitol Building in Washington, D.C. and erected by Purdy & Henderson of New York, 1925–1928. (*Source*: Purdy & Henderson papers.)

to live in homes and work in offices designed according to U.S. norms and tastes. The key point is that by the 1920s the scale of U.S. construction-related influence was becoming more evident throughout Central and South America. Planning initiatives related to land and water transportation, as well as for sanitation and resource extraction, were significant catalysts in fanning the flames of that influence.

Two salient examples from the 1920s that demonstrate this influence are Peru and Chile. By 1919 Peru was entering 'a period of prosperity. The war has enriched the Peruvians who, a little uncertain how to invest their gains, are in many instances buying up lands and old houses and are preparing to rebuild with modern structures possessing all

sanitary conveniences' (*Export News*, **1**, May, 1919, p. 19). In 1920 the Peruvian government embarked on plans to upgrade water supplies, pave roads, centralize sewer lines, expand the capital's nearby port of Callao and build several new major buildings in Lima, whose population was then 170,000 and swelling rapidly with migrants from rural areas. The city was projected to more than double in less than a decade. U.S. engineers, architects and construction companies participated directly in these plans.

Coordinating this work through its Department of Public Works, the Peruvian Government targeted thirty-two cities and towns for new planning ventures. It also fast-tracked these plans, hoping to coincide their completion with the country's Ayacucho Centenary celebrations in 1921–22, although this proved to be overly ambitious. For paving, water and sewage projects, Peru contracted with the Foundation Company of New York, a firm that (as will be shown below) was simultaneously expanding its reach as far as Shanghai. The Foundation Company regraded and resurfaced the capital's principal streets, surveyed an 8-mile long Avenida del Progreso running through a pre-Inca burial mound from central Lima to Callao, laid water and sewage pipelines, and 'opened up new

Figure 4.8. The asphalting of central Lima and many outlying districts in the early 1920s was accomplished by the exporting of American contracting equipment as well as by U.S. civil engineers and planners, who brought a version of civic modernity linked to the automobile. (*Source*: *American Exporter*, 1926, **99**(4), p. 17)

residential districts [e.g., La Victoria, Santa Beatriz and San Isidro] which are being developed and built up along the most modern lines' (Drummond, 1926, p. 17). Because the Foundation Company quickly became the principal user of concrete and cement in Peru, the government also contracted with Foundation to operate the Peruvian Portland Cement Company, which soon doubled its former output (*Ibid*.). Following in the wake of this engineering groundswell was a mountain of American construction machinery, which provided new standards for construction after the Foundation Company's contract terminated. These included steam boilers, pneumatic caissons, concrete mixers, conveyers, cranes, crushers, derricks, excavators, water purifiers, road rollers and 'a host of other labor-saving mechanical devices' (*Ibid.*, p. 133).

In 1922 a U.S. journalist heralded the opening of Lima's first 'modern cable station', affirming (without naming the architect or builder) that 'the record of buildings designed and erected by U.S. firms in foreign countries, and built and equipped in accordance with American principles of construction continues to expand' (*American Exporter*, 1922, **91**, p. 79). And in Peru that expansion continued throughout the 1920s. In 1920 President Leguia ordered his centennial committee to find a suitable, designer and efficient builder to construct a new hotel for Lima, the six-storey Gran Hotel Simon Bolivar, so that it could welcome foreign dignitaries in style for the Centenary. The Fred T. Ley & Company of New York, which was 'engaged in large building operations, particularly in Lima and Callao', was selected to oversee the project (*American Exporter*, 1926, **98**, April, p. 25). As with the cable station and the Foundation Company's operations, to meet an American standard of construction, many local firms were bypassed and instead American manufacturers of building materials were hired to export those products to Lima. For the façade the Sandusky Cement Company shipped its special White Portland cement from Ohio; the Knoxville Marble Company sent its high-grade stone from Tennessee; General Electric supplied a range of electrical products and Otis supplied three elevators. Virtually all the hotel's components were brought from the United States.

In 1929 the planning associated with the port of Callao was an even greater enterprise for Peru's

economy, and here again Peru's president contracted an American firm, the Frederick Snare Corporation of New York, to oversee the erection of the new port operations. Snare proposed building a large breakwater, a new wharf, four new piers (connected by new rail lines to the country's network), two warehouses (with plans for expansion) and a customs house (*American Exporter*, 1929, **104**, February, p. 16).

Further south along the western coast of South America, in Chile, during the late-1920s and early-1930s, other American contractors were similarly engaged in planning work that ranged in scale from individual buildings to whole communities. At Viña del Mar, for example, in 1929 the Fred T. Ley Company was hired by the Chilean government to erect an up-to-date summer home (designed by two Valparaíso architects) for the present and future

Figures 4.9 and 4.10. More up-to-date urban architecture came with the asphalted roads and other infrastructure. These included a cable station and an upmarket hotel (the Bolivar). (*Source*: *American Exporter*, 1922, **91**(5), p. 79; and 1926, **98**(4), p. 25)

Figure 4.11. Aerial view of Callao, the port serving Lima, Peru, as it looked in 1929 and as it was projected to look after the urban planning interventions of the Frederick Snare Corporation of New York. Callao was one of several Latin American cities that tried to attract U.S. engineers, contractors and planners during the 1920s to help upgrade urban infrastructure. (*Source*: *American Exporter*, 1929, **104**(2), pp. 16–17)

Chilean presidents. The *New York Times* asserted that the house 'stands as added evidence of the constantly expanding operations of American builders in foreign countries' (1930, 9 March, XII, p. 7). During 1929 the Ley Company, which by then had branches in Lima, Bogotá and Santiago, completed over $4 million worth of construction work, including banks and schools as well as the work cited above for the Peruvian and Chilean governments. The Ley Company's prestige in South America was further bolstered after it erected the Chrysler Building in New York; in 1933, for example, Ley oversaw the construction of a state-of-the-art, twelve-story office building for *La Nación*, Chile's largest newspaper (*American Exporter*, 1933, **107**, September, p. 17).

However, at least as significant as individual commissions were larger-scale planning consultancies that U.S. firms oversaw in Chile, associated with extracting natural resources from the northern Atacama Desert. As Feliu (2000) has explained, the construction of company towns – enterprises related to the Industrial Revolution – occupied the attention of many commercial entrepreneurs in late-nineteenth and early-twentieth-century Latin America, who were interested in profiting from a host of resources, from sugar, fruit and cocoa to coal, copper and other minerals. In Chile some of the most prominent of these communities, *oficinas saliteras*, were related to nitrate extraction and processing. Antofagasta, planned in 1869, was the *entrepôt* for the nitrate industry, which was initiated in the 1860s but which was greatly expanded in the early years of the twentieth century, reaching its peak in 1915, when there were seventy *oficinas*. In the mid-1920s American capital and technology exerted an even more prominent role in the *oficinas* (Feliu, 2000, p. 337). In his astute analysis of the *oficinas'* planning, Feliu has explained that the Guggenheim method of extraction was introduced near the end of the nitrate boom, in particular at two of the last *oficinas*, Maria Elena (1925) and Pedro de Valdivia (1931).

These communities reflect three of the salient trends associated with U.S. architectural and planning exportation in pre-Depression Latin America. First, they exemplify the so-called 'improvement of uncivilized places' that many American engineers, architects and companies began to train their attention upon because of tempting clients who wanted them to work there. In the case of the *oficinas*, the communities themselves were cut from whole cloth, whereas in cities such as Havana, San Juan or Lima the challenge was to 'improve' the existing fabric by eviscerating, adding and resurfacing. Second, the planning of the *oficinas* demonstrates the adaptation – rather than the wholesale, identical transplantation – of built environment solutions developed in Europe and the United States to local traditions. European and North American prototypes were altered in the harsh Chilean desert. Nonetheless, the morphology of 'American neighbourhoods', with detached residences arranged on curving streets, in contrast to the straighter, narrower and more compact housing for Chilean nitrate labourers, was unmistakeable. Feliu (2000, p. 342) characterized this bifurcated morphology as follows:

The American neighborhoods (so named because most of the residents were North American) explicitly assumed the character of garden city, established in counterpoint to the remainder. Physical separation moved beyond the functional and into morphological and figurative realms. Thus, the settlement did nothing to hide its essentially diverse, stratified nature, particularly common in expatriate American settlements.

Third, the *oficinas* reflect the hybrid patchwork of more monumental, individual structures (for example, movie theatres) interspersed with the dual spatiality of class-laden residential planning and an overriding goal of industrial production. Furthermore, the Chilean desert communities suggest the enduring nature of the 'metropole rivalry' seen throughout Central and South America during the early twentieth century, when American building exporters were locked in a struggle with European counterparts. At issue was persuasion; how to convince Latin American clients that North American standards of industrial progress and spatial propriety were superior to those of the previously unrivalled paradigms emanating from Europe? In the years on either side of the Great Depression, in the dusty, isolated hinterlands of northern Chile, that rivalry was again incarnate, as it had been three decades earlier in the equally remote regions of Sudan. There, at the Atbara Bridge, American bridge builders trumped their British competitors. Thirty years later it was not only bridge builders making the grade, but instead a range of building entrepreneurs: architects, planners, engineers, contractors and materials exporters. Furthermore, by the 1920s this disparate, relatively uncoordinated cast of characters was engaged in construction dramas, from individual buildings to entire settlements, that reached well beyond the western hemisphere.

Exporting American Construction and Planning to Russia

One of the most curious series of construction dramas that reflect the growing pervasiveness and increasing scale of American architectural influence between the two World Wars was played out in the former Soviet Union. Jean-Louis Cohen (1993, 1995) and William Brumfield (1990) have written extensively about several dimensions of this influence. Brumfield's analysis of how Russians perceived American architecture from 1870 to the end of World War I concludes that '"enormous" and "efficient" define just the qualities that Russian observers valued in American architecture' (Brumfield, 1990, p. 43). He specifies how, from the 1870s to World War I, through architectural journals such as *Zodchii* (The Architect) and *Nedelia stroitelia* (Builder's Weekly), there was a black-and-white 'conduit for information

on technical innovations' (*Ibid.*, p. 44). Soon after the Philadelphia Exposition in 1876 Russian architects such as Sergei Kuleshov began to publish their impressions of American urban architecture, and these were supplemented by later descriptions penned by architects such as Aleksandr Dmitriev (*Ibid.*, pp. 47, 59). In the 1890s the editor of *Zodchii*, Viktor Evald, published books and technical reports about skyscraper construction in the U.S. After the turn of the century, Roman Beker trumpeted the virtues of American architectural education in schools such as Cornell, MIT, Yale, the University of Pennsylvania, and the Armour Institute in Chicago (*Ibid.*, pp. 47–56). Brumfield links these measures of American architectural influence to what he sees as 'shared ideals and common standards [where] . . . America is seen as the ultimate standard' (*Ibid.*, p. 64) – he also explains that the onset of World War I brought with it a relenting of the 'visions of growth, progress, and technical development' (*Ibid.*, p. 62). However, Cohen argues that from World War I until at least 1935 there were signs of ongoing interest in American urbanism by Russian observers such as the poet Vladimir Maiakovsky, who travelled to the U.S. in 1925 and wrote disparagingly about the colossal effects he saw there associated with American construction technology (Cohen, 1995, p. 102). In 1926 the Constructivist architect Aleksandr Pasternak argued that by virtue of the skyscraper, 'Americanism [would] leave its mark on the future cities of Russia' (*Ibid.*, p. 124). Certainly that mark in the late-1920s and early-1930s was being made in the landscape of architectural commentary, as Cohen has shown by explaining how fervently Russian architects such as Nikolai Ladovsky, Vladimir Krinsky and Iakov Chernikhov were responding with words and designs to the idiom of the American high-rise, and by how energetically certain Russian architects responded to the 1929 competition for the Christopher Columbus memorial in Santo Domingo (*Ibid.*, pp. 124–133).

Cohen has also explained how, by the early 1930s there was a proliferating Russian interest not only in American skyscrapers, but in broader-scale American city planning approaches, as shown in publications by David Arkin, Alexei Shchusev and L.E. Zagorsky (*Ibid.*, pp. 151–153). Cohen and Brumfield's research, therefore, demonstrates many Russians' sustained fascination with American architecture, construction technology and city planning. What is also clear is how actively certain American industrial entrepreneurs and contracting adventurers in Russia were building upon that foundation of curiosity and inspiration. One of the most vivid and literal examples of that 'constructing upon a foundation' is found 265 miles east-north-east of Moscow where, in the late-1920s, the Austin Company, a successful, Cleveland-based construction firm helped plan and then build the first stage of a new industrial city, Molotov (also known as Gorky and Nijni Novgorod) whose *raison d'être* rested on the production of Ford Motor Company automobiles.

The project's genesis stemmed from many Russians' astonishing admiration for Henry Ford himself, not as a capitalist (as some might first assume), but instead as a revolutionary. 'Russia was a "have-not" nation and any man strong-willed enough to put such a luxury as an automobile into the hands of the laboring classes was held in high esteem' (Scoon, 1970, p. 1).

Even before the October Revolution of 1917 Czarists in Russia were more interested in U.S. automobile technology than that of any European competitors, partly because of how well tank trucks manufactured by the U.S.-based White Motor Company fared in trials over unpaved Russian roads in 1912, and also because of Czarists' suspicions about European businessmen during the War (*Ibid.*). In 1920, when the new Soviet government began to focus on agricultural and industrial production, it used money from then-U.S. Commerce Secretary Herbert Hoover's 'anti-starvation program' to

purchase over 24,000 Ford Motor Company 'Fordson' tractors. In 1923 an ex-Ford employee from Detroit who was deported to Russia for his Communist activities helped to build a small factory in Leningrad (St. Petersburg) where F-15 pick-up trucks were produced (*Ibid.*). Cohen has explained that in the early 1920s Ford had become nearly as popular in Russia as Lenin; by 1924 Henry Ford's memoirs had gone through four editions. 'Ford was as famous as Charlie Chaplin, and the vein of Fordist literature inexhaustible . . . Ford had become Uncle Sam personified' (Cohen, 1995, p. 72). By 1926 Ford was exporting so many Fordson tractors that the company was invited by the Soviet government to send an engineering team to Russia to investigate whether and where it might build a tractor plant. Although these plans were initially stalled, by late 1928, when Joseph Stalin ousted Trotsky and launched a Five-Year Plan of industrial expansion (which included a production target of 70,000 trucks and 30,000 cars by 1932), Ford was in a fortuitous position to gain a firmer foothold in Russia. However, that position was not completely assured until General Motors' six-cylinder Chevrolet was bypassed in favour of Ford's Model A. This occurred after a heated debate in the Supreme Industrial Council during early March 1929 when, at that same meeting, the Council's president M. Quibesheff also decided upon a manufacturing site, 7 miles from the medieval city of Nijni, near the confluence of the Volga and Oka Rivers (Scoon, 1970, p. 2).

A few months before that fateful meeting Soviet officials had selected the Austin Company to design and build not only the factories where American cars would be fabricated, but also Molotov, the city where those factories would be located. Some called it 'the first socialistic city of the world' (Davis, 1932, p. 84). Why Austin? 'Standard factory buildings', a hallmark of Austin's success since 1914, caught the Russians' attention and convinced them that Austin was the right company to build what became the then-largest

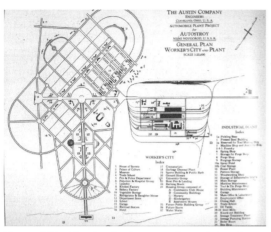

Figure 4.12. The plan for the new industrial city of Nijni Novgorod, designed by the Austin Company, a Cleveland-based firm hired by Soviet planners in the 1920s. (*Source*: Greif, 1978, p. 107)

Figure 4.13. Austin Company officers conferring around a conference table, *c*. 1913. Wilbert Austin (pictured second from the right), the son of Samuel Austin, the company's founder (seated at the head of this table) was responsible for leading the Austin Company into contracting ventures abroad. (*Source*: Greif, 1978, p. 24)

automobile plant in Europe: a structure 1800 feet long and 350 feet wide, equipped with six assembly lines, that was the focus for a complementary workers' settlement to house between 35,000 and 50,000 workers, covering 25 square miles.

Austin's trail from the Great Lakes to the Russian steppes was hardly pre-ordained. It began when the adventurous, itinerant British carpenter Samuel Austin sought his fortune by intending to settle in Chicago after that city's disastrous 1872 fire. Austin founded his company in 1878, when he suddenly fell in love with a young woman from Cleveland and sank roots there instead of in Chicago (Luce, 1959, p.6). Austin's son Wilbert became an engineer and after joining his father in business in 1900, convinced him to undertake the design as well as the construction of buildings for clients. This led to what the company called 'the Austin method of undivided responsibility', and it unwittingly placed the company in a vanguard of firms (such as Truscon, discussed above in Chapter 2 and below, in the context of China) that were commercially and technologically well-situated to benefit from the expansion of the U.S. automobile industry in the

early years of the new century. 'New concepts of mass production that accompanied the automobile industry's early growth led to the Company's development of standardized designs for single-story factories' (*Ibid.*, p. 8).

However, it was not just automobile production that fuelled Austin's rise. Large, open but enclosed spaces were also necessary for fabricating airplanes. One of Austin's projects that brought the company considerable fame was the Curtiss Aeroplane Company in Buffalo, New York which took Austin builders only 90 days to erect during the winter of 1915–16. During World War I Austin began selling its standardized buildings to the U.S. Army in France. As an Army subcontractor, the American Light Railways Company purchased several shops, planing mills, foundries, warehouses and a powerhouse to outfit the Army's operations at Abainville (*Austin Book of Buildings*, 1922, p. 55).

At the end of the War, Wilbert Austin invested more heavily in France, where he secured the company's 'first truly international project', the reconstruction of the Maubeuge glass factories at Rousies (Greif, 1978, p. 149). The early 1920s was a period of mushrooming growth for Austin's international operations. In 1920 the Standard Oil Company of New York purchased nineteen of Austin's standardized factory buildings, ranging in size from 40 feet by 50 feet to 100 feet by 500 feet, used as distribution centres for Standard Oil's expanding operations in Istanbul, Turkey; Bourgas, Bulgaria and Piraeus, Greece (*Export News*, 1, 1920, **1**, March, p. 22).

By 1922 Austin was building actively upon its commercial success in France and the Balkans with a particular, although not an exclusive focus on oil company facilities. '[Since 1920] Austin Standard Factory Buildings have [also] been constructed in England, Canada, Venezuela, Cuba, Mexico, Gibraltar, [Argentina] and Peru' (*Austin Book of Buildings*, 1922, p. 55).[3] Also by 1922 the Cleveland-based firm had expanded within the continental U.S., opening offices in Chicago, New York,

Philadelphia, Detroit, Pittsburgh, Birmingham, Seattle, St. Louis, Los Angeles and Dallas. This geographic diversification not only facilitated Austin's servicing its domestic clients; the continental reach also helped the company satisfy the divergent needs of an international, largely industrial clientele. That the reach could also be trans-continental was demonstrated when Austin was hired to design Molotov, the industrial settlement near Nijni Novgorod. Part of the company's success in foreign arenas can be attributed to what Austin termed its 'completeness' and 'adaptability'. Regarding the former:

A complete shipment for an Austin Standard Building includes practically everything above the floor – fabricated steel, sash, glass, doors, roofing and, if desired, lumber . . . The Austin Company takes care of all routine attached to export shipments, securing cargo space, procuring necessary licenses and other documents. Cable, traffic and other departments are thoroughly organized, and experienced in every export requirement. Quotations are made and correspondence conducted in any language. This coordinated service relieves the purchaser of all divided responsibility. (*Ibid.*)

The company recognized, however, that not all clients would want to hand over complete construction control to a contracted customer. Therefore, to maximize its flexibility Austin created three plans for clients operating abroad.

Figures 4.14, 4.15 and 4.16. Industrialists from the Soviet Union were impressed by the Austin Company's proven track record in building large-scale industrial plants, such as the ones shown here in Buffalo, New York, for the Curtiss Aeroplane Company (figure 4.14), Tampico, Mexico (figure 4.15), and Buenos Aires, Argentina. (*Source: Austin Book of Buildings*, 1922, pp. 4 and 55; Greif, 1978, p. 75)

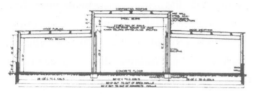

2   Austin No. 2 Standard, for light machine shops,
    foundries, etc.   Width 90 ft.   Length any
    multiple of 20 ft.

Figure 4.17. As the Milliken Brothers Company had
done 20 years earlier, Austin marketed many of its
buildings as prefabricated units that clients could select
from a catalogue that showed a wide variety of types,
using both steel and concrete technologies. This one was
a light machine shop. (*Source: Austin Book of Buildings,*
1922, p. 34)

[Under] Plan A, Austin assumes responsibility for the entire
project – engineering, building and equipment. [Under]
Plan B, Austin will ship all essential material and furnish
an erection engineer who will supervise all construction.
[Under] Plan C, Austin will ship all essential material and
furnish plans, specifications and complete instruction for
erection by local forces. (*Ibid.*)

In the outskirts of Molotov (Nijni Novgorod)
those 'local forces' were proletarian Marxists, or
what some called '*mujiks*' (peasants). In 1928 the
Supreme Industrial Council was impressed with both
Austin's standardized industrial structures and its
efficiency in shipping them from one of America's
chief industrial heartlands. Despite their decade-
long experience exporting standardized buildings
to Europe, Austin executives were initially sceptical
because of the unknown Russian terrain where they
were being lured to build a city. If they could have

foreseen the upcoming Depression in October 1929,
they might not have been so reticent in accepting
so large a commission. Leaving prophecy aside, in
winter 1928 the Council dispatched a delegation to
Cleveland to buttonhole Austin managers directly.
The strategy worked. An Austin Vice-President
was invited to survey the site, on a high riverbank
near three villages, all of whose inhabitants were
resettled and the villages razed. In summer 1929,
the Council created 'Autostroy' (the administrative
unit overseeing Molotov's construction) and signed
the contract with Ford and Austin. Austin's contract
provided the wide scope of designing the entire
settlement; Ford's stipulated that the company's River
Rouge and Highland Park plants near Detroit would
be used as models (Scoon, 1970, p. 3; Wilkins and
Hill, 1964, p. 220). Austin's challenging tasks, then,
included the design and construction of 'all public
utilities, such as the water supply system, storm and
sanitary sewer systems, central power and heating
plant for both plant and city, electric power and light
systems, telephones, in fact everything required by
the modern industrial city' (Davis, 1932, p. 83). The
Soviets imagined that the project would take 4 years.
However, Austin believed it could plan and build the
settlement in 15 months which, if completed on time,
would bring a handsome bonus. Construction began
in August 1930 and was finished in early November
1931; Austin reaped the bonus.

The plans for Molotov's automobile plant were
drafted at first by Albert Kahn in Detroit. Kahn's
concrete reinforcing company, Truscon, therefore
benefited directly from the contract. The plans
were then finished in Cleveland, but the plan for
the surrounding settlement was finalized in Russia
(Davis, 1932, p. 83; Wilkins and Hill, 1964, p. 220).
The joint-venture nature of the enterprise was a
variant on the Austin Company's trademark qualities
of 'completeness' and 'adaptability'.

Six of Russia's foremost architectural societies
and institutions competed for the city's design,

Figure 4.18. Perspective views of industrial buildings designed by the Austin Company at Nijni Novgorod. (*Source:* Greif, 1978, p. 106)

ultimately awarded to the High Technical School, but that design only 'laid down the fundamental requirements of size, area per person [9 square metres] and the number and kind of functions to be provided in the city. [The School] then turned to American architects and engineers to "rationalize" the project, to use the parlance of the moment in Russia' (Austin, 1931, p. 10).

A sense of what contemporaries understood by that word 'rationalize' is found in the way in which a Russo-American engineer, in 1932, described how a well-administered construction office should react to unpredictable building realities.

A large construction office may be compared to the bridge of a battleship in the heat of a naval engagement. Emergencies arise on all sides, breakdown of essential equipment, rush supply orders, failures of men and mechanics to appear or properly carry out orders, disasters of flood and fire, accidents of explosion or collapse. Into the central office pour the vital messages about these situations. They must be immediately overcome. Every detail of expeditious handling must be arranged. In transmitting information, minutes means thousands of dollars and human lives. Communication is the vital nervous system . . . The Russian [offices] totally lacked this. (Gelb, 1991, p. 96)

Austin, then, stood at the helm of the 'battleship Molotov' and assisted their less-organized Russian counterparts in the planning of a new socialist settlement. The 'worker's city' at Nijni Novgorod was laid out using three interlocking geometries: a grid oriented roughly north-south; two major perpendicular roads that sliced through the rectilinear grid (somewhat reminiscent of L'Enfant's Washington, D.C. plan) and created a city centre where the roads met; and four circular arcs that helped enclose the settlement at its peripheries. The industrial plant, detached from the city to the north-east and located south of one of the city's main roads, was composed of a series of factory structures linked by several elliptical roads. Four-storey housing blocks, with 'Communes' placed on the top floor, were erected using reinforced concrete produced according to American specifications, but they were aligned in the city according to Soviet 'microrayon' planning principles (Kopp, 1970; Castillo, 1992). Therefore, schools, community buildings and recreation space were situated near the dense housing blocks. A 'House of Soviets', 'Palace of Culture', hospital, hotel, and department store were placed in a circular cluster at the city's main intersection.

To erect up-to-date American industrial forms and spaces, Austin's builders trained a workforce of approximately 40,000, 40 per cent of whom were women. Under the principles of Stalin's Five-Year Plan, they were conscripted to assist the Americans, but having been engaged previously in rural occupations, they first required instruction in U.S. construction methods. A journalist later described the scene:

Gangs of Russians who had been trained [to use] large American mortar trowels were pitted against Russians using the small native trowel. The greater quantity, if poorer quality of the American style mortaring was demonstrated. All construction workers at the A plant were paid on a piece-work basis so as to reduce the malingering which the American engineers had noticed on their earlier tours of Soviet factories. (Scoon, 1970, p. 4)

One contemporary Austin engineer characterized some of the contracting dynamics in this way:

A majority of 'mujiks' had very little education and no training or experience at all along mechanical lines. They only excelled in . . . excavation. The village carpenters were experts with a cross-cut saw and axe; all other tools, however, were foreign to them. . . . The Mujik, his wife and children, really furnished the labor power. The young people especially were taken as apprentices. This condition, combined with a very high labor turnover, caused a low production of labor, and good workmanship was obtained only under very close supervision. (Davis, 1932, p. 85)

Austin superintendents organized the site of the 'first socialistic city' according to U.S. construction standards. During initial stages,

long lines of workers, their backs laden with sand and gravel came up out of the barges along the river and carried their burden to the railroad cars. Large logs were whipsawed into boards by hand. All kinds of building materials were carried up four stories on the backs of men and women. As the job progressed, all of this was modernized as far as possible. At the dock, materials were unloaded by power cranes, conveyors and skip hoists directly from the barges to railroad cars . . . All buildings were equipped with material hoists. American-made crawler cranes were used in the erection of the 14,000 tons of structural steel . . . Machine operators were sent from America . . . to teach Russian apprentices . . . The whole plant [was] a large trade school. (Davis, 1932, pp. 86, 88)

Nijni Novgorod became a series of object lessons demonstrating to Soviet Russians the 'rationalization' of American construction. Another lesson, one geared to the Austin Company, was that marketing U.S. construction materials and methods overseas could be both challenging and profitable. Wilbert Austin demonstrated that he was learning this latter lesson when, in 1930, he opened a branch office in Canada, followed 8 years later by one in London, when the company erected the British Technicolour laboratory. Allan Austin, Wilbert Austin's son who opened that London office, envisioned an even broader global presence for the company after World War II; in 1955 he established an office in Brazil, followed by the creation in 1960 of Austin International, which operated first from subsidiary

Figures 4.19 and 4.20. Four-storey housing blocks and an industrial building under construction at Nijni Novgorod, erected by the Austin Company. (*Source*: Khvostovsky, 1931)

Figure 4.21. Austin Company advertisement, which graphically reflected the scope of the firm's building operations, from individual structures to entire settlements.(*Source*: Forbes, 1930, from Greif, 1978 p. 118)

branches in Britain, France and Australia, and subsequently in several other European cities, and in Argentina and Japan (Greif, 1978, p. 150). A proper context for these later expansions will be provided in the two chapters that follow. Nijni Novgorod became the key precedent that propelled Austin managers to seize opportunities to stake more transnational claims on construction possibilities.

In terms of what the Russians learned from Nijni Novgorod, the dimensions of the object lessons ranged from individual building elements to complex urban form. At the scale of building tectonics, Austin showed Russian workers how to weld high-quality structural steel members. In 1929, while one large Austin team was working in Russia, other Austin contractors in Cleveland were completing the first 'completely welded steel-framed commercial structure, a four-story building . . . [that] led to the use of welding for the erection of Austin standard design buildings and paved the way for wide use of welding in construction' (Shirk, 1978, p. 14). In terms of construction management, Austin's method of organizing the myriad tasks of construction, from material delivery to building completion, demonstrated to the Russians how they might jettison age-old construction methods in favour of imported American standards. However, given that some Russian workers were sceptical about and/or resistant to some of the material improvements and time/labour-saving methods introduced by Austin managers, the degree to which well-entrenched habits about construction were discarded in favour of American novelties is unclear (*The Constructor*, 1932, **14**, May, p. 28). At the larger scale of the city, American architects and engineers assisted their Russian counterparts in solving the challenges of fulfilling socialist urban functions within capitalist structural shells. Stalin and his confidants were expressing what their South American contemporaries in less socialistic contexts were also sensing in the 1920s and 1930s

– that for cities to reflect their progress and novelty, they should incorporate materials, forms, spaces and places reminiscent of the United States. The advertisements of the Austin Company in 1930 graphically reflect the perceived links between industry, high-rise construction, progress and the American city.

Austin and Ford's commercial ventures were not the only ways in which American architectural and planning influence was being exerted on the Soviet Union in the early 1930s. Visits to Russia by American professionals was another means by which this influence was manifested. For example, just as Austin's contract at Nijni Novgorod was terminating in 1931, the noted Chicago urban planner Jacob Crane travelled to the Soviet Union to provide unspecified technical assistance (*City Planning*, 1931, **7**, p. 124). A year later Robert O'Brien, one of the directors of the Cook-O'Brien Construction Company of Kansas City, Missouri toured the Soviet Union to see for himself the contracting possibilities offered by the Second Five-Year Plan (*Constructor*, 1932, **14**, May, p. 28).

As a prelude to that Plan, Russian officials of the Amtorg Trading Corporation, the Soviet agency established in 1924 in New York City 'for the development of trade and industrial cooperation with American firms and individuals' (Gelb, 1991, p. 321), invited Americans involved in construction, such as Austin, to become more significantly linked to contracting ventures in the U.S.S.R. Because 'municipal economy received more attention' in the First Five-Year Plan, there were financial incentives for projects similar to those which Austin and Ford were doing, but more extensively throughout the Soviet Union (Khvostovsky, 1931).

One significant aspect of these projects is how wide-scale they were in terms of urban and regional development. 'In the main, the opportunities for American contractors are likely to lie in the fields of highway construction, municipal public utility construction or heavy engineering operations such as involve the construction of railroads, power and reclamation dams, canals, etc' (*Ibid.*). Some enterprising American companies were already responding to these incentives while others were being shown by this kind of prediction the possibilities offered by the next Five-Year Plan (Sutton, 1968).

Many American contractors and engineers were in that former category. For example, beginning in 1926 the civil engineer Hugh Cooper, under the terms of a Special Technical Assistance Contract, collaborated amicably with his Russian clients to construct the Dneprestroi hydroelectric dam in the Ukraine. When it was completed in 1931, Dneprestroi was the largest dam in the world, 20 per cent larger in mass than the Nile River Dam and with larger turbines than those at Niagara Falls, New York (*New York Times*, 1928, 21 July, p. 19; Gelb, 1991, p. 321; Rassweiler, 1988). One of the challenges Cooper faced was a shortage of steel, which required him to use wooden bins to hold materials for the American concrete mixers, wooden trusses to support those mixers, and wooden shelters to protect them (*Constructor*, 1932, **14**, May, p. 28).

Another American firm that responded to Soviet clients' enticements was the Longacre Engineering and Construction Company. From 1929 to 1934 Longacre built several six-storey housing blocks in Moscow 'according to the latest American methods,

Figure 4.22. The Dneiper Dam was a massive hydro-electric project in the eastern Soviet Union, constructed by the Hugh Cooper Company. (*Source: Pan Pacific Progress*, 1930, **13**(2), p. 57)

with American technicians and appliances [such as elevators], but [with Soviet labor]' (*New York Times*, 1929, 2 March, p. 1). A third American firm responding to the Soviet lure was the McCormick Company, which designed an American baking plant in Moscow (*Constructor*, 1929, **11**, November, p. 54). Other American engineers 'entirely designed' the city of Magnitogorsk, east of the Ural Mountains (Gelb, 1991, p. 327; Scott, 1942, 1989). However, some of those engineers became so disgruntled with Soviet inefficiency, corruption and false accusations of blame that they returned to the U.S. before their terms expired (Gelb, 1991, pp. 114–115).

Zara Witkin, a young American engineer of Russian descent, exemplified this latter kind of situation. Between 1932 and 1934 Witkin's disillusionment with the realities he experienced in Stalinist Russia collided head-on with his heady idealism about contributing to the revolutionary cause of socialism (Gelb, 1991). A California-bred son of Russian émigrés, Witkin worked as a designer and engineer in Los Angeles during the early 1920s, when he became entranced by propaganda that glorified post-Czarist Russia. During the Depression, which Witkin viewed as confirmation of capitalism's failure, he turned more overtly towards socialism and began to work for Amtorg. At one of his life's major crossroads, he saw a Russian propaganda film in Los Angeles, became smitten with an actress playing the role of a revolutionary peasant, and vowed to find her in Russia, where he decided to contribute his contracting expertise to the cause of the Soviet Union. An expert in American prefabricated construction techniques, the 'talented, energetic and selfless' Witkin began working in Russia in several construction-related capacities. However, 'he came up against the pervasive lethargy, incompetence and outright corruption of Soviet industrial administrators' and within 3 years he became 'the victim of subterfuge, duplicity, laziness, venality, jealousy and stupidity' (Gelb, 1991, p. 7). He carried out several assignments at military construction sites, taught prefabricated construction and helped set construction priorities for the Second Five-Year Plan, but in 1934 his raw cynicism prompted him to return to the United States.

By 1935, a year after Witkin's demoralized self-repatriation, when Stalin's new Moscow plan was being formalized, American influence upon Soviet planners, architects and contractors was more palpable than it had ever been before. In terms of city planning, as Cohen explains,

The principal author of the general plan for Moscow, Vladimir Semenov, [had been] ... attentive to American city planning developments since 1914. In 1935 he reproduced and commented on the sketches published by Hegemann and Peets in *The American Vitruvius*. In the same year, the Russians translated (though not without formulating some reservations in the preface) Thomas Adams's *Recent Advances in Town Planning* which outlined the Regional Plan for New York. (Cohen, 1995, p. 155)

However, as shown above, American planning influence pervaded the Soviet Union, from Ukraine in the west to Nijni Novgorod in central Russia, and at least as far as Magnitogorsk in the east. The examples of the Austin Company, Hugh Cooper, Jacob Crane and Zara Witkin during the years bridging the Depression reflect a spectrum of tangible, technological instances of American influence over planning and construction in a geographically broad, but uncoordinated series of Russian places. That spectrum was brought into sharper focus by Amstorg, the Russian agency promoting greater trade and urging Americans possessing construction expertise to bolster contracting, architectural and planning-related connections between the U.S. and the U.S.S.R. As will be shown below in Chapter 5, as government-sanctioned agencies in the U.S. began operating much more pervasively and strategically after World War II, they (like Amstorg in the U.S.S.R.) created institutional umbrellas under which even

more extensive, transnational, construction-related enterprises operated.

As American contractors enlarged the spectrum of their activities in Russia, they were unwittingly fitting within the kind of pattern that characterized their distant U.S. comrades who had chosen to work in Latin America at roughly the same time. The three salient trends seen there were also evident in Russia: cutting new industrial communities out of a country's whole cloth (as had been done with Chile's *oficinas*); selectively transplanting architectural and planning solutions (as had been done in Cuba and elsewhere); and creating a variegated spatial/functional matrix of up-to-date industrial factories, higher-rise commercial and residential towers, and massive infrastructural interventions.

American Building and Planning in China, 1907–1937

In 1933 one of the countries where the Austin Company exported its construction expertise was China. East of Hangzhou (Zhejiang) and north of Guangzhou (Guangdong), Austin erected a series of buildings for aircraft manufacturing, using (as they had in Russia) 'unskilled local labor under the supervision of Austin Company engineers'.[4] In the midst of growing civil warfare in China caused by Japanese invasions and severe rifts with the Communist Party, the Chinese Nationalist government commissioned the Curtiss Wright Corporation (New York) to assist in the dissemination of aircraft technology throughout those areas of China still under Nationalist control. Three years earlier, when the Nationalists were finishing the plan for their capital city at Nanjing, they had opted for German aircraft technology. This hedging of bets where up-to-date technology was concerned was not unusual in post-imperial China, where construction-related activities intensified between the end of

World War I and 1937, when Japanese military control halted virtually all significant construction throughout China.

American architects, planners, construction companies and real estate development firms were among the growing cast of international entrepreneurs who sought profits from an ever-changing China during this so-called 'republican' period, beginning after the fall of the Qing empire in 1911. American engineers, however, were establishing their presence in China before American architects began to practice there. Among the earliest engineering involvement by U.S. professionals occurred in 1907, when an American import-export firm in Shanghai (Fearon, Daniel & Company) contracted with a new company established by two Danes (Andersen, Meyer & Company) to finance an engineering department on a joint-account basis (*Far Eastern Review*, 1931, **27**, p. 151). That same year the President of Andersen, Meyer travelled to the U.S. and secured the exclusive right to represent the General Electric Company in China. In 1908 Andersen, Meyer parlayed that right into more bountiful cash when it secured its first large engineering contract with the Mukden (Shenyang) Electric Light Works.

Figure 4.23. This etching, showing Chinese workers erecting both Chinese buildings as well as those using foreign building methods, was indicative of a contemporary reality: that in Chinese cities during the 1920s and 1930s building technologies were changing significantly. (*Source*: Ferguson, 1931, p.73)

Andersen, Meyer then expanded its handling of American companies to include many machine and engineering firms, among the most notable of which were involved with building construction (Ferguson, 1931, pp. 73–94). By 1915 Andersen, Meyer

had made arrangements to represent several of the leading American manufacturers of textile machinery and equipment and had sold the first cotton mill completely equipped with American machinery. Since that time there has been a steady flow of orders for new mills and extensions to old mills. (*Ibid.*, p. 152)

During the early years of the twentieth century a small number of American missionaries who had some architectural or construction experience erected buildings for their missions in China. An even more significant American architectural presence was seen at the same time when the Young Men's Christian Association (YMCA) created an International Committee and began designing and building structures abroad that exemplified their moral messages (Cody, 1996*b*). However, the first non-missionary American architect who designed a building in China was probably Charles Paget, who collaborated to build the Arnold-Karberg Building in Guangzhou in 1905 (see above, Chapter 2).

It was not until 1914, however, that an American architect established an office in China. Rowland Curry, a native of Wooster, Ohio who graduated from Cornell University in 1907, moved to Shanghai in 1914 after practicing as an architect in Cleveland for 7 years. In Shanghai at the outbreak of World War I Curry was one of approximately twenty architects in that city, most of whom were British (Cody, 2000). Riding the rising crest of an economic boom, Curry designed banks and other commercial structures, as well as schools and an American Club, for which he often used American materials and structural systems that were increasingly becoming available for purchase in Shanghai, either through agents (such as Andersen, Meyer) or from representatives of the American firms themselves (such as Truscon).

By the end of World War I other American architects and contractors were tempted by Shanghai's promising commercial climate. One of the most noteworthy of the architects who established an office there was Henry K. Murphy (Cody, 2001), some of whose activities will be discussed below. But increasingly Murphy was joined by other Americans with building interests.

An American real estate development company, China Realty, began to compete with similar British and French firms, and by 1920 the Foundation Company, a firm mentioned earlier because of its involvement in Lima's infrastructural improvements, 'entered the China field on a large scale' by participating 'in a big plan to provide Shanghai with model American dwellings' (*Far Eastern Review*, 1920, **16**, pp. 662, 696). Less than a year later the Chino-American Engineering Corporation was established in Peking, 'to engage in general engineering and contracting for building construction and for the production of building materials' (*Far Eastern Review*, 1921, **17**, p. 491).

As important as Shanghai and other cities further north were for demonstrating the rising tide of American architectural influence, Guangzhou was the first testing ground where Chinese politicians consciously tried to apply up-to-date American planning principles (sometimes couched in terms of 'science' or 'efficiency') to a Chinese city that they perceived as inefficient.[5] There were two initial spheres of influence associated with this American connection: an institutional one, in which Guangzhou planners experimented with a commission form of American municipal government; and an influence related to urban space and form, as planners widened several narrow streets of congested Guangzhou and demolished its city wall. Guangzhou's planning experiments in the 1920s were at the forefront of further American planning connections, manifested in four ways: (1) through the actions of largely American-trained Chinese municipal experts, who studied in the U.S. using scholarships from the Boxer Indemnity Fund; (2) through American planning advisors, such as Henry K. Murphy, who were hired by Chinese politicians to provide direct planning assistance; (3) through the formation of professional organizations, such as the Association of Chinese and American Engineers; and (4) through publications in English and Chinese that disseminated information about city planning, urbanism and architecture to a professional audience.

Within a decade after 1911 some Chinese in a position of power began to model their city government administrations on American prototypes and to fashion the physical aspects of some cities with largely American, and to a lesser extent European, precedents in mind (Kai, 1922). The first hints of change came in 1911, as the Qing Empire in north China was dissolving, as Sun Yat-sen's ideas for a new Chinese republic were catching hold and when Cheng Tien-tow, a graduate of an unspecified American university, returned to Guangzhou to direct the municipal Public Works Department (*Far Eastern Review*, 1922, **18**, p. 22). In the first decade of the twentieth century some Chinese began to study engineering, architecture and city planning in the United States because of the Boxer Indemnity Fund (Hunt, 1972; Esherick, 1987).

Cheng advocated to Governor Cheng Chun-shun that he construct a Bund of commercial structures along the banks of the Zhujiang (Pearl) River, similar to Shanghai's district which was then attracting foreign investments (Lee, 1930). The Governor agreed. Cheng, the American-trained engineer, then suggested demolishing the 35 foot thick, 20 foot high and 7 mile-long, 800-year old, brick and stone walls that enveloped older portions of the city. Like some urban planners a half-century earlier who designed the Ringstrasse after demolishing Vienna's medieval wall, Cheng maintained that Guangzhou's walls constricted progress and that integral to the city's development were new, paved roads similar

Figures 4.24. This 1934 photograph of the Guangzhou Bund (waterfront skyline) shows how reinforced concrete and steel frame technologies – many of them from the United States – were altering the visual and commercial complexions of many Chinese cities. (*Source*: *National Geographic Magazine*, 1934, p. 622)

to those he had seen in the U.S. Scholars such as Marc Weiss (1987) and Richard Longstreth (1997) have demonstrated how important automobiles and boulevards were in fuelling California's remarkable property boom in the 1920s. Cheng Tien-tow certainly was aware of the California craze for both cars and boulevards on which to drive them. One of Cheng's colleagues, H.L. Wu, an engineering graduate of Ohio Northern University and the University of Illinois who had also returned to Guangzhou in 1911, agreed with Cheng's ideas but the two were unsuccessful in convincing Governor Cheng Chun-shun to begin dismantling the wall. However, in 1912 a large fire accomplished what the engineers Cheng and Wu had failed to do, providing a rationale for a first wave of demolition and road-building (*Far Eastern Review*, 1922, **18**, p. 22).

Political and military struggles intervened to halt this work until 1918 when China's first Bureau of Municipality was organized to govern the city. Modifications to this Bureau marked an initial sphere of influence, institutional in nature, that was exerted by American planning on Guangzhou, as Sun Ke tried to graft a commission form of Western

municipal government onto a Chinese stem. His efforts came approximately a decade after the first regulations on self-government were established in 1909 at the end of the Qing dynasty, and even more recently after Chinese President Yuan Shikai's abolition of local self-governmental institutions in early 1914.

Four years later in Guangzhou, at first two provincial commissioners were appointed as heads of the Bureau, one responsible for finance and the other for police, both under the direct control of the new Governor Chen Qiongming. However, changes came to the Bureau in part due to the persuasiveness of Sun Ke (also known as Sun Fo), the son of Sun Yat-sen, who had studied city planning and politics at UCLA in Los Angeles and at Columbia University in New York (Keith, 1922*a*). Sun Ke 'was filled with the desire to see Canton placed under a modern administration', and he pleaded with the Governor to alter the hierarchical arrangement of appointees being beholden to a patron by granting the city a charter, more in keeping with contemporary Western (particularly American) notions of municipal government (*Ibid.*). On 23 December 1920 Chen Qiongming agreed to grant the charter, and in March 1921 he allowed a municipal commission government to be instituted, with Sun Ke as mayor, assisted by six commissioners who administered the Departments of Finance, Public Works, Public Safety, Public Health, Public Utilities and Education. One Western journalist explained that 'the sphere of municipal activities is a large one and includes practically everything which pertains to city government in America' (*Ibid.*) The American analogy also applied to the commissioners themselves, since three out of the six had studied municipal government in the U.S. at institutions such as Purdue, MIT and Cornell. Sun Ke also invited three foreign engineers to become honorary commissioners; and one of those was the American architect Charles Paget (*Far Eastern Review*, 1921, **17**, p. 488).

The first problem the administration faced related to which land was governed by the city (initially 23.5 km²) and which was beyond city limits. Soon after the establishment of the Municipality the city's borders were extended to include 61.3 km² and in 1924 the municipal area swelled, mostly towards the east, to 178.4 km², although the population of the municipal area did not increase proportionately.[6] A related planning problem concerned how to facilitate transportation, since the old city centre is just east of where the Pearl River splits into two main branches (at Bai'e Tan), one heading east and the other south-east. The small island (Shameen), where most foreign commercial establishments had clustered during the late-nineteenth century, is also near that intersection, south-west of the traditional city core. During the nineteenth century a subsidiary district (Honam, or Henan), south of the east-running branch of the Pearl River, had been less developed than the land on the northern banks of the river, but easy transportation links between Honam and the central city had not materialized.

Other planning dilemmas faced by Sun Ke and his administrators were how to provide incentives for industrial development, how and where to design five new public parks and a prominent civic centre, and how to build up-to-date urban infrastructure such as steel or reinforced-concrete bridges, sewers, water lines, and gas or lighting fixtures. Massive new construction was suggested by Sun Ke and H.L. Wu, who was appointed the head of the Public Works Department in 1921. One important aspect of the new construction was the revived and intensified effort between December 1918 and December 1920 to demolish the city wall (Lee, 1936, p. 18). Using picks and shovels, 6000 labourers dismantled the wall and reused some of the building materials to construct approximately 20 miles of wide (70 feet by 150 feet), graded, and macadamized roads (*malu*, or '*maloos*' as they were sometimes called in English) that eased drainage, facilitated travel and had a lasting effect on the physical layout of the city. Approximately 6500 buildings were condemned, literally to pave the way for new, American-style boulevards (Kai, 1922).

At least one-third of the condemned buildings were demolished, actions initially resisted by many landowners.

The plan of the city was laid out by the city engineers and the streets were cut through the maize (*sic*) of buildings with ruthless disregard of the protests of the houseowners whose places happened to stand in the way. Only by forcing down this somewhat unpleasant medicine were the improvements made possible. (Kai, 1922)

In part, landowners were irate because of how previous political entities had taken control of their land: by forcing those holding deeds to relinquish them in exchange for vouchers that could be redeemed in local banks. Many of these vouchers proved worthless and deedholders thus traditionally mistrusted those who condemned property. Sun Ke tried to overcome what some foreigners called this 'syndicate system' in favour of 'the American system of condemnation and assessment' (Keith, 1922*b*). As a result, despite initial protests many landowners were not only compensated quickly, but they also turned handsome profits because of rapidly rising land values. Therefore, by the early 1920s, road building according to American practice was a second sphere of influence (in addition to institutional restructuring) exerted by American planning upon the form and dynamics of Guangzhou.

Guangzhou's destruction of its city wall and some of its residential districts should be seen more broadly as the beginning of what was then considered to be a reformed national urban policy. The reworking of Chinese municipal administrations between 1911 and 1922 came as part of national reconstruction (*guojia jianshe*) ardently supported by Sun Yat-sen. Sun's struggle for political power in post-Qing China was matched by his fervent attempts to alter the purposes of many Chinese cities and to prioritize investment so that a national policy of urban reconstruction could spearhead China's development (Thomson, 1969, p. 212). Sun wrote about his programmes in *The International Development of China*, published in 1921 and translated into English a year later. Sun's 'First Programme' was for a 'Great Northern Port' (*beifang dagang*) near Tianjin, a project similar to the 1919 'Chihli Development Plan' proposed by northern Chinese gentry (*shensi*). In part, this port was planned by Harry Hussey, a Canadian architect trained in Chicago who in the late 1910s was dismissed by the Rockefeller Foundation after supervising the design and construction of Peking Union Medical College. Another of Sun's programmes called for an equivalent southern port (at Guangzhou), where he emphasized harbour and residential construction.

Was Sun's 'modern residential city' influenced by Ebenezer Howard's Garden City ideals, as Sun implicitly suggested when he affirmed that Guangzhou was 'an ideal place for planning a garden city with attractive parks' (Sun, 1922, p. 86)? Or was he thinking of more American examples when he advocated the 'remodelling' of all residential construction 'according to modern comforts and conveniences'? It is possible that he thought of precedents from both the U.K. and the U.S. Sun Ke had no doubt seen first-hand many examples of American single-family residences in southern California, where the platting of subdivisions was proliferating at the time, or he might have taken an interest in ways that planners such as Clarence Perry or Grosvenor Atterbury in the New York metropolitan area were experimenting, beginning in 1911, with Garden City ideals at Forest Hill Gardens. In his fund-raising tours to the U.S., Sun Yat-sen had also seen pertinent examples of American housing and he predicted that those residential comforts for China were 'bound to come, either unconsciously by social evolution or consciously by artificial

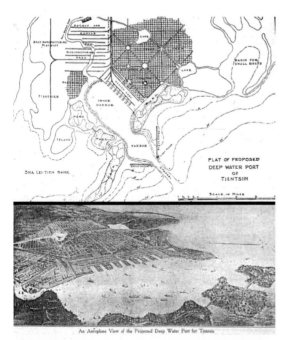

Figure 4.25. This plan for a large industrial port extension of Tianjin, China in the early 1920s was part of Sun Yat-sen's dream for industrial development along China's coastline. The preliminary drawings for the scheme, never fully realized, were by Harry Hussey, a Canadian architect trained at Chicago's Armour Institute of Technology, who travelled to China in 1911 to work for the YMCA. (*Source: Far Eastern Review*, **16**(1), January, 1920, p. 15)

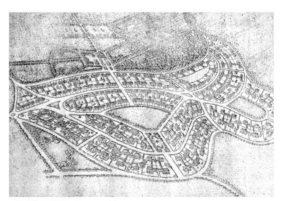

Figure 4.26. When U.S. Chinese planners (joined by one German) began reconfiguring Nanjing in the late-1920s, after Chiang Kai-shek made the city the new Chinese capital, they envisioned large-scale changes, including residential districts like these, patterned after American neighborhood plans. Because of ongoing civil strife and war with Japan, most of these plans were never realized. (*Source*: *Shoudu Jihua*, 1935, n.p.)

construction'. He and his followers preferred the latter alternative. This 'artificial construction' was a further indication, then, that Chinese politicians such as Sun Yat-sen, and students returning from U.S. universities such as Sun Ke, were beginning consciously to adopt certain American planning principles, and then were adapting those principles to try to solve Chinese urban problems.

Sun's reconstruction theories made many unemployed Chinese engineers hopeful that they would be hired to put his theories into practice. One unnamed American engineer suggested that 'the engineering societies of the world should make Dr. Sun their "patron saint", because if he ever got in a position where he could put his plans into effect, there would be work for engineers in China for the next 1000 years' (*China Critic*, **1**, 1928, p. 139).

In the context of Sun's proposals, and in light of the growing numbers of Chinese students returning from study abroad, one organization that demonstrated the ever-intensifying influence of American planning in China was the Association of Chinese and American Engineers, organized in Beijing on 22 November 1919. Beginning with only twenty-five members, the Association's membership mushroomed to 432 by 1927 (*Far Eastern Review*, 1927, **23**, p. 165). In the Introduction of the premier issue of the Association's journal, an unnamed editor elaborated on the organization's genesis and scope. Although the editor did not mention city planning *per se*, much of what he expressed concerning engineering and public works unequivocally also applied to planning practice:

The world is going forward too fast for the people of any nation to think of shutting themselves in from the outside world and expect to keep step with the progress of the times . . . Fortunately, the Boxer Indemnity returned by the U.S. Government has made it possible for a large number of Chinese students to be sent to America to study and graduate in the different branches of engineering in American colleges . . . As a country China is similar in many respects to America and since each year sees more of her

sons educated in the schools and colleges of America, and each year sees a larger number of these students returning to China, it is only natural that the engineers in China and the engineers in America should co-operate and work together in the development of this country along *modern scientific lines* [author's emphasis on 'modern scientific lines']; for China, though old in history and culture is new in her present form of government and in the science of engineering . . . Having studied the same courses in the same colleges and universities in America where the same ideas and ideals were inculcated in the minds of both Chinese and American engineers, it is but natural that there should be, and is, much in common between the large number of engineers educated in America and American engineers now resident in China . . . Many prominent men who have visited China . . . have said that China is well supplied with scholars, politicians and labourers of all classes but painfully short of technical men – men who can bring modern engineering to the service of the nation – men who can build her railways, develop her harbors and ports, construct her canals and control her rivers, who can open her mines, build her steel mills, install her hydroelectric plants, construct her highways, tramways, ships and all the other many and diverse works of modern civilization . . . In hundreds of cities throughout China engineers will be engaged in the building of electric light plants, water-works, sewerage systems, highways and many other civic works which mark the march of a nation along the paths of progress and material prosperity. (*Journal of the Association of Chinese and American Engineers*, 1920, **1**, p. 1)

Which cities? Frustratingly, the author did not specify. However, although Guangzhou was not mentioned by name, the planning activities underway in the city when the above-quoted words were written attest to the correlation between their ideals and Guangzhou's direction where planning was concerned. Guangzhou, then, was one of the major testing grounds for Western-style municipal progress in post-Qing China. The progress was gauged in terms of what the city looked like, how clogged its transportation arteries were, how antiquated its port facilities were perceived to be, and whether it was governed by a warlord or a more Western form of commission government. Within a few short years, other cities such as Tianjin, Shenyang, Xiamen, Shantou, Harbin and Fuzhou had followed Guangzhou's lead (Rasmussen, 1925;

Wu, 1931; Bostwick, 1926). In so doing, they helped set precedents throughout China for destroying traditional walled settlements, widening roads and recladding street façades with more up-to-date architectural features, and trying to finance infrastructural and other improvements along Western lines.

Relatively little is known of Murphy's 1927 plan for Guangzhou, which was approved by Sun in March of that year, and very little of a graphic nature has survived. Two features of the plan received

Figure 4.27. Zhongshan Road, Xiamen (Fujian Province), China. In the mid-1920s, because of street-widening in Guangzhou, other southern Chinese cities also began refashioning their downtown districts: asphalting roads, erecting arcaded shopfronts and implanting electrical systems. Many of these interventions were inspired by what was occurring in U.S. cities. (Photograph by the author)

particular notice: the desire to update Guangzhou's harbour facilities; and the proposal to erect a large, Chinese-style civic centre designed to centralize the operations of disparate municipal bureaus in one imposing building, as had become commonplace in many large American cities as a result of the ideals expressed by Daniel Burnham and others at the turn of the century. This centre was eventually designed in the early 1930s by Lin Keming, a young Chinese architect who had studied in Lyon, France from 1920 to 1926 and who had worked in Paris in the office of Alfred Agache. To plan harbour improvements, Murphy turned to Ernest P. Goodrich, a renowned American civil engineer and city planner who as early as 1907 had helped design harbours in Bogotá, Colombia; Valparaíso, Chile; the Philippines; as well as Los Angeles, Portland (Oregon), Newark, Albany and Brooklyn in the U.S. Goodrich had visited China in 1920 (Goodrich, 1930).

The *New York Times* journalist who reported enthusiastically about the 1927 plan described Murphy's proposals as follows

The Canton of Mr. Murphy's blueprints will be a pleasant contrast to those [of] other cities in China that have come under the influence of the West. It will have some of the glamour of Peking. Like Peking, the entire city will converge toward a splendid central group of buildings, all squared around Chinese courtways, with sloping, up-turned, majestic roofs, with supporting pillars and latticed windows. This will be the civic center . . . From the civic center will radiate four wide avenues: one to the northwest orchard country, past the famous flower pagoda; another to the White Cloud Mountain in the northeast; a third to the riverfront in Tungshan; a fourth to the shore opposite the island of Shameen. Straight down to the river will be the wide central axis, with its arches, and a bridge crossing over to the crowded district of Honam. Care is being taken in the plan not to disturb any of the old temples. Wide thoroughfares through which carts and motor cars pass are necessary, but it is also necessary that a Chinese city should remain Chinese. (*New York Times*, 1927, 13 March, III, p. 13)

Therefore, Murphy took Beijing as his ideal of a Chinese city. However, unlike Beijing, which was planned according to principles codified in the Kaogongji (a famous Zhou dynasty text), where urban form was based upon walls, gates and roads that defined nine equal squares, Murphy's Guangzhou plan was based upon avenues that radiated from a prominent monument. This Baroque planning notion was also favoured by many American planners of the City Beautiful Movement, and since Murphy believed that the 'long vista' was also a fundamental principle of traditional Chinese architectural design, he seemed to synthesize in his Guangzhou plan (although he never expressed this synthesis outright) the urban planning ideals of the City Beautiful Movement with those of axial symmetry in places such as the Forbidden City in Beijing.

Sun Ke was probably Murphy's most pivotal Chinese ally because in his positions, first as Mayor of Guangzhou, then as Minister of Finance of the Nationalist Government in 1927, and finally as Minister of Railways in 1928. Sun was able to argue on the inside of the government for the practical implementation of the plan rather than abstractly debate its aesthetic merits from the sidelines. However, Sun's efforts in this regard initially were thwarted because of continuing economic and political uncertainties. Even after the preliminary approval of Murphy's planning suggestions in 1927, the reality of implementation collided with more pressing problems associated with political stability. It was not until the early 1930s that many of the planning solutions for Guangzhou, such as bridges and a civic centre, were actually implemented. However, in 1927 as hopes for a new civic plan dimmed in Guangzhou, an even more ambitious planning possibility emerged further north.

It was in Nanjing where attempts to create a truly up-to-date city were the most far-reaching. For a brief period of 10 years, from 1927 when Chiang Kai-shek made the city China's capital, until 1937, when Nanjing was massively bombed by the Japanese, the capital was at the forefront of Chinese urban reconstruction and, as in Guangzhou, Henry Murphy played a key role in the city's plan. Nanjing (the southern capital) had been a capital in the Ming Dynasty, from 1368 to 1421, when the capital was then shifted to the northern capital (Beijing). Nanjing was selected by the Nationalists to replace Beijing (or Peiping, as it was then called) in part because of Sun Yat-sen's suggestion as early as 1911. Sun Ke was appointed as an emissary of the Government; he travelled worldwide to seek

the funds for the tremendous program [of Reconstruction] made necessary by the years of civil war . . . The program included flood control projects, port improvements and the planning of the new Nanjing. These plans no doubt will [follow] Murphy's basic idea with Canton, [that being] to prevent the destruction of the native charm of the city through the chance infiltrations of Occidental architecture and ideas of city development. (*New York Times*, 1928, 15 October, p. 25)

Murphy was hired in October 1928 as the chief architectural adviser to the Nationalist Government for the Nanjing Plan, for approximately one year. The news of an American planner involved in the design of a new Chinese capital was widely disseminated (*City Planning*, 1929). Murphy again hired Ernest P. Goodrich to assist him in Nanjing, and Goodrich in turn employed two other Americans, Colonel Irving C. Moller and Theodore T. McCroskey, to assist in solving cartographic and engineering problems (*China Critic*, 1929, **2**, p. 517). When Murphy and Goodrich arrived in Nanjing, city planning work had already been undertaken. The British-trained Liu Chi-wen, who became mayor of the city in July 1928, had immediately begun surveying, dredging waterways, and planning the erection of several public markets and Nationalist monuments. A National Capital Reconstruction Planning Committee (*Shoudu jianshe weiyuanhui*) was organized, Chinese members of which were to work with Murphy and his American cohorts under the administrative control of a Land Bureau, organized in April 1928. Lin Yimin, an American-educated engineer, was the principal Chinese appointed to the Committee, with Zhou Yue and Huang Yuyu as the other two engineering and architectural assistants (Tyau, 1930). Road widening efforts were the most visible manifestation of the Committee's work. Liu Chi-wen was following the precedent set in Guangzhou of 'cutting off the fronts of structures, building new ones and widening the pavement' (Bostwick, 1926, p. 36). He believed that orderly traffic was the basis of an orderly municipality.

In the late 1920s Murphy had his own dreams for Nanjing. The journalist Chester Rowell, who interviewed Murphy as he began his advising work in Nanjing, broadly described Murphy's sentiments:

Of all the officials in China, probably the happiest in his job is Henry Killam Murphy, architect and city planner, whose business it is to do for the capital city of the new China what Major L'Enfant did for Washington, the American capital a hundred years ago. Murphy, too, is dreaming a dream which may not be fully realized until a hundred years after he is dead. But in that dream, and in his work towards its fulfilment, Murphy is happy. And no wonder! At Delhi, in India and at Canberra in Australia, architects are building great European government edifices in the far corners of the earth. But Murphy's job is to build a Chinese capital out of the ancient city of Nanking, and his dream is to make it Chinese. One of his tasks is to convince the leaders of new China that this Chinese capital ought to be Chinese. He has nearly done that. (Rowell, undated)

Zoning was recommended as a basis for developmental control. Patterned upon American zoning ordinances (New York's Zoning Act of 1916 was less than a generation old) and drafted with Ernest Goodrich's assistance, the National Government Enabling Act for Municipal Planning and Zoning empowered municipalities to adopt regulations for land-use control, and Nanjing was divided into eight districts (Tyau, 1930). Three kinds of residential housing were envisioned for the thousands of new residents who began flocking

to the new capital after 1928: 'workers', 'poorer classes', and detached 'villas' for the richer classes and government officials.

The villas were designed with Chinese stylistic features, and organized spatially in ways similar to contemporary American subdivisions, and perhaps more specifically, to Clarence Perry's neighbourhood planning concepts. Perry's first major policy statement about 'the neighborhood unit for the family-life community' was in 1929, just as Murphy was working on the Nanjing plan. Although there is no documented connection between the two, it is certainly conceivable that Murphy, given his strong professional connections to the New York metropolitan area, would have known of Perry's ideas. It is also possible that Murphy suggested these villa designs based upon a housing development he had designed in Coral Gables, Florida in 1926, although here, too, the connection cannot be fully substantiated. In the late-1920s and early-1930s other foreign architects in Shanghai were designing similar kinds of villa projects that reflected Perry's notions about neighbourhood. Columbia Circle, designed by the popular Hungarian architect Ladislav Hudec and financed by the Asia Realty Company (which was directed by the American Frank Raven and incorporated in the U.S.) was a significant example of this trend, where American stylistic ornamentation and nomenclature were invoked as marketing attractions (Cody, 1999b).

In Nanjing, five kinds of zones were distinct from residential: port or industrial development, military or commercial aviation, and a governmental centre. These zones reflected projected growth occurring at the extremities of the existing settlement. Thus, port development was encouraged at the city's north-west corner, while industrial areas and a commercial aviation field would help service the port to the south. A military aviation field was to be located at the south-east corner of Nanjing's centre, servicing the government centre, to the east of the city walls.

Despite rapid population growth, the Nanjing Government's approach to urban development was cautious. 'The feeling is growing that Nanking must get something built soon, or lose prestige', Murphy wrote in mid-February 1930, 'but they don't seem inclined to agree with my optimistic decision that they will need a lot of room for expansion quite soon'. This was probably disappointing to Murphy because it implied that the first government structures would be constructed within the city walls instead of in the 'Capitol Hill' area he had planned. But Murphy's persistence and thrill at being accorded the honors, opportunities and responsibilities in his role as advisor managed to carry him through unsettled circumstances in early 1930.

His first break came in late 1929, when Chiang Kai-shek personally approved of Murphy's plan for a 'Chinese Arlington', a memorial cemetery and five-building complex for 'Heroes of the Revolution' (today's Lingu Si) in the far eastern foothills of Purple Mountain, adjacent to the Government Centre district. Not only did Murphy hope that this was the beginning of a stage of construction in the city area so dear to his heart, but he was also thrilled about designing a memorial pagoda.

Chinese officials in Nanjing continued to grapple with a series of architectural priorities. In January 1930, the importance of gardens and open space was stressed, and comparisons with American and European notions of landscaping were made. The Commission emphasized that boulevards should link urban gardens so that 'the whole city can become a big garden'. New York's Bronx River Parkway was cited as a good example of a 'boulevard' which integrated effective transportation functions with landscaping aesthetics. Trees were planted on the edges of Zhongshan Lu, to emphasize its processional function and to enhance the 'garden-like' aspect of the city centre. This tree-planting campaign launched during the tenure of the Reconstruction Committee was so pervasive that it has had a palpable impact

on Nanjing's distinctively tree-shaded character ever since. The January report also praised the kind of design for an administrative centre on the eastern outskirts of Nanjing which Murphy had proposed the previous Spring, although he was not named as a source and variations of his plan were also considered.

This was not the only case in which Murphy's role can be seen to be less dominant than might be supposed from his own recounting of events. In March 1930, for example, an essay regarding the plan by Heinrich Schubart, a German consultant from the Bauer mission was in contrast to ideas expressed by Lin Yimin in October 1929. Schubart stressed the practical planning considerations implied by attempts to transform Nanjing into a commercial hub, whereas Lin envisioned the plan in more idealistic terms, imagining Nanjing as a paradigm for scientific city planning principles as they were being applied in Europe and the United States.

By 1929 Shanghai had organized a city planning commission similar to Nanjing's (MacPherson, 1990). Dong Dayou (Dayu Doon), a University of Minnesota graduate who had previously worked with Murphy at the Lingu Si complex, was selected as chief architectural adviser to work with Sheng-Yi, Chairman of the Special Municipality of Greater Shanghi Reconstruction Commission. An architectural competition was held to consider a new plan for a 'civic centre' of Greater Shanghai (Da Shanghai), envisioned for an area in north-east Shanghai, between the Bund and the mouth of the Yangzi River to the north-east. Shanghai's civic centre plans paralleled Nanjing's in stylistic terms because an adaptation of Chinese architecture was favoured by the Commission, which hoped 'to make Shanghai the great monument to the new China and an example to the entire country' (China Critic, 1929, 2). As the central government in Nanjing began its attempts actually to build what was drawn on the drafting boards, so too Shanghai government officials began appropriating land for the civic centre and a wide assortment of city planning experts were consulted. One was C.E. Grunsky, a former president of the American Society of Civil Engineers. He was joined by Asa E. Phillips, the American city planner from Washington, D.C., Professor Hermann Jansen of Berlin University and Jacob Crane, the Chicago planning consultant, also advised Chinese officials about their urban plans in 1931, on his way to more extensive planning work in Russia.

By the early 1930s in Shanghai, just as Japan was preparing for massive occupation of the Chinese mainland, several property developers were beginning to erect tall apartment blocks whose units appealed to expatriate and local elites. Publications such as *The Hexagon* and *The China Builder* tried to lure buyers for these flats by proclaiming that Shanghai was finally able to offer American-style, high-rise dwellings as a complement to low-rise alternatives such as terrace housing or detached villas in suburban culs-de-sac (Cody, 1995).

Conclusion

As World War II was germinating in Europe and Asia, American architecture and urbanism – in a multitude of forms, spaces and functions – was being adopted as one of the world's major paradigms of progress. The myriad examples discussed above, from south of the U.S. border to the vast expanses of Asia, reflect a variegated pattern of adaptations derived from U.S. prototypes. Part of that pattern was commercial, as 'Wall Streets' of differing scales and complexions were being erected from Havana to Shanghai. Another element of that pattern was more residential, reflected in detached dwellings on curving streets, as well as in high-rise apartments stacked in steel-framed towers.

A third, no less significant aspect of the pattern was related to industrial structures that epitomized American capitalism à la Ford, Taylor and others. For

Figures 4.28 and 4.29. During the period between the two World Wars, American builders, architects, planners and others involved in the construction trades were exporting on a worldwide basis the components of the up-to-date American city, from simple wharf structures at Ponce, Puerto Rico (figure 4.29) to large-scale urban high rises and infrastructure (figure 4.28). (*Sources: System*, 1910, **18**(3), p. 253; Purdy & Henderson papers.)

example, Truscon had succeeded so well financially by 1935 that it was absorbed by Republic Steel , the world's largest producer of stainless steel. In late 1935 Republic also purchased the Berger Manufacturing Company, an early producer of standardized sheet metal, which in 1934 began to market the 'Berloy Steel-Frame House', a prefabricated dwelling unit that could be built by one person without machinery. In 1936 Republic merged Truscon and Berger's export concerns, hoping to capitalize on the expertise of two proven giants in the commercial field of standardized, prefabricated technologies.[7] The American war effort in the 1940s boosted the export of portable buildings to new levels of sophistication. In 1940 the Butler Manufacturing Company became the licensed fabricator for a 'Panelbilt' construction system that featured a truss-less rigid frame and steel panels 'of such large size that [it] is probably the simplest of all, so far as erection is concerned' (*American Exporter*, 1944, June). During the war the U.S. government used Butler technologies for structures as large as airplane hangars, and subsequently commercial clients followed suit, for reasons that manufacturers and designers had trumpeted since the late 1870s: 'strength in relation to weight, compactness of materials in ocean shipping, simplicity of assembly, fire-safeness, and mobility, i.e. the readiness with which they are enlarged or taken down and re-erected on a new location' (*American Exporter*, 1945, **137**, September). These examples were historically part of the 'foundation for a larger structure' of industrialized building systems that proliferated after 1945 (Cody, 1997). As will be shown in the chapter that follows, other key elements in that larger structure were foreign-aid sponsored, low-cost ('sites-and-services') housing schemes that used precast concrete foundations and concrete block machinery.

Systemitized urban and regional infrastructure was a fourth key component to the pattern, whereby roads, sewers, bridges, power stations and other building blocks in a 'landscape of modernity' (Ward and Zunz, 1992) were exported by those working from American metropoles to disparate peripheries on a global, but still uncoordinated scale.

NOTES

1. I thank Professor Tom Peters, Lehigh University, for bringing Purdy & Henderson's work in Cuba to my attention.

2. Drawing E-1 (September 1927 with June–July 1928 revisions), National Capitol, Microfilm roll #69, Palacio del Congreso, Purdy & Henderson Company archives, New York, New York.

3. In the *Austin Book of Buildings*, 1922, p. 55 the list of clients included Cuban Carbonic (Havana, Cuba), Caribbean Petroleum and Tropical Oil (Colombia), Enamelled Steel Products, Watford, England), Arkell & Douglass (Jamaica), International Steel Corporation (Panama), Atlantic Gulf Oil and New England Fuel Company (Tampico, Mexico), Puerto Rico International Corporation (Puerto Rico), Cape Explosives Company (Cape Town, South Africa), Martini (Buenos Aires), the U.S. Navy (Gibraltar) and the U.S. Army (Verniul and Abainville, France).

4. The Hangzhou plant was built for the Central Aircraft Manufacturing Company, at 'Chien Chiao', 8 miles east of Hangzhou. The Guangdong facility was the Shuikwan Aircraft Works, at Shiu Chow. Information from Austin Company archives, files 1246-H and 1246-K, respectively.

5. A more comprehensive discussion of Murphy's work in Nanjing and Guangzhou can be found in Cody, 1996*a* and Cody, 2001.

6. In 1921 the population was estimated at 788,000; in 1923 it was 802,000 and in 1928 there were 804,000 in the municipal area. See Schinz, 1989, p. 309.

7. Berger Manufacturing Co. was based in Canton, Ohio. See *American Exporter*, 1908, **62**, November, p. 96; *Ibid.*, 1925, **96**, May, p. 46; and *The Constructor*, 1935, **17**, June pp. 6–7.

5 Architectural Tools of War and Peace, 1945–1975

In 1957 the American social commentator Max Lerner, reflecting upon World War II, suggested that

in a world where Americans had to hold their coalition together despite the faltering economies of their allies, and where they had to keep undeveloped economies from succumbing to Communism by default, they found new political uses for reconstruction and investment capital and for the export of technical skills and the tools of war and peace. (Lerner, 1957, p. 885)

Some of those skills and tools concerned buildings and city planning. Which ones? Who helped facilitate the exportation? What were the results? These are three of the main questions that help frame a consideration of American architectural exporting during the 30-year period of peace and war from 1945, marking the end of World War II, to 1975, when the U.S. military withdrew from Vietnam and when oil-rich nations in the Middle East began to wield stronger clout worldwide. After the military victories over Germany and Japan, illusory peace and chilling Cold War ushered in a global wave of work for Americans (and their competitors) involved in construction. That wave swelled with the Marshall Plan and its aftermath in Europe. It then crested in the Middle East as a result of planning schemes associated with petroleum exploitation, in East

Figure 5.1. 'The Servant of Freedom'. This provocative drawing by Boris Artzybasheff (1900–1965) for an advertisement of the Wickwire Rope Company during World War II was accompanied by the assertions that 'The mighty servant of all America is the great construction industry. Now during the war it is helping to crush our enemies. With victory Construction [*sic*] will again serve the peace-time progress of free men'. (*Source: The Constructor*, 1943, **25**(2))

Asia because of U.S. investments associated with postwar exporting of American principles (Zunz, 1998, pp. 159–188), and in South America because of manufacturing investments and burgeoning middle classes (or 'middle masses' as one anthropologist termed them), many of whom yearned for American products, buildings and spaces. Those tastes sparked substantial construction-related investments from private and public U.S. interests. Persistent warfare in some regions, such as postcolonial Southeast Asia, brought other waves of construction (and destruction), the most glaring example of which was the Vietnam/American War.

Previous chapters have established how, in the 60 years from the 1870s to the 1930s, the foundation for American architectural exporting after World War II had been laid broadly and deeply. Whether operating alone or in commercial concert, disparate constellations of American builders and designers were establishing a stronger presence in settings beyond U.S. borders. In so doing, they were building

part of the infrastructure for significantly more pervasive, global involvement by U.S. professionals associated with architecture, engineering and construction (commonly, and hereafter referred to as 'AEC') in the years after Nuremberg and Hiroshima. It is now appropriate to explore how the rest of that infrastructure came to be put in place.

Henry Luce's famous *Life* editorial in February 1941 that coined the phrase 'the American Century' 'challenged Americans to recognize that their own welfare was dependent on the world's freedom and to rise "spiritually and practically" to their status as citizens of the world's "most powerful and vital nation"' (Zunz, 1998, p. ix). One dimension of that practicality concerned the built environment. Some scholars have argued that between 1945 and 1970 'most international construction was American' (Strassman and Wells, 1987, p. 23). Many of those builders, such as the Milliken Brothers, either faltered or were absorbed by larger corporate entities. Others – such as the Austin Company, Morrison-Knudsen or Parsons, Brinckerhoff – stayed the course and rode the international waves of construction after the War. Some architects, engineers and builders acted as what one might call 'private hands', venturing beyond U.S. borders either independently or for private companies, as many of their American predecessors had done before mid-century. However, as will be shown below, one of the distinguishing features of post-World War II architectural exporting was how U.S. governmental institutions began to play more significant roles, becoming what one might term 'public gloves' in bolstering the transfer of American architectural skills – and its tools for war and peace – to countries where those institutions exerted increasing influence. In so doing, the protective 'glove' of the U.S. government facilitated American architectural exporting by a proliferating number of 'private hands'.

One of those institutions was the U.S. military, which played a catalytic role for American construction-related initiatives on a worldwide scale. Near the end of World War II the U.S. government began setting the stage for profound American architectural influence abroad when it intensified the activities of the Army Corps of Engineers, established in 1802. In the early-1940s, as the ranks of the U.S. military swelled, so too did domestic, military-financed construction. As Donald Albrecht has written,

In [1940–41] Army camp capacity quadrupled through the rapid construction of standardized barracks, mess halls and other structures. These simple buildings, marching like soldiers toward the horizon, captured a wartime ethos of conformity and consensus that later proved valuable to many who traded their Army fatigues for gray flannel suits. (Albrecht, 1995, p. xvi)

That 'horizon', towards which those 'simple buildings' marched, stretched from Europe to Asia and beyond. By summer 1945 in the islands of the western Pacific the Army Corps of Engineers was shipping prefabricated hospitals from the U.S. mainland and 'carving whole new communities out of the jungle' (Saunders, 1945, p. 124). In Guam, for example, military engineers

backed up by the tools that typify American construction genius – huge trucks, power shovels, and the peerless bulldozers – have changed the Guamanian landscape for keeps. They hacked landing strips out of the jungle, built 300 miles of paved highways, put together nearly 10,000 Quonset huts, constructed thousands of other buildings, developed a water supply system and deepened and enlarged the harbor. (*Ibid.*)

In North Africa the Corps planned and constructed airfields, roads and new ports. Sometimes the Corps of Engineers was acting like a planning agency (Reybold, 1943), a role it had also played in World War I, but not as intensively in the late-1910s as during and after World War II. The mushrooming U.S. defence infrastructure of the early 1940s 'provided its own argument for continued defense production' (Davidson, 1995, p. 185), some of which

Springboard to Victory

Figure 5.2. Prefabricated buildings and landing mats for aircraft being assembled by workers in the South Pacific during World War II. The U.S. Steel Export Company, which published the drawing showing the airplane, boasted that 'when the conflict is over, [we] will supply trademarked U.S. steels for every peacetime commercial and domestic need'. (*Sources: American Exporter*, 1942, **131**(6), p. 46; 1944, **135**(5), p. 62)

was siphoned off to nations allied with the U.S., which welcomed financial assistance in the form of military construction at the onset of the Cold War (Anders, 1954).

However, some non-governmental exporters were drawn into the public glove not because of the U.S. military, but instead due to the scale of economic support earmarked by the U.S. government for non-military foreign aid and development programmes (Cleveland *et al.*, 1960, p. 109; Rimmer, 1988, p. 768). There were three main catalysts for these programmes. The first was the Bretton Woods (New Hampshire) agreements of 1944, which established the International Monetary Fund and the International Bank for Reconstruction and Development (i.e., the World Bank) (Van Dormael, 1978). Bretton Woods was followed in 1947 by the Marshall Plan, which provided significant foreign aid for war-torn Europe until 1953 (Ellwood, 1992; Diefendorf,1993). The third catalyst was President Harry Truman's Point Four Program of 1949, which established the Technical Cooperation Administration to bring 'the benefits of our [U.S.] scientific advances and industrial progress available for the improvement and growth of undeveloped areas'(Truman, 1949, quotation; Daniels, 1950; Bernstein, 1970).

Even before Bretton Woods, however, a prelude to U.S. foreign aid programmes also served as a catalyst for American AEC expansion to regions worldwide. In 1934 the Export-Import Bank of Washington, established by President Franklin Roosevelt, began to show its muscle with respect to lending funds for industrial redevelopment. Especially in South America, the Export-Import Bank financed a multitude of planning-related construction projects during the war, from railways and reclamation works to steel mills and power plants. One important component of these agreements stipulated that credit funds used to purchase equipment for the works in question had to be spent exclusively for goods or services from U.S. companies (*American Exporter*, 1941, **128**, p. 130; *Engineering-News Record*, 1943, **136**; Ross, 1943; Dulles, 1944; Pugh, 1957). This caveat to 'buy American' often served as a precedent for subsequent aid programmes. For example, in the World Bank's first 8 years roughly two-thirds of the money it loaned was spent in the U.S. itself for construction equipment and materials. There was an inherent preference, therefore, for those firms most familiar with American technologies (*Engineering-News Record*, 1953, **151**). Another *quid pro quo* condition, this one related to the Marshall Plan, came in the form of 'counterpart programmes' where, 'as a condition for receiving Marshall Plan funds, each recipient nation was required to put up a specified amount of its own currency in a fund to be used for roughly the same purposes as the dollar grants' (*Architectural Forum*, 1955, **102**, January, p.102).

These conditions, which often benefited U.S. companies and the U.S. balance of payments, have made it easier for critics of American-influenced economic globalization to see selfish, nefarious ulterior motives behind many U.S. foreign aid programmes. When contemporary architectural analysts reflected upon what they saw regarding the connection between American building and industrial expansion by American businesses, some of those motives are clearly apparent.

> Our industry and commerce are expanding in search of new sources of raw materials, new markets for finished products. To serve increased travel and trade, hotels and stores are springing up along the new commercial routes. (*Ibid.*)

Among the companies that acted upon the implications from heightened trade and travel were Sears, Roebuck and the Hilton International Hotel chain, both of which began expanding their overseas operations in the early postwar period (Wharton, 2001; *Architectural Forum*, 1995, **102**, January p. 110). Other retailers and hoteliers followed suit.

However much they might have been criticized later, these construction-and planning-related ventures by the Export-Import Bank, the Corps of Engineers and other government entities were also highly critical in three main ways for American

Figure 5.3. 'Boston Beach', a hotel and resort designed and built in Jamaica, British West Indies, by Rader Associates, an American firm, in the early 1960s. American architectural exporting of hotels and other building types associated with travel and leisure grew substantially in the post-World War II economic climate. (*Source*: Rader Associates)

architectural exporters. First, by establishing precedents, especially by virtue of military-related rationales, the projects financed by the Bank and the Corps prepared some planners, contractors, engineers and architects for subsequent projects. If the 'wartime ethos of conformity and consensus' helped prepare soldiers to function in a conservative postwar U.S. society, that same ethos helped prepare a spectrum of American architectural exporters to work hand in glove with U.S. government agencies that funded projects abroad. At one end of that spectrum were individual professionals such as Albert Mayer and Julian Whittlesley, helping to plan Chandigarh, India; Neutra and Alexander, working in Guam; and Jacob Crane, whom we met in the previous chapter consulting in China and Russia in the early 1930s, and who after the war began studying tropical housing in Southeast Asia. In 1955 the *Architectural Forum* called the work of these individuals 'deeply humane enterprises' (*Architectural Forum*, 1955, **102**, January, p. 102). At the other end of the spectrum, shouldering 'the lion's share of work . . . helping underdeveloped nations realize their potentials',

were large engineering and construction firms such as Knappen, Tippetts, Abbett & McCarthy (based in New York and later known as TAMS), which between 1950 and 1955 worked on $3.7 billion in projects spanning a dozen countries (*Ibid.*). Other individuals and firms operated between these two ends of that metaphorical spectrum.

Second, those projects sparked by U.S. federal money were sometimes responsible for erecting tangible foundations of transportation, public health and/or electric power-related infrastructure in foreign countries that the U.S. deemed to be either real or potential allies. After the war, wealthier middle classes from many of those countries then invested in either individual buildings or larger settings – for example, office structures, residential enclaves, retail centres – that were often tinged with palpable U.S. influences. Both the infrastructure and the American-inspired architecture tethered to it were imposing manifestations of a postwar perspective about progress and prosperity. Metaphorically welded to each other, the infra/archi/structure was 'imposing' in two senses; imposing (physically) in terms of its

Figure 5.4. A hydroelectric plant under construction at Bokara, India, where women workers assisted in the transformation of a pre-industrial landscape. The facility was designed and built by the International General Electric Co. of India, with assistance from the Harza Engineering Co. of Chicago. (*Source: Architectural Forum*, 1955, **102**, January, p. 102)

Figure 5.5. Eldorado housing project in Santiago, Chile, built with financing from IBEC, the International Basic Economy Corporation. Large cranes lowered steel forms onto concrete floor slabs. For a closer view of the process, see figure 5.12. The configuration of the houses was similar to many residential subdivisions that were then being planned and built throughout the U.S. (*Source*: Broehl, 1968, p. 198)

scale and imposing (subconsciously) in terms of its intrusive impact.

In 1955 when *Architectural Forum* published a probing article about the trends it saw in U.S. building abroad since the War, it began by gushing that

Our architects and planners are creating whole new towns from teeming India to tiny El Salvador. Our engineers and contractors are building new dams and power plants in Turkey and Afghanistan, new refineries in Sumatra and Ceylon, new highways in Colombia, new hospitals in Iran and Peru. We have opened gleaming new embassies and consulates in a dozen capitals, big luxury hotels in a dozen more. (*Architectural Forum*, 1955, **102**, p. 99)

When the *Forum*'s anonymous author then asked 'what is the significance of this tremendous activity?', the first measure he/she stated was that

we are building up the basic welfare of other nations, creating climates unfavorable to communism, readying countries for industrialization and democratic independence, making them prosperous enough to buy more of our products. (*Ibid.*)

This consuming constellation of nations, therefore, was finding itself in the producing universe of the United States. The *Forum*'s author then observed that as the

big extractive industries of oil and steel became even bigger clients overseas than they are at home . . . they also illustrated the great swing in capitalism, away from the old idea of simple 'exploitation' toward new ideas that he who creates unprecedented prosperity among new groups of people creates thereby new *markets* for his product. To get better workers meant building a great deal besides production facilities, administration facilities, executive housing; it meant housing . . . for thousands of native workers, schools . . . and community centers, hospitals, churches, stores, and recreation centers for new towns often in the wilderness. (*Ibid.*)

In the previous chapter, we have seen how some American builders had already shown an awareness of this final point in the 1920s, from the *oficinas* in southern Chile to an automobile-producing city in central Russia. By the mid-1950s, what the writer

Figure 5.6. Exterior view of the CADA supermarket in Caracas, Venezuela, as well as an interior scene in Mérida, Venezuela showing Andean mountaineers purchasing food in a way typical of many contemporary North American shoppers. Both retail stores were part of a constellation of U.S. derivatives constructed with money from IBEC. (*Source*: Broehl, 1968, p. 102)

above called the 'swing in capitalism' was having even more widespread ripple effects in the realm of American architecture and construction overseas.

The third reason that these government-sponsored programmes were so significant for Americans involved in AEC was that the experiences of designing and building abroad taught some (although some might argue all-too-few of them) lessons about non-American architecture and culture.

[As] our planners and builders have ranged far and wide, [and] have spread wealth and knowledge, they have also learned a few things about other climates, methods and materials – and other peoples . . . In many cases they have been able to show in concrete and steel that the kind of system practiced in America produces not only wealth, but technical and administrative abilities as well, and the willingness to share these assets with others. (*Ibid.*)

This writer did not specify which 'few things' American planners and builders had learned, but significantly concrete and steel – those linchpin materials of the early twentieth century that had figured so prominently in previous cases of American architectural exporting – were singled out as the goods that provided the object lessons about American technical, administrative and (seen above through a rosy lens) knowledge-sharing skills.

In the past decade some scholars have begun to analyse the myriad effects of these ventures in specific cultural contexts. Therefore, regarding France (Cohen, 1995; Gournay, 2001), Germany (Diefendorf, 1993), the Netherlands (Ibelings, 1997), and Japan (Zunz, 1998) it is now possible to understand with sharper precision some of the cultural and technological dynamics associated with American architectural exporting in the years after World War II. Evidence largely culled from contemporary journals further enriches, and sometimes confirms or amplifies these scholars' research results. This evidence also permits us to see how the thrust of American architectural exporting dynamics and operations changed over time. It is likewise possible to map, spatially, with greater clarity which countries and regions were targeted by which U.S. private hands and public gloves, and, chronologically, when that targeting shifted. This changing geography of American architectural and planning influence, with concomitant changes in focus by the actors in the drama that brought American AEC professionals to the far corners of the globe, is part of what will be elaborated below.

'You Too Can Be Like Us': American Materials, Spaces and Skills to Europe, 1945–1958

Many U.S. contractors convinced themselves that because of what they deemed to be pressing needs for economic recovery after the War, Europe would provide fertile ground for U.S. construction expertise and materials. In June 1948, when the U.S. government launched the European Recovery Program (i.e., the Marshall Plan), the economic tools for achieving the Program's goals seemed to confirm those expectations. These tools included 'loans, grants, investments, production and productivity' (Ellwood, 1993, p. 84; Siegfried, 1952). And those tools were well sharpened and put to use pervasively throughout Europe. As far as Europe's built environment was concerned, in the first 15 years after the War many building practitioners borrowed, translated and/or transformed several American construction and design ideals, particularly regarding prefabrication, mechanization and suburbanization (Cohen, 1995, pp. 159–203). The dynamics of these transformations varied with their cultural contexts; French Levittowns were not equivalent to Stockholm suburbs (Gournay 2001, 2002; Parsons 1992).

Specific interests within the nations of Europe tended to diverge following the Second World War. France, for instance, was fascinated by problems of productivity and industrialization, while Russia imitated the skyscraper, and British architects became interested in the American landscape, popular culture, and technique in general. (Cohen, 1995, p. 183)

However, by the 1950s many Europeans were also witnessing certain common trends in the expanding propagation of the U.S. built environment as a hallmark of a consumer-driven, consumptive future. In exhibits, publications, radio broadcasts, cultural centres, academic programmes and personal communications, the American way of life was consistently trumpeted as a standard to which most 'free' peoples should aspire (Pells, 1997; Loeffler, 1998; Wagnleitner and May, 2000). As one scholar has graphically described that trumpeting,

. . . Private-sector [businessmen] spread the message of People's Capitalism; to head for the developing world with their rolled-up back issues of *Life* magazines as missionaries once did with their Bibles. And that is exactly what thousands of U.S. artists, industrial designers, intellectuals and businessmen did. They travelled from Leipzig to Bangkok like old fashioned door-to-door salesmen, harvesting sales contracts as if they were souls and shepherding converts to capitalism out of the darkness of socialism, communism and inefficient, tradition-bound economies toward the absolutely guaranteed promised land of skyscrapers, supermarkets and shopping malls. (Haddow, 1997, p. 17)

Other scholars have shown that this acceptance of American materials, forms and spaces stemmed in part from longstanding cultural affiliations – albeit not always cultural congruencies – between North America and Europe (Hogan, 1989; Ellwood, 1992; Ibelings, 1997; Pells, 1997, pp. 2–22). The anti-communist, propaganda message that accompanied the physical materials was as much cultural and political as it was economic and unequivocal: 'You Too Can Be Like Us'.

By the early years of the Cold War, U.S. policy-makers drew on this long tradition of anti-imperial rhetoric [concerning the U.S.] to argue that freedom was everywhere endangered by a red imperialism of unprecedented power and ambition that was headquartered in Moscow . . . The American Century was more typically broadcast as a philanthropic endeavor to share the blessings of freedom and democracy. (Appy, 2000, p. 2)

Invoking the famous metaphor of the 'media is the message' from Marshall McLuhan's *Gutenberg Galaxy* (1962), the literal building blocks of that democracy were among the tangible media that conveyed the lofty, freedom-loving message.

To understand better some of the dimensions of that message, it is useful to listen to contemporary commentaries about, and trade literature geared towards, AEC professionals. For example,

Architectural Forum, which had ignored virtually all the manifestations of architectural exporting outlined in the chapters above, published a fifteen-page article in early 1953 titled 'U.S. Architecture Abroad', mainly featuring the work of the Foreign Buildings Office of the Department of State, established in 1946, which had evolved from the Foreign Service Buildings Commission, created 20 years earlier (*Architectural Forum*, 1953, **98**, pp. 101–115; Robin, 1992; Loeffler, 1998). Owned by Henry Luce, one of the key proponents of 'the American Century', *Architectural Forum* also served as 'a forum for Cold War rhetoric' (Loeffler, 1998, p. 7). With proud fanfare that was not entirely matched with historical accuracy, the unnamed author of the article proclaimed:

We are known the world over for the quality of our exports . . . Now, at last, we are beginning to export some of our best architecture as well. This, of course, is a good deal more important than exporting tractors; Americans have never felt self-conscious about the quality of American machinery – but we have felt very unsure of ourselves in the past where architecture was concerned . . . No country can exercise political world leadership without exercising a degree of cultural leadership as well. Whether consciously or not, the U.S. Government has now made U.S. architecture a vehicle of our cultural leadership. That is the fundamental importance of [this] story. (*Architectural Forum*, 1953, **98**, p.101)

Other 'stories' in *Architectural Forum*, *Engineering News-Record* and other journals also make it clear that between 1945 and 1953 there were three principal activities in which American architects and planners became directly engaged in Europe: (1) planning and constructing U.S. military installations; (2) designing and overseeing the construction of substantial infrastructure projects such as oil refineries, steam plants or reclamation works; and (3) serving as consultants to clients who sought advice about U.S. construction machinery. By the early 1950s several U.S. companies involved with AEC were thriving under the aegis (i.e., the 'glove') of the U.S. government-sponsored Marshall Plan. As Europe crawled with members of the U.S. construction industry by late 1948, architects went abroad to advise on the planning of industrial plants and housing, to give the benefit of their experience in expanding the U.S. wartime industrial machine. In the early stages of the Marshall Plan . . . U.S. architects advised on better than half of the projects. (*Architectural Forum*, 1955, **102**, p. 99)

However, not all professionals immediately fell in line behind U.S. government initiatives where construction was concerned. For example, in a 1948 official statement, the American Society of Civil Engineers expressed its concern about government-sponsored building initiatives overseas, affirming that the U.S. government should only 'prepare designs, plans, specifications, or engage in supervision of construction of projects for foreign governments [when] the national interest demands such actions' (*Civil Engineering*, 1950, **20**, p. 335). The reality, however, was that several engineering companies received a significant corporate boost by virtue of their postwar European construction and planning work: Parsons, Brinckerhoff and TAMS (New York); Stone & Webster (Boston); Morrison-

Knudsen (Boise, Idaho); Fluor (Los Angeles); and Bechtel (San Francisco), to name just six of the largest companies which in the early 2000s are still actively engaged in overseas operations.

In July 1953, four months after *Architectural Forum*'s first reflection about 'American architecture abroad', *Engineering News-Record* published a synopsis of how American construction firms were faring in Europe by virtue of the Marshall Plan (*Engineering-News Record*, 1953, **151**, 30 July). The scope associated with those firms illustrates how, in just 5 years, increasing numbers of American building products and experts were helping not only to 'reconstruct' Europe after military devastation, but also to 'reconfigure' several European industrial and/or urban landscapes (*Engineering-News Record*, 1953, **151**, 17 September). Several tables below not only summarize that scope, but also flesh out the skeleton of American architectural exportation by specifying projects and companies related to the enterprise.

In January 1955 *Architectural Forum* published

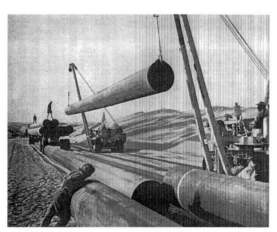

Figure 5.7. The Trans-Arabian Pipeline, constructed in the early 1950s by the Bechtel Corporation of San Francisco, was one of many ventures undertaken by American oil companies throughout the Middle East after World War II. (*Source*: *Architectural Forum*, 1955, **102**, January, p. 106)

Figure 5.8. Oil loading terminal at Khor Musa, Iran. In addition to the engineering of the pipeline itself, entire communities were designed and built to service the needs of booming petroleum production throughout the region. Town planning of this ilk had certainly occurred prior to U.S. involvement [Crinson, 1997], but in the post-World War II period American engineers, architects and planners had a cachet that attracted many local clients. (*Source*: Rader Associates)

a second, more expansive essay, what it called a 'broad panorama of some of the best examples of jobs designed, financed or built by the U.S. around the world. These structures, and the men who made them, are the face of America abroad' (*Architectural Forum*, January, 1955, **102**, p. 99). However, the complexion and expressions on that face sometimes changed according to context. So many variations prevailed throughout the European continent alone that it was difficult for both of the unnamed *Engineering News-Record* and *Forum* analysts to generalize too extensively. Nonetheless, *Engineering News-Record* suggested that 'by and large Europe has been more inclined to embrace the products of U.S. construction equipment manufacturers than the services of U.S. technicians. Even here, U.S. participation is frequently through foreign manufacturing affiliates or subsidiaries' (*Engineering-News Record*, 1953, **151**, 30 July). The analyst's individual country reports reveal the extent to which that equipment was being used, the tangible results the Plan was spawning, and

the degree to which several European home-grown companies related to industrial and infrastructural development were using their own technicians to adapt American products when they were transplanted across the Atlantic.

For example, in Great Britain *Engineering News-Record* reported that 'U.S. know-how and equipment have built the British oil refining industry from nothing to over 20 million tons capacity since the war; but in contrast, even on the airbases destined for our use, British engineers and contractors were in charge. Oil refineries were beyond British ability to build. Airbases could be handled in our stride' (*Ibid.*, p. 57). In other construction arenas, although in 'special and small cases' Americans were retained on jobs that Britons could handle, more frequently American builders tended to establish a 'subsidiary organized as a limited-liability British company' (*Ibid.*, p.59). Those American firms handling construction work in the U.K. as of 1953 are shown in Table 5.1 below.

In stark contrast, however, was how U.S.

Table 5.1. AEC companies from the U.S. operating in the U.K., 1953.

Name of Company	Type of Work	Location; Client Company
Foster-Wheeler	chemical/oil refineries	—
Kellogg International	chemical/oil refineries	—
E.P. Badger & Sons (div. of Stone & Webster)	chemical/oil refineries	Kent; Anglo-Iranian
Procon	chemical/oil refineries	Stanlow; Shell
Lummus	chemical/oil refineries	Grangemouth, Scotland Forth Chemical
	chemical/oil refineries	Stanlow, England Cabot Carbon
	chemical/oil refineries	Coryton; Vacuum Oil
		Stanlow, England Shell
	chemical/oil refineries	Kent; Anglo-Iranian
Richard Hawley Cutting (Cleveland)	U.S. military installations	—

Source: Engineering-News Record, 1953, **151**, 30 July.

construction companies fared in France, where (despite U.S. military assistance during the War) they found the country to be 'practically forbidden territory'. The most effective way to operate was to create limited partnerships with French-owned firms, which is how Morrison-Knudsen, Fluor, Vacuum Concrete (Philadelphia) and Preload (New York) operated. In this way, the U.S. companies were not only allowed to work in France itself, but they could also extend their corporate reach to former (or present) French colonies, such as Algeria. Within France, American companies fared more successfully when they assisted French firms in building military facilities. In the early 1950s the U.S. Air Force created the European Command Joint Construction Agency, which integrated under one commercial umbrella the work of three American contractors (Raymond Concrete Pile Co., Brown & Root, and Walsh Construction) on nine airbases throughout the country. Besides those four principal firms, the Air Force hired a cluster of other U.S. consultants to work on projects of more limited scope.[1]

However, as France intensified its reconstruction agenda there were at least four other ways in which American construction and regional planning techniques began to influence French practitioners (Cohen, 1995, pp. 162–77). One was by dint of French émigré architects who had settled in the U.S. during the War and were intrigued with innovations they witnessed there, from micro-level prefabrication of building components to macro-scale planning on the order of the Tennessee Valley Authority.[2] A second measure of the influence was seen in the activities of the French Ministry of Reconstruction and Town Planning, which disseminated vast amounts of information about U.S. construction and planning paradigms. A third way that influence was manifested was through exhibits of American architecture and planning mounted in and around Paris shortly after the War. A fourth way came as a result of guided tours – 'productivity missions', as

they were called in English – of important U.S. sites organized in the late 1940s and early 1950s for French architects, builders and urbanists. These examples suggest how, in just 5 years after the War, the tangled web of American architectural influence on a country such as France was riddled with knots and loops.

Italy was yet another convoluted context that presented an entirely distinct set of challenges for Marshall Plan administrators, primarily because of the degree to which opposing Communists had mounted fierce propaganda against the Plan. This, in turn, inspired Plan adherents to mount 'a truly mass program using every method possible . . . to reach Giuseppe in the factory and Giovanni in the

HARKNESS AND PLAN AMID RUBBLE

Figure 5.9. John Harkness, an American architect who assisted local planners in Isernia, Italy to rebuild and reconfigure a city ravaged by World War II. (*Source: Architectural Forum*, 1945, **102**, March, p. 107)

fields' (Ellwood, 1993, p. 84). One major component of that programme concerned Italy's construction sector, because planners believed that a palpable way to demonstrate Italian-American cooperation was by building houses, roads, hydroelectric plants, gas pipelines and railways; rebuilding devastated towns and cities (*Architectural Forum*, 1945, **82**, March, pp. 107–111); and 'pre-building' for projects that could arise either on newly reclaimed land or on terrain previously susceptible to flooding (*Ibid.*, p. 85; *Engineering-News Record*, 1953, **151**, 30 July, p. 60). In this regard, 'the welcome mat [was] out for the Americans' because the 1948 'treaty of commerce and friendship provided for a footing of equality with Italian firms in either public or private construction'

(*Engineering-News Record*, 1953, **151**, 30 July, p. 60). This led to a wide spectrum of activities by U.S. firms involved with AEC, as Table 5.2 demonstrates.

In Greece between 1947 and 1953 American AEC firms exerted very strong influence over the country's rebuilding efforts, in part because of large appropriations from the Marshall Plan, coupled with an extremely weak domestic construction industry. One of the most significant American firms erecting new infrastructure in Greece was Knappen, Tippetts, Abbett & McCarthy, established in 1942. One of the firm's chief partners, Theodore Knappen, had collaborated with the U.S. Army during the war (building bases in the Caribbean) when he worked for Parsons, Brinckerhoff (Bobrick, 1985, pp. 99–101).

Table 5.2. AEC companies from the U.S. operating in Italy, 1953.

Name of Company	Type of Work	Location; Client Company
Arthur G. McKee Co.	steel mill	Cornigliano
(Cleveland) and Armco International (Middletown, Ohio)		—
Kuljian Corporation (Philadelphia)	steam power plant	Palermo; Spiti Co.
Gibbs & Hill (NY)	electric power plants	Genoa and Piacenza; Società Edison
	electric power plants	Naples Società Meridionale di Elettricita
Gilbert Associates (Reading, PA)		Civitavecchia;
		Società Termolettrica Tirrena
		Torino Società Idroellettrica Piemonte
		Società Termolettrica Tirrena
Ebasco Services (NY)	steam power plant	Torino Azienda Elettrica Municipale
Giffels & Vallet (Detroit)	automobile factory expansion	Torino; FIAT Motors
Foster-Wheeler and M.W. Kellogg	oil refinery	Porto Marghera I.R.O.M.
Vacuum Concrete (Philadelphia)	precasting concrete	Mucone and Volturno hydroelectric plants

Source: Engineering-News Record, 1953, **151**, 30 July.

When the Marshall Plan was announced, Knappen and his partners targeted war-ravaged Greece as a country needing substantial engineering assistance. The company's engineers rehabilitated the Corinth Canal, the port at Piraeus, and designed new hydroelectric dams (Balbiani and Brown, 1983, pp. 7–8).

Greece then 'became the launching site for new contracts secured in nearby nations with important economic goals of their own', such as Iraq, Turkey, Iran, Libya and Lebanon (*Ibid.*, p. 8). In 1950, the firm employed the same strategy of anchoring itself substantially in one location – in this case, San Juan, Puerto Rico – and then spreading its wings more regionally from that base. As the company characterized it,

Greece had served as a visible example, available to scrutiny from its neighbors, of the merits of engaging an energetic and ambitious American consulting firm that appeared able to adapt readily to local customs and work pattern in its engineering assignments. San Juan was to serve somewhat that same purpose for TAMS in the Caribbean and in Central and South America. (*Ibid.*, p. 11)

Table 5.3. U.S. AEC companies operating in Greece, 1953.

Name of Company	Type of Work
Johnson, Drake & Piper (NY); Guy F. Atkinson (SF); Starr, Park & Freeman (NY)	rehabilitation of railways, highways, bridges
Grove, Shepherd, Wilson; J. Rich Steers Co. (NY)	reopen Corinth canal
Knappen, Tibbetts, Abbett & McCarthy (NY)	port rehabilitation, irrigation projects, ten reclamation projects, dams and power plants
Ebasco Services	steam power and hydroelectric power plants
Burns & Roe; Foundation Co. (NY)	steam power plant

Source: Engineering-News Record, 1953, **151**, 30 July.

In their summary of conditions in 1953, *Engineering News-Record* analysts underscored that the preceding four countries – Greece, Italy, France and the U.K. – probably had the greatest potential for American construction firms. (However, *Engineering News-Record* did not predict that in only a few years construction companies from the latter three of those nations would compete vigorously with Americans, as will be shown below.) In 1953 *Engineering News-Record* also suggested that other European countries might well provide fertile ground in the future, even if 'there are no American [contractors] working within their borders [due to] local competition, capital shortage and a lack of sufficiently large contracts'(*Ibid.*, p. 68). The countries comprising this category were Austria, Belgium, Denmark, Finland, Portugal, Spain, Sweden, West Germany and the Netherlands. Recently, however, scholars who have analysed postwar architectural contexts in the latter two of these countries have found substantial U.S. influence there even without there having been large contracts and major capital investments.

In West Germany, a decade after the War's end, U.S. advisors exerted 'considerable influence on housing construction' (Diefendorf, 1993, p. 140). For example, in the Ruhr Valley, eight housing projects for miners were established using 'counterpart funds' under the Marshall Plan. Other residential settlements were planned in at least seven other German cities, under terms of the Economic Cooperation Administration (ECA), which stipulated that funds would only be released if construction costs 'were held down through the use of standardized building techniques', one of the hallmarks of Bauhaus-inspired housing recommendations that had been stalled in Germany with the rise of Nazism (*Ibid.*, p. 141). Instead, as is well known, several German architects such Walter Gropius and Mies van der Rohe emigrated to the U.S. and exerted phenomenal influence on U.S. architects through their affiliations with Harvard and the Illinois Institute of Technology. After the

War, American architects such as William Wittausch, Vernon De Mars and Bernard Wagner joined a specially-designated housing mission established under the ECA, which selected housing designs from among 725 entries submitted by German architects and promoted the use of prefabricated construction materials, some of which came from the United States (*Architectural Forum*, 1955, **102**, January, p. 104). In this way, 'the ideology of modernism [that had] moved from Germany in the 1920s to America in the late1930s [was sponsored by the U.S. to return] to Germany after the war in the ECA competition' (Diefendorf, 1993, p. 142).[3] Housing economists also assisted Germans to initiate competitive bidding for housing contractors and financing plans for home-buying based on procedures of the Federal Housing Administration. In Berlin during 1956, to counter Soviet-initiated housing erected in East Berlin along the Stalinallee – what the *Architectural Forum* dubbed 'grimly monumental showpieces' – the U.S. sponsored an International Building Exhibition north of the Tiergarten, where U.S. construction techniques in various stages of completion were shown in 8,000 permanent dwelling units erected especially for the exhibition (*Architectural Forum*, 1955, **102**, January, p. 104).

Regarding the Netherlands,

in the first few years of the [Marshall Plan] 600 million guilders was allocated to the building industry . . . for the building of houses, farms and factories, repair of roads, bridges and railway lines, reforestation, redistribution of land . . . and the construction of dykes around the future Flevo Polder . . . Money . . . was also used to fund two new industrial projects: a rolling mill for Hoogovens in Velsen, which supplied part of the American car industry's steel requirements, and the Americentrale power station in Geertruidenberg. (Ibelings, 1997, p. 10)

And as occurred in France, Dutch 'delegations [building industry productivity teams] were invited to come to the U.S. and see for themselves the latest developments' (*Ibid.*, p. 17).

By the mid-1950s, many of those developments were becoming more widely disseminated, in the forms of adapted transplantation, throughout a recovering Europe (Pells, 1997). One of the American government-sponsored institutions doing the disseminating was the U.S. Information Agency, established in 1953, which 'inherited the tasks pioneered by the Office of War Information during World War II: the dissemination and interpretation of information' (Haddow, 1997, p. 11). However, because that Office also became involved in 'dis-information' (i.e., propaganda), the U.S.I.A. was sometimes tainted by association.

Another government-sponsored disseminator of information about U.S. developments, including those in the building industry, was the Department of Commerce. Well before World War II this Department had been a strong ally of U.S. building interests. Soon after its creation in 1903, the Department's Bureau of Foreign and Domestic Commerce published *Daily Consular Trade Reports*, which often summarized building-related developments that American Consular officials stationed around the world wrote about for the benefit of U.S. citizens involved in the building industries. In 1954 the Department helped organize a series of trade fairs in foreign countries to promote a broad spectrum of American products.

The Department promised corporations that it would ship their products to the foreign fairs, set up exhibition booths for them, provide translators for their business representatives, and prepare the ground with trade 'missionaries' – businessmen sent abroad ahead of the fairs to explain what American products could do, [and] how they could be purchased. (Haddow, 1997, p. 13)

The housing exhibition in Berlin described above was an event that demonstrated a similar intent. Probably the most significant of these fairs took place in 1958, when the American architect Edward Durell Stone was chosen by the American Institute of Architects to design the U.S. pavilion for the World's Fair in Brussels (Haddow, 1997, pp. 70–92; Stone, 1962).

'Lighthouses in a Sea of Ignorance': Object Lessons in the Middle East, Africa and Asia 1945–1958[4]

One of the most unusual U.S. trade fairs occurred in Kabul, Afghanistan in 1956, when the featured exhibit was the largest geodesic dome that Buckminster Fuller had ever designed up to that point (100 feet in diameter), erected in two days using local labour. 'Putting the dome together demonstrated to locals that innovation need not be expensive, arcane or threatening' (Haddow, 1997, p. 61). Ironically, given what occurred almost half a century later, on 11 September 2001, 'photomurals of the New York skyline presented an Oz-like vision of the United States, and a Cinerama show outside pulled in curious onlookers' (*Ibid.*).

Immediately after World War II American contractors, architects, planners and engineers did not limit their ventures to Europe. President Truman anticipated U.S. involvement in promoting American technology to underdeveloped countries as well as to war-torn Europe when he announced his Point Four Program in 1949. For example, 'American advisers employed by Point Four have . . . set up model farms in India and health programs in Iran . . . Money from this program has also paid for a two-year technical and economic survey supervised by the engineering firm of [TAMS] for the government of Burma' (*Architectural Forum*, 1955, **102**, January, p. 101). And in Afghanistan from 1947 to 1955, Morrison-Knudsen oversaw the construction of two large dams. By 1955 this Boise-based company had over $560 million worth of foreign contracts, ranging from south and central Asia to northern Africa. These projects included the erection of the Gal Oya Dam in Sri Lanka (Bleifuss, 1951), military bases in north Africa for the U.S. government, and the Karadj hydroelectric power dam north-west of Teheran, Iran.

By the early 1950s Africa was already lagging with respect to U.S. architectural, engineering and construction influence, with only a few exceptions. As Truman attempted to implement Point Four in the context of ongoing U.S. military expansion during the late-1940s and early-1950s in North Africa, Americans planned and erected airbases in Libya and Morocco. However, most planning work was given to European practitioners because colonial connections were still bringing primarily European planning influences to Africa. One contemporary observed that 'by long custom and by the economies of contact with Europe, the jobs go northward, not to the west' (*Engineering-News Record*, 1953, **151**, 30 July, p. 75; Hamilton, 1956).

One exception to this 'jobs go northward' rule was Liberia, which held traditionally close political and cultural associations with the U.S., where American planners in 1953 updated the port of the capital Monrovia and erected the city's waterworks and sewerage system. A second exception was Ethiopia, where the American ally Haile Selassie employed U.S. highway planners to try to knit his empire together in a more American way by using asphalt to move vehicles more efficiently across the East African desert. Table 5.4 provides a relatively comprehensive summary of initiatives in which U.S. firms were directly involved.

In the Middle East during the same period (1945–1955), American AEC professionals competed keenly with, but often more successfully against, Europeans and by the mid-1950s the U.S. was exerting a highly significant planning role from Turkey to India, especially in the fields of infrastructure development and regional development planning. Planners were especially needed because of the implications stemming from petroleum development that intensified in the region after the War. Dams, highways, ports, new settlements and related facilities needed to be threaded into programmes of economic development. Furthermore, as the temperatures dropped during the Cold War, many saw the Middle East as a testing ground for capitalism on the Soviet

Table 5.4. AEC companies from the U.S. operating in Africa, 1953.

Name of Company	Type of Work	Location; Client Company
'PUSOM' (Porter & Urquhart; Skidmore, Owings & Merrill)	design U.S. army bases	Morocco
Atlas Constructors (Morrison-Knudsen, Bates & Roger, Ralph L. Mills, Blythe Bros., Nello L. Teer)	design U.S. army bases	Morocco
Knappen-Tippetts-Abbett-McCarthy	design U.S. army bases	Morocco
J. Rich Steers; Grove, Shepherd, Wilson & Kruge; Mackenzie, Bogert & White (N.Y.)	naval air facility	—
'C-S-S' W.L. Crow Construction; J. Rich Steers (New York); Shepard Construction (Atlanta)	naval air facility	Wheelus Air Force Base, Tripoli, Libya
Raymond Concrete Pile (New York)	new port planning	Monrovia, Liberia
Firestone Tire & Rubber	roadbuilding, sanitation, housing	Monrovia, Liberia
Hazen & Sawyer (NY)	waterworks and sewage system	Monrovia, Liberia
U.S. Bureau of Public Roads	roadbuilding	Ethiopia
Knappen-Tippetts-Abbett-McCarthy	railway system extension	Mozambique
Foster-Wheeler (NY)	oil refinery	Standard Caltex Durban, South Africa
Arthur D. Little, Inc. (Cambridge, Mass.)	survey low-cost housing materials and construction; demonstrate construction machinery	Egypt

Source: Engineering-News Record, 1953, **151**, 30 July.

Union's southern flank where American techniques of industrial development could become not only bases for monetary profit but also object lessons in the contemporary quest, as the U.S. Chairman of the Middle East Commission of the Committee on International Relations put it, to 'demonstrate to the people concerned, who will make the decision between our way and the Russian way – whether they know they are making it or not' (Thornburg, 1949).

However, as retrospect shows, by choosing 'our' way, the governments ruling the peoples of the vast lands between the Mediterranean Sea and the Indian Ocean were also casting their lots with U.S. interests that did not – despite lofty hopes to the contrary – sufficiently understand the cultural contexts in which they were operating. This might justifiably apply to most other regions where American architectural exporters were working soon after the War. It might also apply to many U.S. architectural exporters encountered in previous chapters, who chose to export architectural commodities and technologies without fully meeting the more difficult challenges related to adapting those products and methods to unique environments. As the aforementioned Chairman Thornburg perceptively asserted,

what the American engineer does in the Middle East during the years 1948, 1949 and 1950 will be an important factor in determining the fate of the world for many years to come. (*Ibid.*, p. 331)

He was hoping that American engineers would be able to resist being painted with the same brush as those (largely) British and Russian

salesmen, contractors and engineers [in Iran] who loaded the country with such costly installations of so little use to the country. Whatever the feeling that the foreign experts should have protected these inexperienced governments from the folly of their own politicians, the fact remains that it was the governments themselves who ordered these plants built. Under the harsh principle of *caveat emptor* the blame is their own if what they bought proved to be useless or even worse than useless. (*Ibid.*, p. 335)

However, American builders in Iran did not escape the wrath of those Iranians who saw through the 'worse than useless' constructions commissioned by their government. The challenges that Thornburg passionately wrote about in his 1949 article were unfortunately never fully addressed, either by indigenous governments, the U.S. government, or America's AEC professions. Large projects, huge investments, imposing structures and broad-scale policies throughout the Middle East did not compensate for pervasive discontent with the assumptions of choosing either 'our' [U.S.] way or the Soviet way instead of an 'Islamic' way.

Another U.S. commentator who reflected a conventional outlook about what the U.S. was trying to do in the region said

The Middle East is a fertile field for the American method

Harold T. Smith, American engineer in Iraq, gives ENR his opinion on . . .

How U.S. Firms Will Make Out in Iraq

Figure 5.10. Harold T. Smith, an American engineer who helped drill miles of wells in Iraq during the 1950s. In a prescient comment, Smith asserted that 'to operate in the area, Americans, business and government alike, have got to accept certain political realities'. (*Source: Engineering-News Record*, 1959, **157**, January, p. 44)

and the American machine – [because] the quantities to be moved are big enough to warrant big machines [and] the jobs to be done warrant big organization. (*Engineering-News Record*, 1953, **151**, 30 July p. 85)

One of those growing organizations was the World Bank, whose sponsored planning work in the Middle East could be found in Iraq (for irrigation work), Turkey (for highway construction), Lebanon (for dam construction), Pakistan (for modernizing Karachi's harbour) and Iran (for long-term health, education and agricultural plans) (*Engineering-News Record*, 1953, **151**, 30 July; Larkin, 1949, p.25). As was the case in Europe, some of those organizations were private firms while others were subsets of the U.S. government (see Table 5.5 below).

Examples of the private firms were Parsons, Brinckerhoff (planning the new Turkish, coal exporting town of Zonguldak on the Black Sea as well as highways in Bahrain); Thompson-Starrett (planning the new Turkish resort town of Cesme on the Aegean); Harza of Chicago (designing dams in Iraq and India); Knappen, Tippetts, Abbett, McCarthy of New York (erecting dams along the Tigris River in Iraq); Morrison-Knudsen (building

Figure 5.11. In this photo of President Eisenhower, taken in 1959 near the end of his presidency, the link between U.S. foreign aid to the Middle East and the region's construction needs was taken for granted. (*Source*: *Engineering-News Record*, 1959, **157**, December, p. 26)

dams in Afghanistan and Sri Lanka); Harland Bartholomew (providing planning services for municipal water supply and sewerage systems in Pakistan); Bechtel of San Francisco (building roads, harbours and generating stations in Saudi Arabia);

and Fluor of Los Angeles (planning the U.S. airbase at Dharan, Saudi Arabia) (*Engineering-News Record*, 1953, **151**, July 30).

Exporting American Architecture to the 'Far East', 1945–1955

In the early 1950s most of the so-called 'Far East' was not clearly within the focus of most American AEC professionals. In part this was because of so many other 'public glove' opportunities stemming from the programmes described above; by 1955 the U.S. government had still not decided upon the extent of aid to provide this vast region through the government's newly-created Council

Table 5.5. AEC companies from the U.S. operating in Turkey, 1955.

Name of Company	Type of Work	Location; Client Company
Skidmore, Owings & Merrill, architects	hotel	Istanbul Hilton
Parsons, Brinckerhoff, Hall & McDonald	new port construction	Zongaldak, Black Sea
Morrison-Knudsen	dam construction	Seyhan Dam, near Adana
Thompson-Starrett	resort city planning	Cesme
Ralph Parsons Co. (Los Angeles)	oil refinery	Raman
Metcalfe Construction; Gordon Hamilton Contracting	seven U.S. bases	Army Corps of Engineers; bases at Adana, Balikesir, Bandirma, Batman, Diyarbakir, Eskisehir and Merzifon
Southwestern Engineering (Los Angeles)	mineral flotation plants	Turkish government; at Ergani, Easter Chrome
Western Knapp Co. (San Francisco)	mineral flotation plants	Ergani
McNally Pittsburgh (Pittsburgh)	mineral flotation plants	Soma
Hamilton Overseas Construction	coal mining tunnelling	Zonguldak
Koppers Company (Pittsburgh)	coal mining tunnelling	Zonguldak
Frederick Snare (NY)	coal mining tunnelling	Ergeli Coal Mining Administration
Paul Weir (Pittsburgh)	coal mining tunnelling	Ergeli Coal Mining Administration
Charles T. Main (Boston)	dam and hydroelectric plant	Sariyar Dam
Stone & Webster (Boston)	power transmission lines	Catalgazi-Istanbul

Source: Architectural Forum, 1955, **102**, January.

of Foreign Economic Policy (*Architectural Forum*, 1955, **102**, January, p. 101). Another reason for those professionals' hesitancy to either act or invest was due to what they perceived as mixed signals.

Depending upon where you look, attitudes in the Far East range from 'why don't you come over?' to 'not much room here', to 'no Americans need apply' . . . In general the Far Eastern situation might be summarized this way: The supply of capital is fair in spots. Common labor is plentiful, skilled labor scarce (but the natives are very quick to learn).

Materials are generally available, machinery badly needed. Technical help – plentiful and generally good in special fields. Attitude – mostly good. Local governments – rather surprisingly stable. (*Engineering-News Record*, 1953, **151**, 30 July pp. 99–100)

This brief assessment at the end of the Korean War, and less than 4 years after the establishment of the People's Republic of China, would soon be ripe for amendment.

Table 5.6. AEC Companies from the U.S. operating south and east of Turkey, 1955.

Name of Company	Type of Work	Location; Client Company
Construction Aggregates (Chicago)	swampland reclamation	Lake Huleh, Israel
	highway surveying	Beersheva to Eilat, Israel
Chemical Construction Co. (NY)	fertilizer plants	Haifa, Israel
Lock Joint Pipe Co. (NJ)	concrete pipes	Central Israel
Edward Durell Stone, architect	hotel	Savoy Plaza, Istanbul
Knappen, Tippetts, Abbett & McCarthy	surveys for irrigation	Tigris-Euphrates, Iraq
Harza Engineering Co. (Chicago)	hydroelectric dam	Bekhme, Zab River, Iraq
Edwards, Kelly & Beck (NJ)	highway system	Iraq
Edmund J. Whiting, architect; Severud-Estad-Krueger, engineers	medical centre	Shiraz, Iran
Parsons, Brinckerhoff	highway planning	Bahrain
Chauncey Riley, architect (NY)	research laboratories, housing, dining halls, theatre, library, gymnasium, shopping centre	Awali, Bahrain
Morrison-Knudsen	two dams and one canal	Afghanistan
Kuljian Corp. (Philadelphia)	newsprint plant	Pakistan
Harland Bartholomew (St. Louis)	municipal water supply & sewage	Pakistan
Morrison-Knudsen	gas pipeline	Karachi, Pakistan
Bechtel International (SF)	electrical systems, harbours, roads, airport	Saudi Arabia
	refinery and town	Aden, Yemen
Michael Baker, Jr. (PA)	public works construction	Saudi Arabia
Fluor Corp. (Los Angeles)	U.S. airbase	Dhahran, Saudi Arabia

Sources: Engineering-News Record, 1953, **151**, 30 July, and *Architectural Forum*, 1955, **102**, January.

Table 5.7. U.S. AEC companies operating in India, 1953.

Name of Company	Type of Work	Location; Client Company
Ebasco (NY)	paper mill thermal power station	Nepanang, India Tata Power Co., India
Harold T. Smith (Wash., DC)	tube wells	Northern India
Kuljian Corp.	thermal electric plant	Patna (Bihar), India
Lummus Co. (NY)	two oil refineries	Bombay, India
Merritt-Chapman & Scott	pipelines	Bombay, India
Adams, Howard & Greeley (Boston)	town planning	India
Mayer & Whittlesley (NY)	town planning agricultural institute	Chandigarh, India Allahabad, India
Koppers Co. (Pittsburgh)	steel plant	India
American Cyanmid	fertilizer plant	Bulsar, India
Harza Engineering Co.	dam	Maithon, Damodar Valley, India

Source: *Engineering-News Record*, 1953, **151**, 30 July.

The Challenge of Opportunity in Latin America: Gringos and the 'Middle Masses',[5] 1945–1958

If the Middle East and western Asia were financially intriguing for American AEC professionals in the early 1950s, the region that received even keener attention of both private AEC hands and public U.S. gloves was Latin America (Whyte and Holmberg, 1956). Table 5.9 reflects how much private investment was targeting Latin America (37 per cent of the total) versus other regions. It also shows that both manufacturing and petroleum industries were receiving higher levels of investments relative to other kinds of industries.

Given the intense commercial linkage between North and South America that had existed since at least the early nineteenth century, this connection was more a ratification of a longstanding relationship than it was a newly-found arena for American AEC operations. During the war, because of military base construction, Central and South America had

witnessed the U.S. Army expanding its presence throughout the continent. At the end of the war one of the 'public gloves' that continued to finance many of these projects was the Export-Import Bank, which often focused on transportation planning such as road and rail construction, environmental planning such as drainage and sewerage works, or low-cost housing projects that often used American prefabricated component technologies (*Engineering-News Record*, 1943, **136**, pp. 145–152; *Architectural Forum*, 1946, **85**, July, pp. 10–13; *Ibid.*, 1948, **89**, October, pp. 14–16).

One site that exemplified Export-Import Bank initiatives was Volta Redonda, Brazil, where a new 3-mile long, steel mill was created, a new model community planned, and a new railway built to bring products more easily to export facilities. The Brazilian President Vargas took personal interest 'in making Volta Redonda a show place . . . The town has been laid out with curving streets, fine plazas and park areas, and carefully planned landscaping. The town will [have] electricity, gas and treated

Table 5.8. AEC Companies from the U.S. operating in the 'Far East', 1953.

Name of Company	Type of Work	Location; Client Company
Knappen, Tippetts, Abbett & McCarthy	two-year engineering survey	Burma
Knappen, Tippetts, Abbett & McCarthy	consultation for development	U.N., Korea
Litchfield, Whiting, Panero, Severud & Associates (NY)	hospital and health centres	Burma
J.G. White Engineering Corp.	economic development planning	Indonesia
U.S. Bureau of Reclamation; J.G. White Engineering Corp.	hydroelectric dam	Wu Sheh, Taiwan
Guy F. Atkinson Co. (S.F.)	river development	Tenryu River, Shizuoka Province, Japan
Ebasco Services	concrete arch dam	Kyushu Electric Power Co., Japan
Hawaiian Dredging Co.	land reclamation	Tokyo harbour, Japan
Guy F. Atkinson Co.; Harza Engineering; Marsman Construction Co.	hydroelectric dam	Ambuklao, Philippines
Foster-Wheeler Corp. Philippines	oil distillation	Caltex Bauan, Batangas Province,
Oscar Van Kohorn & Co. (NY) Rayon Corp.	rayon factory	Ma-ao, Negros Or. Province, Philippines
Hawaiian Dredging; J.H. Pomeroy (S.F.); Bechtel (S.F.)	U.S. airstrip and naval base	Subic Bay, Philippines
Utah Construction Co. (S.F.) & Water Supply Co., Australia	dam	Eildon Weir; Victoria State Rivers Comm.
Morrison-Knudsen	canal	Goulburn-Warranga No. 2 Main Channel, Australia
John L. Savage	dam	water supply to Sydney Warragamba Dam; joint venture with Sydney Metropolitan Water, Sewerage & Drainage Board
John L. Savage; U.S. Bureau of Reclamation	hydroelectric dam	Adaminaby Dam, Snowy Mountains, N.S.W.
Kellogg International Corp.	oil refinery	Kwinana, Western Australia; Anglo-Iranian Oil Co.
Braun Transworld Corp.	oil refinery	Melbourne, Victoria
Raymond Concrete Pile Corp. and Merritt-Chapman-Scott (NY)	port expansions	Auckland, New Zealand
Morrison-Knudsen	tunnel construction	Wellington-Wairarapa Railway, New Zealand
Preload Company	concrete reservoirs	several New Zealand cities

Source: Engineering-News Record, 1953, **151**, 30 July.

Figure 5.12. Prefabricated U.S. housing components being fitted into place on a construction site in South America. (*Source*: Broehl, 1968, p. 198)

water' (Ross, 1943). The US\$ 75 million agreement at Volta Redonda mandated, as was often the case with Export-Import Bank projects, that credit funds could only be utilized for the purchase from the U.S. of all equipment (Bunge, 1958). This stipulation locked recipient countries into an ongoing economic

relationship with American construction technologies as well as with those who knew how to operate and export those technologies.

Other offices of the U.S. government also acted as catalysts for planning schemes. One example was the International Cooperation Administration, which provided funds for development planning and (like the Export-Import Bank) was 'partial to U.S. companies'. A second example was the State Department, which sponsored travelling exhibitions devoted to U.S. architecture and planning that toured South America in the late 1940s. This professional endeavour had previously occurred as early as the 1920s when the International Committee of the American Institute of Architects sponsored similar exhibitions throughout the continent.[6] Shortly after its establishment in 1945, the World Bank also became a major source of revenue for American planners, as was the case in the Middle East. In 1951 in Bogotá, for example, the Colombian Minister of Public Works applied for a large loan to finance the construction of a long railroad line, bridges, housing and a 'pilot plan . . . to find a normal size and shape for the capital city which as been growing very irregularly for 400 years' (*Engineering-News Record*, 1951, **147**, 29 November). In the same year El Salvador was awarded a large World Bank Loan to construct a new airport, pave roads 'from border to border' and build a \$30 million 'TVA-type power project', planned by the J.A. Jones Construction Company of Charlotte, North Carolina (*Engineering-News Record*, 1951, **146**, 8 February, p. 54). By 1953 the World Bank was financing other electric power generating projects, at least partially patterned after the Tennessee Valley Authority, in Brazil, Chile, Mexico and Uruguay (*Engineering-News Record*, 1953, **151**, 17 September). Therefore, TVA planning assumptions, along with those technologies tied to the TVA, were being fanned to foreign shores by World Bank loan schemes.

If these 'public gloves' were actively stroking the South American continent at the behest of American

Table 5.9. U.S. private investment abroad, 1950–1953.

Countries receiving Investments	(US$, billions)
Western European dependencies	0.593
Western European countries	2.367
Canada	5.257
Latin America	6.001
All other countries	2.085
TOTAL	16.303

Targets of Private Investments by Type of Industry

	1950 (US$ millions)	1953 (US$ millions)
Agriculture	589	658
Trade	762	1,046
Mining and smelting	1,129	1,934
Public utilities	1,425	1,499
Petroleum	3,390	4,931
Manufacturing	3,831	5,242
Other	662	994
TOTAL	11,788	16,304

Sources: U.S. Department of Commerce; Office of Business Economics. (Reproduced in *Architectural Forum*, 1955, **102**, January, p. 101.)

planners, many U.S. 'private hands' were also energetic in the 1950s where South American AEC business was concerned. Probably the most important of these was IBEC, the International Basic Economy Corporation, established by Nelson Rockefeller in 1946, and operating 'on the premise that a private American business corporation that focused on developing the 'basic economies' of developing countries could turn a profit and encourage others . . . to establish competitive businesses', such as supermarkets and other American retailing schemes.[7] IBEC became most active in Venezuela and Brazil, although it advised clients about burgeoning development plans in Iran as well. In 1950 Rockefeller constituted an eleven-man panel of New York municipal service experts headed by Robert Moses to visit and then make planning

recommendations for São Paulo that encompassed mass transit, highways, parks, water supply systems and land reclamation (*Engineering-News Record*, 1951, **146**, 8 February, p. 54). Similar initiatives occurred in Caracas, Venezuela (Gonzalez, 1996). IBEC continued to operate in both Brazil and Venezuela throughout the 1950s.

Competition and Adaptation, 1957–1960

The summaries of projects listed/described above demonstrate how broadly some American AEC firms and individuals were reaching for overseas work in the first decade after World War II, as either gloved or bare-handed entrepreneurs. Although the

Table 5.10. AEC companies from the U.S. operating in Latin America, 1955.

Name of Company	Type of Work	Location; Client Company
Knappen, Tippetts, Abbett & McCarthy	highway construction	Bolivia
Harza Engineering & J.A. Jones Construction Co.	hydroelectric dam	El Salvador
Stone & Webster	thermoelectric power	Sao Paulo, Brazil
Kuljian Corporation	power plant	Caracas
IBEC: George Dudley, Edward Echeverria, architects & Robert Burlingham, planner	post-earthquake rehabilitation of towns	El Salvador
IBEC	housing construction	El Salvador and Puerto Rico
IBEC: Venezuela Basic Economy Corporation	shopping centre	Suburban Caracas, Venezuela
U.S. Public Health Service: Edward Durell Stone and A.L. Aydelott, associated architects	hospital construction	Lima, Peru
Skidmore, Owings & Merrill	town planning, schools, houses in a refinery town	Venezuela
U.S. Steel (Orinoco Mining Co.)	new town planning for mining towns	Puerto Ordaz and Ciudad Piar, Venezuela
Squibb Pharmaceutical Co.	laboratories and offices	Cali, Peru; Colombia; Brazil; Cuba,
Abbott Laboratories	laboratories and offices	Caracas, Venezuela
Sterling Drug Company	laboratories and offices	Brazil; Columbia
General Motors	expansion of facilities	Montevideo
Ford Motor Company	expansion of facilities	Sao Paulo, Brazil
Chrysler	expansion of facilities	Mexico
Hilton Hotels Welton Becket, architect (Los Angeles)	hotel construction	Havana, Cuba
Intercontinental Hotels Holabird & Root & Burgee (Chicago)	hotel construction	Tamanaco Hotel, Caracas, Venezuela
Intercontinental Hotels Holabird & Root & Burgee (Chicago)	hotel construction	Tequendama Hotel; Bogota
Bank Building & Equipment	bank construction	Mexico; Cuba; Honduras; El Salvador; Quito, Ecuador

Sources: Architectural Forum, 1955, **102**, January; *Engineering-News Record*, 1954, **152**, 13 May, p. 60.

tables above provide quantitative data about many of these companies and persons, they do not provide information about the numbers of Americans (and others) involved in AEC work abroad, which is shown in Table 5.11.

Data in Table 5.11 confirm some of the points made above regarding American AEC activities abroad during the immediate postwar period. For example, remarkably there was only one U.S. citizen involved in engineering and construction work in central and southern Africa, and less than 1,000 in the Far East, despite there being more than 25,000 foreign nationals engaged in AEC-related work in that region. Instead, judging by these data, American AEC professionals were more engaged in Middle Eastern/North African, Latin American and European projects.

Table 5.12 is also useful in specifying members of the cast of American AEC players who were venturing abroad during this period.

Table 5.12 suggests several points. First, despite its compiler's hopes that this would provide a comprehensive snapshot of 'firms practicing abroad', the differences one finds between the names in the previous, more detailed tables and this list suggest an elusive comprehensiveness. There were other

Table 5.11. American business and overseas employment in Engineering and Construction (number of firms: 49).

Geographic Region	U.S. Citizens	Foreign Nationals
Latin America	1,086	16,843
Middle East/North Africa	1,400	16,680
Far East	814	25,760
Europe	1,004	6,737
Canada	589	10,336
Central/Southern Africa	1	126
TOTAL	4,894	76,482

Source: Overseas Training Project, Maxwell Graduate School of Citizenship and Public Affairs, Syracuse University, 1957. Reprinted in Cleveland *et al.*, 1960, pp. 102–103.

Table 5.12. U.S. AEC firms operating abroad, 1955 and 1960.

Firm	1955	1960
Atlas Constructors	X	X
Bates & Roger Construction	X	X
Bechtel Company	X	X
Catalytic Construction Company	X	X
Cayuga Construction Corporation	X	X
Chemical Construction Corporation	X	X
Compania Constructora Groves-Drake	X	–
Construction Management & Engineering Associates	X	–
Corbetta Construction Company	–	X
George A. Fuller Company	X	X
Gahagan Overseas Construction Company	X	X
Graver Construction Company	X	X
*Harrison & Abramowitz, Architects	X	X
*Holabird, Root & Burgess	X	X
A. Johnson Construction Company	X	X
J.A. Jones Construction Company	X	X
Leonard Construction Company	X	X
Loewy Construction Company	X	X
MacDonald Construction Company	X	X
Maxon Construction Company	X	X
Metcalf & Eddy	X	X
Montgomery Construction Company	X	X
Oman Construction Company	–	X
Preload Construction Company	–	X
*Raymond & Radio Architects	X	–
*Skidmore, Owings & Merrill, Architects	X	X
Smith Engineering & Construction	X	–
Smith Construction Company	–	X
Stone & Webster Engineering Corporation	X	X
Taylor Construction Company	X	X
Treadwell Construction Company	X	X
Utah Construction Company	X	X
Volpe Construction Company	X	X
Walsh Construction Company	X	X
West African Constructors, Inc.	–	X
Western Contracting Company	–	X
Wright Contracting Company	–	X

Notes:
X indicates a firm was listed.
* indicates architects.
According to the above there were 29 firms in 1955 and 34 in 1960.

Source: Angel, 1955–56, pp. 22–108; and Angel, 1959–1960, pp. 52–148.

companies and individuals whose activities abroad slipped through the compiler's nets as he trawled for evidence of Americans operating abroad. Note, for instance, the difference between Angel's figures about the number of AEC firms overseas (29 in 1955 and 34 in 1960) and those provided by Syracuse University (49 in 1957). Therefore, one needs to be wary about deducing too much from these less-than-complete statistics.[8] Second, many more contractors and engineers were practicing abroad during the 1950s than architects, an observation confirmed by the more detailed tables above. This in turn reflects a conclusion drawn in earlier chapters: that by and large the 'E'[engineers] and 'C' [construction industry personnel] of the acronym AEC prefaced the activities abroad of the 'A' [architects]. Third, the large number of repeating names in the 5-year period imply that once operating abroad, many firms chose to continue to make a go of their ventures. The exceptions to this tendency are clearly obvious. However, the persistence of these firms' operations also suggests one of the conclusions drawn in previous chapters: that some of the most successful American firms practicing abroad – both prior to mid-century and after – were those that stayed in their foreign locales as long as feasible, despite differences and mounting challenges. In the words of one patriotic U.S. marketing expert:

The key to success in foreign operations can be summed up in a single sentence. Study the markets and act in accordance with the differences you find, in dignity and to the equitable advantage of all concerned, for the benefit of your company and your country – for firm and for flag. (Rundt, 1960, p. 13)

Another contemporary urged flexibility in this way:

American business has been learning, often very painfully, that what is good in Toledo or Terre Haute is not automatically going to be successful in Tunis or Timbuktu. (Cleveland *et al.*, 1960, p. 109)

Even when flexible, tenacious or 'gloved' by

U.S. government programmes, American AEC professionals after the mid-1950s began to run 'full tilt into vigorous competition', mostly from their European counterparts but also in Latin America from indigenous companies, who had largely learned how to build and manage their businesses from Americans (*Engineering-News Record*, 1957, **155**, p. 25). After surveying fifty major construction firms conducting business internationally in 1957, the *Engineering News-Record* concluded that Germany, France, Italy and the U.K posed the most serious challenge to U.S. firms. Although 'large public works projects were once considered to be strictly an American specialty', Germans were gaining ground not only in their own country, but also in the Middle East and South America; the French in the Middle East and North Africa; Italians in South America, the Middle East and North Africa; and the British in Commonwealth countries (*Ibid*).

Engineering News-Record listed several reasons for this change of fortune: lower labour costs and cheaper construction materials in Europe, more favourable credit terms from banks and stronger colonial ties from clients, as well as more pro-active involvement by European embassy officials in scouting potential projects. In other words U.S. embassies, consulates, chambers of commerce or other agencies were not perceived to be functioning as well as those of some European competitors (*Construction Review*, 1961, **7**, January, p. 4). In response to competition, many American AEC firms abroad began to reduce their profit margins and accept foreign currency, affiliate more readily with European partners, and use European materials more frequently. These responses reflected many American AEC firms' awareness of the need to be more adaptable with respect to their practices. For example, the journal *Iron Age* admitted that many U.S. companies 'fear they are losing out permanently in foreign markets', but suggested that 'there's still opportunity for companies willing to shift with changing conditions overseas' (*Iron Age*,

1959, **183**, p. 16). And as one American contractor working in Mexico bluntly expressed it, 'It is best not to stick your well-polished Yankee neck out in a Latin country. The faster you become Mexicanized, Brazilianized or Argentinized, the better your relationship with government officials and local businessmen will be' (*Engineering-News Record*, 1958, **156**, 4 September, p. 114). Many companies also employed two additional retaliatory measures: work as much as possible with 'public gloves' (such as the International Cooperation Administration) and highlight more aggressively to potential clients the strengths of American AEC firms. In 1957 there seemed to be four of them: Americans' 'ability to get a job done fast, their use of better equipment, greater availability of supplies and fast delivery of materials'

(*Engineering-News Record*, 1957, **155**, 14 November p. 27). In other words, American standards related to efficiency, materials and management were seen as hallmarks of American building practice. However, just as those ideals were being touted in local contexts, a U.S. House of Representatives subcommittee in Washington began to express serious concerns about the 'inadequate, indifferent and incompetent' ways in which International Cooperation Administration funds were being administered (*Engineering-News Record*, 1958, **156**, 3 July p. 84).

But competitors did not pose the only gnawing challenge to American AEC firms that tried to survive overseas in the late-1950s. Other economic, political and cultural realities sometimes flew in the face of Americans' assumptions either about how to operate an international AEC office efficiently, or to what extent they could place politics on the sidelines of their concerns. For example, in Latin America, although some believed that 'the U.S. construction man's main concern is with economics, not politics', it sometimes proved to be impractical (as in Cuba, Haiti, Colombia, Venezuela or Argentina) to ignore violence, kidnapping, insurrections (i.e., 'terrorism' in the lexicon of the early 2000s) against existing regimes that had allowed Americans to practice there in the first place.[9] Furthermore, because of the

LOCAL CONTRACTORS—having gained experience from working with foreign firms —are increasing in numbers and capacity.

STEPPING INTO the field of global construction, the European constructors are eagerly competing with U.S. engineers and contractors for jobs at all points in the world.

Figures 5.13 and 5.14. These two cartoons reflect some of the trepidation American contractors were feeling in the late 1950s, as they faced ever-stiffer competition from both local entrepreneurs and European building firms. (*Source: Engineering-News Record*, 1957, **155**, November, p. 26)

instability of many regimes, currency devaluations, financial kickbacks and personnel changes of leadership were frequent, thus sometimes weakening personal connections between American contractors and, for instance, powerful Ministers of Public Works (*Engineering-News Record*, 1958, **156**, 4 September, p. 113).

In the Middle East, too, during the late-1950s the political landscape was sometimes tumultuous, as oil revenues began to fuel more significant construction investments. Iran was a case in point.

Figures 5.15 and 5.16. These images of a proposed master plan for Teheran, Iran are from a 1966 consultancy report produced by Victor Gruen Associates, Los Angeles, in conjunction with Abdul-Aziz Farman-Farmian of Teheran. They urged the adoption of European and American modernizing ideals for commercial and residential living, in an extension of the city along an east-west axis. (I thank Prof. Vincent Costello, Faculty of the Built Environment, University of the West of England, Bristol, for bringing this document to my attention and providing me with a copy)

In 1953 the Shah, with covert U.S. military assistance, overthrew Mossadegh and then turned increasingly to U.S. engineers, architects and planners for advice about urban, regional and industrial development. The Shah's 'Plan Organization' was buttressed financially by Point Four Program and World Bank loans, and it comprised major railroad, highway, port, telecommunication, and dam construction, much of which was planned and directed by AEC personnel from the United States (Marashian, 1958). This involvement, as well as other kinds of projects such as shopping centres planned by Victor Gruen (Costello, 1998) and residential developments designed by other investors, linked the U.S. inextricably with the Shah. In the late-1950s many Americans might have hoped to design and build their projects in Iran while ignoring regional politics, but 20 years later the bond between U.S. builders and the Shah proved to be catastrophic for American interests in the region.

By the late-1950s some American AEC professionals thought they had learned several lessons about operating overseas. In 1958, to help the aspiring AEC exporter avoid potential pitfalls, *Engineering-News Record* (1958, **156**, 27 March, pp. 31–34) suggested the following: (1) investigate carefully the physical and other dimensions of a project before leaping into it; (2) try to specify a contract that brings a bonus for beating the target date; (3) sometimes prepare to 'first build a city' for workers of all kinds engaged on the project; (4) employ a minimum number of well-chosen Americans and hire more local subcontractors and 'an influential cousin', both because of lower costs and because 'it creates a more favourable attitude on the part of foreign national and local governments'; (5) feed local workers to make them healthier and more 'efficient'; (6) carefully monitor supply lines and local economic conditions; and (as noted above) (7) try to avoid politics because 'stepping into local or national politics is a sure way to buy difficulties'.

Aid, Oil and Construction, 1960–1975

By the early 1960s, as U.S. national politics shifted and John F. Kennedy replaced Dwight D. Eisenhower as President, foreign aid initiatives proliferated. Some of these created relatively small-scale organizations that operated worldwide, such as the Peace Corps created in 1962 or the International Executive Service Corps instituted in 1964. Other U.S. government institutions arising from aid expansion, however, were larger-scale ventures that operated within particular regions, such as the Inter-American Bank in South America, or the Development Loan Fund (started by Eisenhower), which initially doled out the lion's share of its monies to South Asia, the Middle

East and East Asia, respectively.[10] Some of these are summarized in Table 5.13.

Beginning in the early 1960s the nature of many lending institutions also began to change, as organizations disbursed more loans than grants and encouraged even greater linkages between U.S. firms and local investors (marking the beginning of joint-venture operations) especially in the housing field. This change occurred as Kennedy attempted to consolidate foreign aid operations in the Agency for International Development (A.I.D.) (*Engineering News-Record*, 1961, **159**, 8 June, p. 17). The net result was

unprecedented financing for construction projects of all kinds, for big long-term development programs from the Andes to the China Sea. The money is there for roads,

Table 5.13. U.S. foreign aid's monetary implications for AEC Firms, 1960.

Aiding Institution: International Cooperation Administration

Country	Project/Contractor	Amount of Loan/Grant (US$ millions)
Vietnam	national highway (Route 1) Contractor: Johnson, Drake, Piper	30
Korea	fertilizer plant Contractor: McGraw-Hydrocarbon	33
Taiwan	Shimen Reservoir Contractor: Morrison-Knudsen	19
Taiwan	power, transport, public works & industrial projects Contractor: J.G. White Engineering	3
Afghanistan	Kandahar Airport construction Contractor: Morrison-Knudsen	4
Thailand	roads and bridges Contractor: Raymond International	9
TOTAL		98

Aiding Institution: Development Loan Fund

Country	Project/Contractor	Amount of Loan/Grant (US$ millions)
Spain	earthmoving equipment/reclamation	7.7
Spain	power plant and dam/Tagus River	3.9
Greece	Acheloos hydroelectric project	31
Yugoslavia	Kosovo power plant	9
Yugoslavia	Trebisnjica hydroelectric plant	15
Sub-total Europe		*66.6*

Table 5.13. U.S. foreign aid's monetary implications for AEC Firms, 1960 *(continued)*

Country	Project/Contractor	Amount of Loan/Grant (US$ millions)
Libya	Tripoli power plant	5
Morocco	Mechra Klila Dam	23
Tunisia	pulp factory	6
Sudan	textile plant, Khartoum	10
Sub-total Africa		*44*
Argentina	railways and highways	24.8
Ecuador	Pan-American and national highways	10
Honduras	highway development	5
Peru	Aguaytia-Pucallpa highway	4.5
Sub-total Latin America		*44.3*
Iran	municipal development, sewage, etc.	9
Iran	highway development	33.5
Iran	railway terminals	3.6
Iran	airport improvements	7.2
Pakistan	Karachi water and sewage system	5.5
Pakistan	Karnafuli hydro project	17.5
Pakistan	West Pakistan water development	15.2
Pakistan	Karachi commercial jetstrip	4.8
Pakistan	railway rehabilitation (depots, etc)	31
Pakistan	tubewells	15.2
India	thermal power station, Damodar	30
India	railway developments	7
Sub-total Central/South Asia		*179.5*
Malaya	deepwater port in North Klang Straits	10
Malaya	roads and bridges	10
Vietnam	Saigon-Cholon water system	19.5
Philippines	roads and bridges	18.6
Philippines	cement plant	3.7
Taiwan	Shimen dam	21.5
Indonesia	port and harbour development	6
Sub-total Far East		*89.3*
TOTAL		423.7

Source: Engineering-News Record, 1960, **158**, 9 June, p. 20.

waterworks, dams, railroads, power stations, schools, hospitals, urban development, housing, and ports. (*Engineering News-Record*, 1961, **159**, 28 September, p. 22)

However, problems persisted for AEC professionals trying to cement linkages with local investors, tap into increased funding, or actually implement projects abroad (*Engineering-News Record*, 1963, **161**, 31 January, p. 15). Although the U.S. State Department both increased the number of commercial officers in embassies and built new facilities abroad, many European countries continued to be even more proactive in this regard (*Construction Review*, 1961, **7**, January, p. 4). The U.S. situation was more hit-or-miss, exemplified by the kind of request issued by Secretary of State Dean Rusk to all U.S. foreign service posts in September 1962:

I am requesting that your principal aides be alert to, and seek out export opportunities for American business; that you develop the necessary contacts in order to be 'in the know'; that your Mission shows foresight in advising U.S. business not only of impending bids, but also on construction and development projects long before they reach a definitive stage.[11]

Complications also arose both from divergent cultural norms regarding laws and contracts, and the lack of realistic estimates or specifications before planners and contractors submitted a project bid.

However, by the mid-1960s incentives for international work by AEC professionals continued to escalate. Many Western Europeans continued to be fascinated with U.S. norms regarding housing, shopping and working (Ibelings, 1997, pp. 30–56; *Construction Review*, 1964, **10**, January, p.4; *Nation's Business*, 1964, **52**, p. 76; *International Commerce*, 1966, **72** , p.12). Furthermore, the European Common Market relaxed some of its rules about bidding, which encouraged more American firms to work across the Atlantic (*Engineering-News Record*, 1964, **162**, 14 May, p. 25). In the mid-1960s U.S. engineering companies and planning consultancies also began changing

internally, from partnership-based corporate entities to more internally-specialized entities with functional branches, such as structural engineering, town planning, and service engineering (Rimmer, 1988; Logcher and Levitt, 1979, pp. 7–13).

By 1966 AEC professional organizations began conferring publicly with U.S. government officials about how to overcome bureaucratic encumbrances and further increase incentives to engage in international work (*Engineering News-Record* , 23 June 1966, p. 15; and *Construction Review*, 1966, **12**, October, p. 9). Despite the challenges in accomplishing that work, however, the reality persisted throughout the 1960s that if American AEC professionals sought work abroad, then it was usually more beneficial for them to attach their projects to a federally-sponsored 'public glove' than it was to go it alone as an entirely 'private hand'.

The net result – despite challenges and with incentives – was that more AEC companies opted to internationalize their operations. This is clearly borne out by the data in Tables 5.14 and 5.15, which show a growing set of AEC professionals relative to earlier years. From the mid-1960s to approximately 1970 one of those incentives came in the form of military contracts resulting from the escalation of the Vietnam/American War (*International Construction*, 1964, **3**, September, p. 16).

By the early 1970s, however, AEC professionals working abroad again experienced heightened competition. This was largely due to significant decreases in U.S. military spending abroad, better technical skills of foreign workers, and 'a growing nationalism that is leading [foreign countries] to handle most standard construction themselves' (*Engineering News-Record*, 1972, 23 March, p. 173). This in turn implied that, in order to survive constantly-shifting conditions, AEC exporters had no choice but to be flexible with finances, keen with competition, and inventive with international operations. One way they could demonstrate that

Table 5.14. American AEC firms operating abroad, 1966.

Firm	1966
*Adrian Wilson & Associates	X
Vern E. Alden	X
*Amman & Whitney	X
Atkinson & Company	X
Austin Company	X
Bechtel Corporation	O
*Alexander Bernhard Associates	X
C.F. Braun	X
*Marcel Breuer & Associates	X
*Brown, Daltas & Associates	X
Brown & Root	X
Burns & Roe	X
Butler Manufacturing Company	X
Catalytic Construction Company	O
Chemical Construction Company	O
Christiani & Nielsen	X
*Daniel, Mann, Johnson & Mendenhall	X
Ebasco Services, Inc.	X
H.K. Ferguson Company	X
Paul Hardeman, Inc.	X
Jones Construction Company	O
Levitt & Sons	X
*Litchfield, Whiting, Browne & Associates	X
*McGanby, Marshall & McMillan	X
Merritt-Chapman & Scott Corporation	X
Metcalf & Eddy	O
Metcalfe-Hamilton	X
Morrison-Knudsen	X
*Pedersen & Tilney	X
Procon Incorporated	X
Rader & Associates	X
Raymond International	X
Reynolds Construction Company	X
Rust Engineering Company	X
Sanderson & Porter	X
*Stanley Engineering	X
Stearns-Roger Corporation	X
Stone & Webster	O
Tecon Corporation	X
Teer Company	X
*Tippetts-Abbett-McCarthy-Stratton	X
Walsh Construction	O
White Engineering Corporation	O
Wright Contracting Company	+

Notes:

X   indicates firm was neither listed in 1955 nor in 1960
    – i.e. first listing.
O   indicates firm was listed in 1955 as well as 1960.
+   indicates firm was listed in 1960, but not in 1955.
*   indicates architects.
Total number of firms = 44 (including 12 architects).

Source: Angel, 1966, pp. 8–147.

Table 5.15. U.S. Contractors' Earnings Abroad, 1969.

Name and Location of Company	Earnings (US$ millions)
1. Kaiser Engineers, Oakland, CA	613.5
2. Bechtel Corporation, San Francisco, CA	340
3. Procon, Inc., San Francisco, CA	337
4. Lummus Company, New York, NY	300
5. Brown & Root, Houston, TX	261
6. Arthur McKee & Co., Cleveland, OH	244
7. Boise Cascade Corporation, Boise, ID	216
8. M.W. Kellogg Company, New York, NY	205
9. Stone & Webster Engineering, Boston, MA	200
10. Foster Wheeler Corporation, New York, NY	162
11. Rust Engineering Company, Pittsburgh, PA	161
12. Dillingham Corporation, Honolulu, HI	151
13. Badger Company, Cambridge, MA	150
14. Ralph M. Parsons Company, Los Angeles, CA	136
15. Stearns-Roger Corporation, Denver, CO	93
16. Fluor Corporation, Los Angeles, CA	91
17. Morrison-Knudsen, Boise, ID	69
18. Austin Company, Cleveland, OH	66
19. Raymond International, New York, NY	58
20. Dravo Corporation, Pittsburgh, PA	57
21. Daniel Construction Company, Greenville, SC	55
22. J.A. Jones Construction Company, Charlotte, NC	41
23. Vinnell Corporation, Alhambra, CA	40
24. Guy F. Atkinson Co.-Walsh Construction, SF, CA	34
25. Edward J. Gerrits, Miami, FL	33

Source: Engineering-News Record, 1970, 5 November, pp. 80–81.

ingenuity was to concentrate more on labour-intensive construction techniques that could be used more easily in so-called 'developing' countries (Howenstine, 1972, p. 6). A second way to be both ingenious and responsible was to 'have a special regard for local traditions and for cultural, religious and other factors' related to construction (*Ibid.*). And a third way to be both responsible and compliant with changing U.S. regulations was to conduct environmental reviews of capital projects, in line with the National Environmental Policy Act of 1969, which also applied to A.I. D.-funded projects. However, the degree to which this sensitivity was actually achieved is unknown.

What is much clearer is how voraciously American AEC interests responded in 1974–75 to

Middle Eastern clients (citizens of the Oil Producing Export Countries, or OPEC) who found themselves suddenly awash with approximately US$100 billion in petro-dollars as a result of sharp rises in oil prices. In 1975 alone, Iran announced the creation of new towns at Ahvaz and Bandar Shahpur (for which Skidmore, Owings & Merrill of Chicago was hired to do the planning); Saudi Arabia commissioned over 100,000 new housing units, and Egypt began planning the rehabilitation of three towns in the Suez Canal zone (*Engineering-News Record*, 1975, 9 January). Competition was again fierce among U.S. and European construction interests to be awarded these, and other jobs related to the world's newest centre of gravity for planning and building activity (*Engineering-News Record*, 1975, 24 April, pp. 13–17; *House and Home*, 1975, **48**, October, p. 9).

Conclusion

The 30-year period after the conclusion of World War II brought phenomenal changes to U.S. architectural and engineering interests that had an eye for international work. In searching for the roots of American architectural globalization in the four preceding chapters, one finds myriad examples but only hints of large-scale coordination. After the War, as the U.S. government became much more actively engaged in promoting AEC work abroad for U.S. companies and individuals, the infrastructure of investment was in place. The architectural tools of war and peace were sharpened and exported. They were also shepherded along and promoted by a significantly larger number of U.S. professionals working in much more diverse kinds of construction sites. As will be seen in the next chapter, American AEC interests were well-entrenched on a global scale by the late-1970s.

At the beginning of this chapter, three questions seemed sensible to be posed about the exporting

of American architectural tools of war and peace from 1945 to 1975. The first of those asked which skills and tools were exported? Five of them seemed to predominate: large-scale infrastructure, prefabrication, mechanization, creating suburban forms/spaces, and promoting efficiency, speed, reliability and standards. In all these respects U.S. companies were facing sharper competition – already by the late 1950s and certainly by the mid-1970s – from both Europeans and native companies throughout the world, who learned from U.S. precedents and then challenged the precedent-setter.

The second question asked who helped to make the transfer of skills and tools easier to occur? Here, there are four separate, but often intertwined answers: U.S. government programmes (what I have been calling 'public gloves'); large U.S. companies, 'private hands' (sometimes working alone); and indigenous companies/individuals in far-flung contexts that attached themselves to a groundswell of building. A proliferating mosaic of possibilities emerged for American AEC interests in the three decades after the War. Some of those grew out of the U.S. government's efforts to use its dollar-muscle to promote exporting and thus offset a balance of payments problem. The government sustained a series of foreign aid programmes, bolstered its foreign consular presence, invigorated the international scope of the Department of Commerce, and encouraged private companies to compete, in capitalist manner, with a growing number of non-AEC companies/individuals on a worldwide scale. Those companies adapted in the face of uncertainty. They learned to employ new strategies, such as specializing in one area/country and then spreading out from that base, and creating new corporate entities, such as limited partnerships and joint-ventures.

The third question asked what were the results of this transfer of tools and skills? Given the numbers of firms and projects cited above in this chapter's tables, the answer to this question at first might seem to approach infinity. However, they might well be clustered under three main umbrellas. The first is the umbrella of industrial production and energy exploitation. Repeatedly between 1945 and 1975, American AEC companies were hired to harness water for power, build factories, erect bridges and highways, and reconfigure existing landscapes so they could accommodate new industrial uses, places and activities. Many objected angrily to the changes; others profited handsomely by them. American companies claimed to be primarily concerned with economics and less obsessed with politics, although that became practically impossible. The second umbrella was one associated with capitalistic consumption. American-inspired retail stores, shopping centres, recreation areas and residential districts were consistently found in clients' contracts as they sought builders – often American ones – to translate American functions to foreign places. That translation was not word-for-word. Instead, the transplants became variants, the home-grown became foreign-bred, as there were repeatedly local adjustments being made to transplanted American prototypes.

NOTES

1. As *Engineering News-Record* reported, those U.S. consultants and their projects in France were: Parsons, Brinckerhoff, Hall & MacDonald (engineers), and Walker & Poor (architects) on bases in Evreux and Dreux (Normandy); Seelye, Stevenson, Value & Knecht (engineers) and Frank Grad & Sons (architects) on bases at Chaumont, Chambley, Toul and Laon; Cutting Associates (inspection work) at bases in Etain and Phalsburg; Atlantic Engineers (Amman & Whitney and Guy Panero, architect) at bases of Chateauroux and Chambley; MacKenzie Bogert & White (designers) at a depot in Saran; Daniel, Mann, Johnson & Mendenhall (designers) for unspecified airfields; Fluor (designers) for unspecified hospitals, supply stores and petroleum storage facilities; Dumont, Greer and Associates (designers) for the new U.S. Army headquarters near Paris; Foster-Wheeler (architect-engineer) for petroleum storage facilities at Donges, Melun and Verdun; Vacuum Concrete (contractors) for erecting prefabricated concrete slabs and columns for a factory in Bordeaux.

2. Cohen (1995, pp. 162–177) details many of these instances, which include Maurice Rotival's suggestion that a 'Rhine Authority' be created along the lines of the Tennessee Valley Authority.

3. For an astute analysis of U.S. architectural and planning influence in postwar West Germany, see Diefendorf, 1993, especially pp. 106–107 (for historic preservation) and pp. 181–221 (for planning issues).

4. Quotation from Thornburg, 1949, p. 339.

5. 'Middle Mass' is taken from the anthropologist John Gillin who, in a 1955 article, characterized the incipient Latin American middle classes in this way. Quoted in Whyte and Holmberg, 1956, p. 21.

6. For the International Cooperation Administration, see 'Competition tightens overseas', *Engineering-News Record*, 1957, 14 November; for the State Department, see 'Houses USA', *Architectural Forum*, 1947, **86**, pp. 81–88.

7. Quotation from *A Guide to Archives and Manuscripts* at the Rockefeller Archive Center, NY, p. 10; also see Broehl, 1968; Persico, 1982, p. 35; Kramer and Roberts, 1976, pp. 55–58.

8. Even as late as 1961, statistics were 'lacking to show how much construction has been undertaken by U.S. firms in foreign countries'. *Construction Review*, 1961, **7**(4), January, p. 4.

9. For example, in 1958, Cubans loyal to Fidel Castro burned equipment of one U.S. construction company and kidnapped U.S. citizens of another (*Engineering-News Record*, 1958, **156**, 4 September, p. 113). A few months earlier in Haiti, after a 'political blowup', labour groups 'bore down on [a U.S. contractor] with money demands' (*Engineering-News Record*, 1958, **156**, 27 March, p. 31).

10. For the Development Loan Fund, see *Engineering-News Record*, 1960, **161**, 9 June, p. 19.

11. K.L. Kollar, 'Exporting consulting engineering' (1963), quoted by P.J. Rimmer, 1988, p. 768.

6

The American Century's Last Quarter: Exporting Images and Technologies with a Vengeance, 1975–2000[1]

By the mid-1970s, because of the 'boom years of the Vietnam era and the growth of international construction, particularly in the petrodollar Middle East . . . foreign markets were becoming a staple of the big builder's construction diet' (*Southern Exposure*, 1980, **8**, p. 101). However, domestic markets increasingly contributed to that diet as well. This was evident from the early to the late 1980s, as a major U.S. recession provided incentives for many AEC professionals to globalize their architectural operations, and as smaller firms and family-owned subsidiaries became subsumed within larger corporate conglomerates. In the last quarter of the

American Century, foreign/domestic hybrids (i.e., joint ventures and limited partnerships) increasingly characterized the nature of U.S. international construction activities. What other kinds of dynamics were operative regarding the exporting of American architecture during this final generation of the twentieth century? This central question frames what follows. The answers are myriad:

1. further involvement in overseas construction activities by the U.S. government, but with professionals' consistent complaints about efficiency;

2. more intense competition from both overseas and within the U.S., as more players entered the field;

3. shifting geographies of focus, as the Middle East throughout the 1980s waned considerably and as other regions, Latin America and particularly East Asia, waxed constructive;

4. increasingly sophisticated technical responses to the sharp challenges posed by foreign work;

5. deeper sensitivity to the cultural contexts in which AEC firms from the U.S. practiced; and

6. pervasive indications that the United States – through architecture being erected by U.S. architects, builders and/or clients overseas – was exporting concepts and recognizably U.S. spaces. The concepts included citizens' workshops (Gould, 1999), and 'New Urbanism' (*Architecture*, 1996, April, p. 77); the spaces concerned entertainment areas in 'fantasy cities' (Hannigan, 1998), and suburban subdivisions in cities worldwide.

To flesh out the fuller dimensions and implications of this bony skeleton, it is prudent to examine both the 'diet' and the gluttony of increasingly globalized American architecture during the period after the boom of the Vietnam era, and after the gush of the petrodollars. Some of that gluttony is evident from counting the dollars.

Consider these facts: from 1962 to 1978, Bechtel companies' annual revenues grew from $237 million to $4.6 billion, an increase of 1,840 per cent. The Fluor Corporation grew from $111 million to $2.8 billion, Brown & Root from $186 million to $4.4 billion, J.A. Jones from $107 million to $1.1 billion . . . Virtually every major U.S. contractor has entered the foreign contract sweepstakes. (quotation from *Ibid.*; see also Fluor, 1978; Angel, 1979; Covell, 1996; Mote, 1997; Covell and Salamie, 2000)

One firm running in that sweepstakes was Diversified Design Disciplines (3D), based in Houston since its inception in 1955. In 1973, 3D pondered whether to retrench in response to a projected, domestic U.S. slump, or instead to internationalize its operations. The firm hired William Bonham, an entrepreneurial U.S. architect working for an international hotel developer. Bonham believed that 'architecture and engineering – at least as they have been practiced for the past fifty years in the U.S. – are sort of dinosaurs' (*Engineering-News Record*, 1978, 9 February, p. 18). He further maintained that in the mid-1970s 'we are coming into an era that will require new responses in the way we building professionals do our thing'. To handle unprecedented, exceedingly complex projects, Bonham and 3D directors set out 'to develop a new breed of professional', which they likened to breeding a new kind of cat: 'good architects and good engineers who think like businessmen' (*Ibid.*, p. 19). Such professionals, 3D believed, should be beholden to what the firm called one-point management responsibility, meaning that clients could direct their inquiries to one point in the complex mix of construction experts involved in any project. However, 3D also believed that their company's professionals should also be comfortable with working in a multidisciplinary team that offered project management 'for the entire design-construct process – master planning, architecture [exterior and interior], engineering [of all kinds], graphics, contract service, landscaping and programming' (*Ibid*). 3D changed its name to 3D/I ['International'] and initially targeted Saudi Arabia and the United Arab Emirates. In the former case the firm designed Buraidah New Town, north-west of Riyadh; six new towns in the east of the Kingdom for the Arabian-American Oil Company; several hotels and expansions of conference centres as well as rehabilitations of palaces. In the United Arab Emirates, 3D/I designed the Galadari Corniche Complex and Inter-Continental Plaza, both in Dubai. This 'diet' of construction swelled the company's girth considerably, from a volume of $780 million in 1974 to $3 billion in 1978.

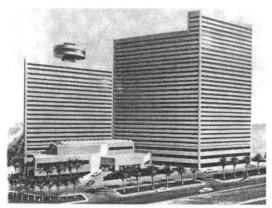

Figure 6.1. Galadari Corniche project in Dubai, erected by the American firm of 3D/I in 1978–79. Several American architectural firms sought commissions in the oil-rich Middle East during the 1970s. Many of those commissions, like this one, were testimonials to retardataire architectural modernization, taking forms from a European modernist aesthetic and disseminating them to other contexts. (*Source: Engineering-News Record*, 1978, 9 February, p. 18)

Another American architectural 'horse' in the late-1970s petrodollar-fuelled sweepstakes was HOK + 4, based in St. Louis. Hellmuth, Obata & Kassabaum was established in 1955 and by the late-1990s had become the largest architecture/engineering firm in the U.S., with 1,800 employees practicing in twenty-four offices worldwide in 1997.[2] In the early-1970s HOK helped plan and build the University of the West Indies, a project funded by the Agency for International Development (A.I.D.). This positive experience prompted by a U.S. government 'public glove' helped inspire the firm to leap further afield in the mid-1970s, in particular to Saudi Arabia, where Gyo Obata designed, and HOK erected, King Saud University in Riyadh (completed 1984). As King Graf, HOK's Vice Chairman, observed in 1990,

The OPEC countries were booming then and American design firms were all over the Middle East, competing with the British, French, Japanese and others. The American firms, I believe, were quickly recognized for listening to clients, responding to their needs including budget and schedule control, and providing design solutions that were efficient and architecturally exciting. (Graf, 1990)

In September 1974, when George Hellmuth received an unsolicited, pre-qualification questionnaire from the Saudi Minister of Education, he personally and swiftly responded by travelling to Riyadh. The client had invited seventeen other firms to submit proposals, and HOK realized that to win the job, in addition to being graced with good luck, it would have to work expeditiously (multiple trips over 9 months) and creatively, employing 'western technology . . . [and using] contemporary architecture reminiscent in massing and detail to the traditional Najd architecture of Central Arabia' (*Engineering-News Record*, 1976, 11 November, p. 22). The firm also established a consortium composed of a series of critical limited partnerships, primarily with three U.S. engineering companies but also with the U.K. architectural firm of Gollins Melvin Ward, all four of whom were among the seventeen competitors.[3] The winning of that bid ultimately led to other joint ventures in Saudi Arabia, as well as to wider global initiatives by the firm in the 1980s. For example, in 1981 the firm designed the World Trade Center in Taipei, which opened the door more widely to East Asian clients. HOK thus searched for a suitable regional base,

making a number of trips to explore the Asian/Pacific region . . . We met contractors, consultants, local architects, potential clients, government officials, people at the American Embassy (especially the commercial officer) and we were enthusiastic about what we found. We then asked ourselves, if we had an office in the Far East, where should it be? Hong Kong came up best because it is well-located in the region, has a large English-speaking population, a British legal system and was an air transportation hub. (Graf, 1990)

HOK opened its Hong Kong branch in 1983, and by 1997 it was the largest American office in Asia, with nearly 100 employees.

If 3D/I and HOK + 4 exemplify a corporate side of American architecture abroad in the late-1970s, then the construction odyssey of Ralph Yeakel suggests a more personal, episodic side to these globalizing architectural trends. Yeakel, a Philadelphia native who started in construction as a ditch-digger and who acquired incurable wanderlust and 'builderlust', began working abroad in 1965 when he signed on as an assistant concrete superintendent for Bechtel, building a nuclear power plant in India. Yeakel reflected in one dynamic person the six, intertwined, operative dynamics regarding latecentury U.S. building abroad: U.S. government involvement; competition; varying geographic focus; changing techniques of practice; more acute sensitivity to culture; and the exporting of American concepts and ideas along with spaces and forms.

With an almost romantic sense of mission . . . [Yeakel] is a veteran member of America's foreign legion of expatriate construction men, a master of the bulldozer and the crane, and [what is called] a 'process constructor' . . . He has devoted most of the past twenty years to helping such countries as South Korea, Pakistan, Venezuela, India, Iran, and Saudi Arabia build oil refineries, fertilizer factories, steam and gas plants, nuclear generators, and pipelines. (McQuade, 1980, p. 96)

Yeakel believed that contracting abroad was more an art than a science, and he loved pursuing that art. 'What he finds most compelling about his business is the experience of building, first hand, in remote parts of the world' (Ibid., p. 100). As Yeakel expressed it,

Construction satisfies me as no other activity does. Movement, power, accomplishment, excitement, broad vistas, towering heights – all that captures man's imagination is there . . . It is a series of many little and some big steps. You . . . open bank accounts, construct housing for supervisors, build camps and warehouses and staging yards for laborers, sort through hundreds of potential subcontractors to come up with a reasonable list, then sell this list to the client, set up customs clearances, work permits and visas [and] organize survey teams. (Ibid., pp. 98, 100)

However, tempering the pursuit of this 'art' were niggling challenges. Yeakel was scornful, for instance, about his own government's shortcomings concerning international construction, citing 'disincentives' created by U.S. government bureaucrats that

hindered American AEC professionals in their underbidding of European and Asian competitors: inefficient salesmanship by U.S. embassies, high taxation for expatriate builders, and opening the bidding for constructing U.S. military installations overseas to international, rather than exclusively U.S. companies. Yeakel was also blunt in his disdain for foreign bureaucracies, cynically calling some of them 'a proctologist's delight: a collection of perfect assholes' (Ibid., p. 100).

U.S. Government Assistance in the Face of Competition

Despite several fervent attempts by the U.S. government in the immediate postwar period to provide what I characterized in the preceding chapter as 'public gloves' for AEC professionals from the U.S. to practice abroad, by the mid-1970s those attempts were sometimes falling short of their intended goal. Although

in 1976 the U.S. construction industry ranked first in the field of overseas contracts [16%], by the end of the decade it ranked only fifth [5%]. The leading four countries were then Japan, South Korea, West Germany and Italy, in order of volume done overseas. The U.S. contractors were largely squeezed out of the lucrative Middle East business that had been fuelled mainly by the 'petrodollar surplus' resulting from the oil crisis of 1973. (quotation from Stallworthy and Kharbanda, 1985, p. 12; see also Hodge, 1982, p. 24)

The main reasons for this lagging stemmed from rising labour costs in the U.S., more coordinated efforts by foreign competitors' governments, and more stringent U.S. regulations and procedural requirements, which weakened 'productivity'.

However, despite this lagging and 'squeezing out', U.S. design firms still managed to hold 42 per cent of the world's design market in 1979. Two of the reasons they did so was by creating jointventureships with local firms and by hiring larger numbers of foreign engineers (*Engineering-News Record*, 1979, 13 December, p. 30). Both strategies helped them circumvent adverse tax and onerous regulatory policies (*Engineering-News Record*, 1979, 6 December, p. 26). Furthermore, in the late 1970s 'top U.S. design-only architectural firms' also reported increasingly large foreign earnings. In 1978 the American Institute of Architects (A.I.A.) noted that those top design-only firms were working in 147 countries and earning $708 million (most of it coming from the Middle East) and roughly twice the amount reported in 1974. In 1977, among the 448 design firms, 45 per cent were involved in overseas work. However, others quantifying the trends towards transnational practice by the AEC professions (Angel, 1979) tallied slightly different numbers. In 1979, for example, according to Juvenal Angel, there were 130 U.S. firms practicing abroad in the AEC domain, with

only twenty of those listed as architects. Their names and project locations are listed in Table 6.1.

'The World Bank, regional development banks, and the OPEC countries remain the strongest possibilities [as providers of overseas work], while the U.S. A.I.D. and military construction programs have been scaled down considerably' (American Institute of Architects, 1978, p. 1). The A.I.A. also found two noteworthy trends that presented targets of potential opportunity for American architects: the growing number of 'turnkey contracts' (i.e., 'conglomerate packages that include planning, design, construction, materials and equipment, and initial operation management services'), and 'new types of architectural services, such as project management and management information systems design. Because of advanced U.S. technology and expertise, American architects are being sought out,

Table 6.1. American architectural firms practicing abroad, 1979.

Name of Firm	Project location
Airways Engineering	Greece, Saudi Arabia
Allied Architects, Engineers, Planners	Lebanon
Amman & Whitney	Bangladesh, Ethiopia, France, Greece, Iran, Pakistan
William W. Bond	Belgium
Marcel Breuer & Associates	France
Leo Daly Company	Hong Kong, Indonesia, Singapore
Daniel, Mann, Johnson & Mendenhall	Brazil, Spain, U.K., Malaysia
A. Epstein & Sons International	France, Nigeria
Granite Management Services	The Netherlands
Hellmuth, Obata & Kassabaum	Saudi Arabia
Henningson, Durham & Richardson	Italy, Korea, Spain
Lyons Associates	Indonesia, Thailand
W. F. Pedersen & Associates	Italy
Pope, Evans & Robbins	Indonesia
Rader & Associates	Iran, Jamaica, Panama
Skidmore, Owings & Merrill	Hong Kong
Soule Steel Company	Indonesia
Urbanographers Associated	Brazil, France
Wilsey & Ham	Mexico
Adrian Wilson Associates	Indonesia, Saudi Arabia

Source: Angel, 1979.

not only as designers, but as specialists, managers, and overseers' (*Ibid*.). This 'expert' quality of American architects seems to have endured; one Hong Kong analyst affirmed in 1999 that Americans' 'expertise' was 'the key to U.S. architects' success in winning jobs [in Hong Kong]' (Lui, 1999, p. 47). However, the specific nature of that 'expertise' can be elusive, in the sense that U.S. architects might be renowned for manufacturing expertise, whereas Japanese architects are noted for their structural design, or European architects for their mastery of designing buildings' envelopes (Katz, 1999).

A.I.A.'s analysis in 1978 of recent trends pointing to a growing international market came in response to 'an increasing number of requests from A.I.A. members and other design professionals for information about overseas work' (*Ibid*.). The analysis – more an introduction for the curious than a 'definitive encyclopedia [because] facts and statistics are likely to change as soon as they go into print' – was published as *The Architect's Guide to International Practice*, commissioned by the Institute's International Affairs Committee and prepared by the Government Affairs Committee, which worked closely with several U.S. government agencies. The seven-part *Guide* provided an overview of the trends as well as synopses concerning legal considerations, overseas representation and association, financial considerations, U.S. Government agencies, world market profiles (by far, the *Guide*'s longest part), and international development institutions. The 'Introduction' provided a concise summary of what was attracting American architects overseas in the late 1970s as well as what was challenging them when they did so.

Overseas work is enticing for many reasons. Profit potential and growth opportunity are not the least by any means; foreign contracts in certain areas can be extremely lucrative. Another attraction is the glamour and prestige that comes with international work. A firm that has one or two overseas successes to its credit is soon likely to develop worldwide

recognition and prominence. Finally, there is the creative stimulation and challenge associated with working for clients in countries where culture, tastes, lifestyles, and climates are different and projects are usually larger, more complex, and perhaps unlike any encountered in domestic work. Add to all of this, a sense of the exotic and a touch of adventure, and the appeal of overseas work is obvious. (*Ibid*.)

But there was another side to the story. Profits, prestige, and creative opportunity notwithstanding, foreign work had (and continues to have) its decided disadvantages for American AEC professionals. One of those is that the benefits do not come easily. As one veteran put it, 'It's no place for the faint-hearted'. The *Guide* then listed some reasons: risky and relatively high financial costs associated with setting up and maintaining a branch office ('costs of doing business overseas have practically doubled over the past decade'); intense competition (particularly from the U.K., Germany, Japan, Canada and Australia); and 'the frustration factor. Everything seems to be more complicated, arduous, costly and time-consuming' (*Ibid*., p. 2).[4] To modulate 'the frustration factor', the A.I.A. suggested learning more from several U.S. government agencies, depending upon what thrust an architectural firm was deciding to adopt in its foreign venture: A.I.D., Housing & Urban Development, and the Overseas Private Investment Corporation (*Ibid*., p. 107; Sumka, 1989).

In 1980, two years after the A.I.A.'s *Guide* was published, the federal government began to address international AEC professionals' problems even more proactively. Furthermore, after President Reagan's election in 1982 this public-private collaboration received an even stronger boost. The cooperation was forged largely between the U.S. Commerce Department and the International Engineering and Construction Industries Council [IECIC], an organization established in 1967 'to deal collectively with the mutual interests and problems of project designers and builders abroad' (Hodge, 1982, p. 24). Those designers and builders were represented by four national organizations: the American Consulting Engineers Council, the Associated General Contractors of America, the National Constructors Association and the American Institute of Architects. IECIC gave 'these groups a liaison with government agencies, financial institutions and private organizations concerned with foreign investment and development projects' (*Ibid.*). As shown in previous chapters, the Associated General Contractors and the American Institute of Architects had begun to focus on international aspects of their members' work as early as the 1910s and the 1920s, respectively. However, in cases the focus dissipated. By the early 1980s and with the help of the IECIC, American architects, builders and engineers engaged in international practice began to find some concrete assistance from both the Commerce Department and the International Trade Administration.

The IECIC's sixth annual conference (1982) reached two conclusions. First, the organization resolved to communicate more directly and clearly with the U.S. government with an eye towards jointly 'forming legislation', and other Administration policies to assist AEC professionals wanting to practice abroad (*Ibid.*, p. 25).[5] Secondly, the IECIC committed itself to 'creating a database' along with the government so that AEC professionals interested in practice abroad would have an easier time communicating with one another. Throughout the 1980s the lines of communication remained open between the federal government and the Council, which continued to play a proactive role in finding ways for the government to assist private firms to compete successfully with overseas construction-related companies (Phillips, 1984; Saunders, 1987). During the final quarter of the century, the U.S. Commercial Service Program, administered by the Commerce Department, continued to provide this kind of assistance, both domestically and through a selected number of U.S. embassies and consulates.

Shifting Geographies of Focus

Evidence from previous chapters as well as data presented above in this chapter point to consistent regional variation with respect to U.S. architectural exporting. Therefore, it should not be surprising to find a continuation of this pattern during the final quarter of the twentieth century. In 1978, when 'demand [was] especially heavy in the oil-rich countries of the Middle East' (A.I.A., 1978, p. 1), many firms obviously trained their attention on that region. However, as the flow of petrodollars slowed, and as decision-making became less centralized and contracting procedures became more complex (*Ibid.*), other nations beyond the Middle East began to vie for attention and sought up-to-date construction assistance, which meant they were looking to the U.S. as well as to firms from countries competing successfully with the U.S. companies (Strassmann and Wells, 1988, pp. 9–12 and 22–58; Warf, 1991, pp. 151–155).

A decade later, when computer technology was just beginning to have marked effects on architectural practice, one noted architectural theorist characterized the situation concerning U.S. architectural exporting in this way:

An important question that ought to be answered by America, therefore, is what happens to forms that are transferred from one place to another? An obvious effect of such a transfer is fragmentation and relativization. The New World, in fact, no longer consists of integrated systems based on defined values but has become a seemingly chaotic multitude of scattered bits. Thus it makes the possibility of choice manifest. (Norberg-Shulz, 1988, p. 8)

Three of those many choices were what forms to transfer, where to transfer them, and for which clients to work. Summaries compiled by *Engineering-News Record* help to provide a clearer sense of this shifting geography. In 1980, for example, when 81 U.S. firms ranked among the top 150 international designers (using the criterion of how much was billed), they earned 58 per cent of their fees billed in Latin America, 52 per cent in the Middle East, and 50 per cent in the Far East. Only in north and west Africa, where French firms continued to benefit from colonial ties, did they rank second. Although *Engineering-News Record* did not correlate U.S. firms to specific countries, its listing of the top ten countries where the top 150 design firms worked suggests that oil-rich countries still predominated in terms of contracted work. Those countries and the number of firms from the top 150 working there are shown in Table 6.2.

From 1980 to 1983 the Middle East continued to predominate world construction markets, despite the Iranian Revolution of 1979 and other regional unrest. However, by 1982 when the U.S. and Western European economies plunged into economic recession, that region's 'dominant position [was] being challenged by developing markets in Asia and Latin America' (*Engineering-News Record*, 1982, 22 April, p. 114). U.S. design, engineering and increasingly construction management firms continued to predominate in terms of gross dollars billed, with U.S. design firms pulling in 34 per cent of the total in 1980, 37 per cent in 1981, and 34 per cent in 1982 (*Engineering-News Record*, 1981, 30 July,

p. 34; 29 July, 1982, p. 22; 28 July, 1983, p. 39). By 1981 economic development throughout East Asia was turning it into 'construction's hottest foreign market, where the value of new contracts climbed 21% above 1980's level' (*Engineering-News Record*, 1982, 22 April, p. 115). Many of these contracts were for hydroelectric power plants, road construction and urban infrastructure (*Engineering-News Record*, 1982, 29 July, p. 25). But AEC professionals from the U.S. continued to design and build along a spectrum of projects. As the noted architectural journalist Ada Louise Huxtable wrote in 1981, when she reflected upon an 'American Architecture for Export' exhibition in New York,

what strikes one most are the extremes of this exotic overseas work. At one end is a slender, teardrop-shaped, gold glass office tower with intricate reverse curves, designed for a development in Singapore called the Golden Mile, that is the epitome of suave, luxurious, high-fashion, high-tech commercial construction. At the other pole are 750 units of concrete block housing costing $7.50 a square foot, erected in record time for the government of Cyprus to serve refugees from the 1974 Turkish invasion ... Stylistically sophisticated symbols of economic development are a response to the changing economies and politics of the Islamic countries and the Third World, including the inevitable desire for symbols of progress. (Huxtable, 1986, p. 296)

In Latin America, which displaced Europe as the fourth-major design market, U.S. design firms acquired 49 per cent of the continent's new billings, with most of the new construction occurring in Mexico, Venezuela and Argentina. However, by 1983 the worldwide economic recession was causing a shift in geographic focus. Although the Middle East continued to be a significant terrain of activity for U.S. firms (43 per cent of the total U.S. foreign contracts), Asia drew fewer American companies, who lost out largely to Japanese and Korean contracting and design firms (*Engineering-News Record*, 1984, 19 July, p. 55).

By the mid-1980s, Asian contracting firms were competing strongly and successfully with U.S.

Table 6.2. Markets attracting the top 150 design firms, 1979.

Country	Number of 'Top 150' Firms working in that Country
Saudi Arabia	110
Egypt	68
Nigeria	52
Brazil	47
Canada	43
Indonesia	42
UAE	42
Mexico	41
Iran	38
Kuwait	37

Source: Engineering-News Record, 1980, 31 July, p. 27.

companies in East Asia, although many Asian consultancies continued to face challenges 'breaking into the club' (Rimmer, 1988). Although East Asia continued to attract many U.S. builders and designers (who scooped up 29 per cent of all billing in 1985, for example), it was largely Latin America that lured U.S. companies (increasing their share there to 65 per cent of the total) and it was the Middle East where U.S. firms lost ground, dropping from 38 per cent in 1984 to 31 per cent in 1985 (*Engineering-News Record*, 1986, 7 August, p. 28). By 1989 'tower cranes looming over construction sites [were] becoming one of the [East Asia] region's most pervasive images', and increasingly Japanese and Korean contractors were moving into the breach, ahead of 'a handful of U.S. companies who set foot in the door' (Goldstein, 1989, p. 39). In reality, by 1990, where real estate investment and construction were concerned there were many doors open to the East Asian region, from coastal cities to distant hinterlands. Some analysts called the investment surge 'meteoric' (*World Property*, 1990, **4**, April, p. 48), while others marvelled at the

Figure 6.2. Mobil Oil in Lhasa, Tibet. During the late-1980s many East Asian cities experienced a building boom fuelled by remarkable foreign investment. As that boom percolated beyond urbanized coastlines to inland cities such as Lhasa, the effects of investment and architectural exportation were palpable, as shown here by the juxtaposition of a trademark of a transnational oil company near the Potala Palace. (Photograph courtesy of André Alexander)

'Asian floodtide' that was luring 'seemingly limitless offshore investment potential' (*Ibid.*, pp. 3, 55.).

In East Asia during the early 1990s, then, the appeal of the designs produced by U.S. architects (more than contractors and engineers) in the so-called 'tiger economies' of the region – notably Japan, Korea, Taipei and Hong Kong – shifted some of the U.S. geographic focus concerning construction once again to that region. In its 1992 survey, *Engineering-News Record* called Asia 'the epicentre of construction' (*Engineering-News Record*, 1992, 24 August, p. 34). Renowned U.S. architects and firms such as Michael Graves, Peter Eisenman, Steven Holl, Morphosis, the Cambridge Seven and RTKL began working more fruitfully in Japan and then throughout the region (Schmertz, 1990; Lui, 1999).

Simultaneously in Europe, U.S. architects began to command greater attention from clients on that continent, while the lead-up to the European Economic Community (1992) encouraged U.S. real estate investors and contractors to seek opportunities in Europe while the U.S. domestic economy was again heading for the doldrums (*New York Times*, 1990, 20 May, Commercial Property, p. 14; *Engineering-News Record*, 1990, 31 May, p. 25; Dolan, 1990).

In 1980, only a handful of pioneering U.S. architects were working abroad on projects in Europe and Japan. Between 1988 and 1989, however, American practitioners reported increasing their foreign billings by 247%, from $17 billion to $59 billion . . . Firms in the vanguard of this movement have been taking advantage of the affluent Thatcher years, securing commissions in London's new generation of development in the city's easternmost section. The skyline once dominated by St. Paul's Cathedral will soon be punctuated by towers designed by Skidmore, Owings & Merrill, Cesar Pelli & Associates, and Swanke Hayden Connell' (quotation from *Architecture*, 1990, **79**, September, p. 57; see also Knevitt, 1990; Dixon, 1995; Dietsch, 1990; Dean, 1990)

Many U.S. firms considered the U.K. to be the springboard to western Europe, just as they viewed a newly reunited Germany to be a potential launching pad to Eastern European markets (*Builder*, 1992, **15**, January, p. 275).

Data from surveys and professional trade journals help to define the geography of American architectural exporting in the quarter of century from *c.* 1978 to 1993. Analysts seeking to secure a grip on annual movements of AEC companies operating overseas often used monetary figures to allocate rankings, and then compare (as I have done, above) the relative performance of U.S. builders or designers *vis-à-vis* European and/or Asian competitors. However, what is missing from this macro-level picture of the international building profession – and what is perhaps most bluntly portrayed by an adventurous engineer such as Ralph Yeakel, depicted near the beginning of this chapter – is the more microscopic view of American architectural exporting during the explosive final quarter of the twentieth century. To appreciate that finer grain of detail, it is best to leave most of the statistics behind and instead to shift the focus again onto a more human-scale geography.

Low-Tech to High-Tech: Distinguishing U.S. Architects Abroad

In 1988 Erich Theophile, a 34-year old American architect, began working in Nepal as a programme director of the Kathmandu Valley Preservation Trust, an organization based in Cambridge, Massachusetts that was working with the Nepalese government to preserve the country's architectural heritage. 'Here you reinvent the wheel', Theophile observed, reflecting upon 5 years of experience in Nepal. In addition to helping to restore temples, he also rehabilitated the house where he lived and helped design a spiritual retreat (*New York Times*, 1993, 21 January, p. C-10). Other American architects and builders who did not quite fit within a corporate architectural structure were similarly active in

many countries worldwide in the final quarter of the twentieth century. However, their numbers are not as easy to cite because their activities have not been comprehensively documented. Whether as Peace Corps volunteers, missionary architects, relief agency builders, emergency contractors arriving after natural calamities, student interns measuring and drawing historic buildings, or other kinds of low-tech volunteers involved in construction, American architectural exporting was enriched by the more low-tech approach of architects such as Eric Theophile.

Although they didn't know one another, Theophile had a kindred spirit in the American architect Tom McCracken who, from 1984 to 1986 in China, designed the Hopkins-Nanjing University Center for American and Chinese Studies, which Nanjing authorities had approved 2 years earlier. McCracken's experience in China was as rewarding as Theophile's in Nepal, although building an up-to-date American educational centre from scratch was qualitatively different than restoring temples. However, McCracken also found himself frustrated, not because of what he could not do in China that he could in Baltimore, but because 'the education, training and experience I rely on daily here [in Maryland] do not equip me to do basically the same type of job overseas. I'm dealing in somebody else's world and the rules change' (*Johns Hopkins Gazette*, 21 January, 1986, p. 3).

While McCracken and Theophile were having their adventures in Asia, other kinds of rules were beginning to change for all U.S. architects working overseas. Some of these rules were more technological than political, and they have had enormous economic and cultural implications. One significant change occurred in 1978, when the Federal Communications Commission for the first time permitted commercial fax machines (marketed first by the Xerox Corporation in 1966) to connect directly to telephone lines. This, in turn, permitted those who could afford such machines (still expensive commodities in the late-1970s) to send and receive fax communications from foreign countries. Digital fax machines helped reduce the price of this technology dramatically, so that by the late-1980s many businesses (AEC firms among them) were using the fax regularly to transmit and receive information (Sih, 1993).

One example that demonstrates how the fax machine helped make American architectural exporting more efficient concerned I.M. Pei's Pyramide at the Louvre. When Yann Weymouth, one of Pei's Paris-based colleagues, began experiencing problems supporting the structure's key glass panels, he and Tim Eliassen, an engineer in Massachusetts, 'began faxing each other sketches of the project. Fax allowed a cross-Atlantic discussion of design concepts and cut down the time needed to work out problems by months' (*Newsweek*, 1988, Pacific edition, 4 July p. 31).

Innovations in fax technology were followed in the early 1990s by video conferencing and internet communications which have been monumentally significant in helping to unknot the logistical tangles of practice abroad (*Newsweek*, 1988, 4 July, p. 31; *New York Times*, 1991, 21 February, p. D-1; Tombesi, 2001). That significance will be explored below in the context of a recent project involving a collaboration stretching from East Asia to North America to Europe.

Hong Kong's Cheung Kong Center, 1995–1999

In the early 1990s Li Ka-shing, one of Hong Kong's most powerful industrial entrepreneurs, began planning the erection of a new 62-storey corporate headquarters for one of his flagship companies, Hutchison Whampoa Property Group (Chan, 1996).[6] In 1995 he chose one of central Hong Kong's prime locations, at the corner of Garden Road and Queen's

Figure 6.3. Cheung Kong Centre, located between the Bank of China (L) and the Hong Kong-Shanghai Bank (R) in Central, Hong Kong. This flagship skyscraper of Cheung Kong, the company owned by Li Ka-shing, one of Hong Kong's richest billionaires, was designed by Leo A. Daly Company, an American firm, with the assistance of many other firms operating in a globalizing orchestra of construction. (Photograph by the author.)

Road Central, a 2-acre site sandwiched between two of Hong Kong's most illustrious architectural icons: Sir Norman Foster's Hong Kong-Shanghai Bank (1985) and I.M. Pei's Bank of China (1989).

The Hilton Hotel and Beaconsfield House stood on the site, but Li Ka-shing bought and demolished both properties to build the Cheung Kong Center. Adjoining the site are two of Hong Kong's seventy-five declared monuments: to the west, the former French Missions Building (1917), now Hong Kong's Court of Final Appeal; and further south, St. John's Cathedral (1849). In erecting any new construction at the Cheung Kong site, the client and his architect had to ensure the structural integrity of these two historic structures (Chan, 1995).

In selecting the architect for his office tower, Li turned to Leo Daly, an American whom he had known since the mid-1970s when the two worked on a project together in North Point, Hong Kong.[7] Leo Daly said he secured the Cheung Kong commission 'the old fashioned way. Li Ka-shing asked me to come over and we had lunch' (*Hinge*, 1999, **59**, p. 52). The Leo A Daly firm (hereafter LAD), established in

1915 and based in Nebraska, is the third largest architecture & engineering practice in the U.S. After World War II it was one of the earliest U.S. architectural firms to expand its operations abroad. In 2000 LAD had ten offices in the U.S. as well as branches in Dubai, Madrid and Berlin. The firm opened its Hong Kong office in 1969 and during much of the 1970s employed as many as eighty architects at a time to handle commissions either in Hong Kong or within East Asia. However, by 1994 the office had been scaled down dramatically, only hosting five architects when Leo Daly himself won the Cheung Kong commission.

Li Ka-shing wanted a premier office tower for one of Hong Kong's most prestigious sites.

The challenge was to create a structure that stands in harmony with its distinguished neighbors and yet states its own commanding presence. The urban impact of the tower's footprint was a major consideration, as well as the appearance of the tower's simple classic form in such a complex context. (*Ibid.*)[8]

That form, an 'unblemished rectangular pillar' (Hammond, 1999, p. 41), derives from a square plan and contrasts starkly with many architectural neighbours. The simple geometric form derives in part from the straightforward geomantic prediction made to Li Ka-shing by his *fengshui* master, who told him the square, oriented at an angle on the site, would bring him good luck. Li also chose Pelli as the main consulting architect to LAD because of how impressed he was with both the Canary Wharf and Petronas Towers projects that were already bringing Pelli's office such notoriety.

Besides *fengshui*, LAD faced several other initial challenges with this premier commission. As a result, the firm not only had to expand its design profile internally, but also needed to assemble a construction-related orchestra of diverse and far-flung talents, as listed below.

In 1995, to oversee design on this high-profile project, LAD hired approximately a dozen designers working for such well-known firms as SOM and KPF. Stimulated by the idea of working with Cesar Pelli and energized by the idea of designing a corporate icon for Li Ka-shing, these designers quickly became part of an in-house 'design studio' at LAD. The fact that LAD's staff in Hong Kong had been scaled down to a handful in 1994 made it possible for the firm to expand so fast, and to move so efficiently in a concerted direction on the Cheung Kong project. A cutting-edge kind of 'emerging design practice' became a hallmark of the new LAD in Hong Kong.

Table 6.3. Design and construction professionals associated with Hong Kong's Cheung Kong Center.

Project Team	Company	Location
Consulting Design Architect	Cesar Pelli	New York
Structural Engineer	Ove Arup & Partners (HK) Ltd	U.K./H.K.
E & M Consultants	Flack & Kurtz Asia, Ltd	U.S.A.
	Parsons Brinckerhoff (Asia)	H.K./U.S.A.
Landscape Architect	Belt Collins Hong Kong Ltd	H.K.
Curtain Wall Consultant	Israel Berger Associates	New York
Main Contractor	Paul Y. – Downer Joint Venture	H.K.
Curtain Wall Contractor	Permasteelisa Hong Kong	H.K./Singapore
Lighting	HM Brandston & Partners	New York

Source: Asian Architect and Contractor, 1999, **28**(10), p. 17.

Figure 6.4. Cheung Kong Centre's curtain wall, showing its 'linen steel' cladding and fibre-optic lighting. (Photograph by the author)

Figure 6.5. Cheung Kong Centre's main lift lobby. (Photograph by the author)

These new LAD designers confronted three principal design issues: how to maximize the rentable floor space; how to retain, with distinction, the appearance of a classical geometric form in a complex urban context; and how to develop the character and connectivity of public spaces at the tower's base (*Building Journal*, 1989).

Subsumed within these broad issues were also stimulating technical challenges: (1) how to design a distinctive and progressive curtain wall (using 'linen steel' and silver-reflective glass, which resulted in an eye-catching latticework); (2) how to illuminate distinctively the exterior wall surfaces day and night (employing fibre optics, which resulted in dazzling effects); (3) how to integrate a series of elevators

(which resulted in sleek banks of the fastest lifts in Hong Kong at 9 metres/second); and (4) how to provide advanced telecommunications that would anticipate corporate needs for at least 20 years (making the Cheung Kong Center one of the most high-tech office towers in Hong Kong).

Having assembled energetic design and technical teams in Hong Kong, LAD began to confront the question of how to achieve design and construction harmony. The client was supremely engaged with the project from the outset – helpful because of his frequent input but also daunting because of his constant demands for a high degree of efficiency in meeting rigid deadlines. Under this pressure, conflicts and time-wasting needed to be minimized.

Two linked trends helped bring this about: the growing dependence upon the internet and solid understanding of the technical matters related to the complex commission

Internet technology helped foster some of the requisite harmony. Rapid communication was a logistical joy, whether between LAD and Pelli regarding the curtain wall, LAD and Brandston concerning the lighting, or LAD/HK and LAD/DC for design and technical backup. The internet was especially critical in the latter scenario because although LAD was expanding its Hong Kong branch, it could also marshall talent from nearly 800 architects under the firm's payroll in the U.S. From spring 1996 to fall 1997, as much as 75 per cent of the project's work was handled by LAD's office in Washington, DC whereas beginning in Winter 1997–98 the situation was reversed. LAD in Hong Kong could work all day and then send questions and drawings via the internet to workstations in Washington that were just being turned on. LAD in Washington could then contribute substantially while the architects in Hong Kong were asleep, thus virtually doubling the amount of work produced in any given day. Synergy was also achieved between LAD and Pelli's office, which had developed a particular 'linen steel' for the curtain wall at both Canary Wharf and the Petronas Towers (Tam, 1999). Similarly with Ove Arup, harmony was enhanced by the fact that these large companies each had both local office branches and larger corporate facilities on other continents. However, the internet also played a key role in helping to coordinate between companies, such as when Permasteelisa (Singapore main office) needed to consult Brandston in New York and other lighting consultants in Australia about building a mock-up of the curtain wall in Singapore, to monitor the effects of the innovative fibre optics being employed at Cheung Kong.

A depth of technical know-how, therefore, also facilitated the desired harmony. Although this was certainly true of many of the consultants' offices, technical savvy was especially important regarding the American players in the project's orchestra. To be 'high-tech' the building had to cater to the needs of future high-technology, which meant it had to provide space for future, as well as present cables. To meet this need, LAD was able to call upon its past experience with Microsoft in the design of high-tech parks in locations such as Reston, Virginia. LAD/DC could therefore efficiently answer many of the IT-related questions posed by the designers in Hong Kong. Similarly, regarding electrical and mechanical questions, experts from Flack & Kurtz, Israel Berger and Van Deusan (elevator consultant) in the U.S. could call upon a wealth of experience with high-rise construction to answer quickly most of the questions raised by the smaller contingent of designers in Hong Kong.

At the very least, there were four major lessons to be learned from the Cheung Kong Center's design and construction scenario. First, because the project was high-profile, both local and long-distance partners were perhaps more willing to go the extra mile than they would have been if the project had been, for example, a more conventional high-rise structure in a western Chinese city. If either local or long-distance partners can attach themselves to a highly visible and publicized project, then in some respects they might be more tolerant of annoyances. Second, time-distance became more critical than space-distance (Mitchell, 1999). The internet helped bridge both kinds of distances, but the client's repeated demands to finish the project rapidly, to optimize rental incomes, still posed formidable challenges regarding time. Third, foreign-based firms (especially in the U.S.) were most helpful in facilitating research and development, whereas local firms were most adept at production. In addition to U.S. firms, long-distance partners in Singapore, Australia and the U.K. also researched and developed aspects of the project in significant ways. The Cheung

Kong Center, then, is an example of how, increasingly at the end of the twentieth century, globalization of design was becoming as globalized as commodity markets. Tombesi (2001), in analysing what he calls the 'new international division of labour in architecture', notes that the percentage of U.S. firms transferring drawings electronically rose from 35 per cent in 1996 to 83 per cent in 1999 (Dalal, 2000). Finally, one can witness in the Cheung Kong Center project that there is an increasing blurring of the distinction between 'local' and 'foreign' firms. We might well be witnessing the localizing of global architectural firms, where those previously global firms will need to become localized in order to survive.' Then they'll either 'sink or swim'.[9]

The Cheung Kong case implies that there is no single, foolproof recipe for design collaboration in Asia. Instead, those architects engaged in projects with multiple partners find themselves practicing in a smaller world, but also coping with a larger universe of problems (Rowe, 1996, pp. 220–230, and Boyer and Mitang, 1996, pp. 11–12). These include some of the age-old architectural difficulties associated with budget restrictions, client demands, building materials or contracting headaches (Cuff, 1991, p. 75). For many decades, design and construction collaborators have been facing these(and other) kinds of challenges as they confront the unpredictable realities of building in Asia (Scott-Stevens, 1987; Lee and Walters, 1989).

One such challenge concerns communication. In the recent past fast-developing internet technologies have made some aspects of communication easier, quicker and less expensive. Ironically, however, communicating with partners can also still be daunting because ease of communication also implies a proliferation of that communication (Baden-Powell, 1993, pp. 81–82). This is sometimes due to larger numbers of partners engaged in more globalizing construction dynamics, and at other times because of cultural differences, time-zone vagaries and linguistic

barriers. If it is true that 'the profession does very little to prepare would-be architects for the crowds of participants who will want a say in their projects' (Cuff, 1991, p. 74), then it is also the case that often, because of the scale and logistical complications related to international design collaboration, there are 'crowds of participants' that many architects either need or want to bring into their projects. In Asia where crowds are perhaps more the norm than the exception, design collaboration often leads to a full orchestra of players in the dramatic symphony of construction.

American architects practicing in Asia, therefore – whether they are 'low-tech' (such as Theophile and McCracken, working in Nepal and China respectively in the 1980s) or more 'high-tech' (such as the LAD Company in the late-1990s) – need to be sensitive conductors of a symphony whose music changes with each new project. Sometimes the result is harmony, while at other times discord prevails. Designing, building and collaborating in Asia, where architects often 'need to be guided by those who understand nuances and interpretation', the difficulties can be great but they are often not only profitable, but also 'worth it because [the effort is] so invigorating' (Pedersen, 1999).

Conclusion

During the 1990s increasing numbers of American architects, lured by both profit and invigoration, decided to take the uncertain plunge into practicing abroad (*Engineering-News Record*, 2000, 4 December, pp. 30–58). So many have done so, in fact, that new companies in the U.S. have emerged to help firms assess the risks of venturing overseas before they take that plunge (*Engineering-News Record*, 2000, 19 June, p. 25). However, those firms that have already invested the energies, personnel, dollars and patience in establishing transnational practices, have also learned to be cautious and optimistic, visionary and down-to-earth. In the twenty-first century, however, their presence abroad, and the spaces or forms they have helped erect in their quest for profit and invigoration, have also led increasingly vocal, anti-globalization critics to charge that American architects are colluding with capitalist clients in bringing American paradigms to non-American contexts.

In the early twenty-first century as in the early twentieth, American forms in non-American spaces often provoke reactions, some of which might be desired by clients wanting to be identified with the United States, others of which are either unintentionally offensive or necessarily unpredictable. As the architect Jaquelin Robertson said after working in Iran in the 1970s, 'the export model we have been sending out is not working very well, and most of the world has a bad case of cultural indigestion' (quoted in Huxtable, 1986, p. 297). One might plausibly argue that in the last three decades that indigestion has got even worse.

This book has shown that the transplantation of American architecture has as much to do with importing as it does exporting. 'Whether something is an export or an import is an abstraction, depending on what part of the process you are looking at. What matters is the value it contributes to the whole, not where it came from' (*International Herald Tribune*, 1996, 5 October, quoting the *Far Eastern Economic Review*). In making historical sense of the cultural indigestion to which the architect Robertson referred, I have been concerned with both the processes and products of American architectural exportation, as well as with the values – cultural as well as economic or political – related to the whole.

Figure 6.6. Shanghai's Sassoon Park villas, advertised as being akin to Manhattan residences near Central Park.

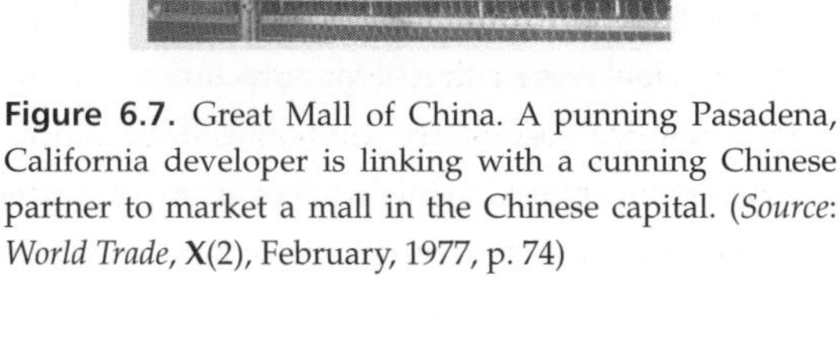

Figure 6.7. Great Mall of China. A punning Pasadena, California developer is linking with a cunning Chinese partner to market a mall in the Chinese capital. (*Source: World Trade*, **X**(2), February, 1977, p. 74)

Figure 6.8. Chinese entrepreneur Li Qingfu in front of his company headquarters, modelled after the U.S. Capitol. (Photograph by Ritzu Shinozaki)

Figure 6.9. Kentucky Fried Chicken in Shanghai and California Beef Noodle King. The globalization of American fast-food is one of the most obvious examples of architectural exportation in the early twenty-first century. Less obvious, but also pervasive is the appropriation of the prototypical brand by local entrepreneurs who seek to capitalize on name- and form-recognition to create a profitable hybrid. (Photograph above by the author; photograph below by Wang Gang Feng)

As was shown in Chapter 1, from the 1870s to the early twentieth century the products seem to have loomed larger than the processes because of the hubris associated with U.S. building exporters' abilities to compete with European rivals in capturing niches within foreign markets. The Philadelphia Exhibition of 1876 was a crucial catalyst in galvanizing attention by domestic and foreign merchants in the burgeoning power of American technology. U.S. military victories in 1898 were other defining actions that provided an imperial basis for architectural exportation. American building material exporters and engineers, more quickly than architects, began to understand the

potentials of practicing abroad, engaging in what Zunz (1998) has called the 'brokering and using' the knowledge they were gaining. One of the main keys unlocking the door of American architectural exportation was made of steel. In those disparate places where American steel was fashioned into structures – from the Pencoyd Company's Atbara Bridge in the Sudan to high-rise towers related to the Milliken Brothers in Havana, Buenos Aires or Capetown – that product unleashed a chain reaction of social and architectural processes, only some of which have been explained above. The precise dynamics of those historical processes – which technologies persist in different cultural contexts, the degree to which local AEC workers accept, reject or modify American architectural imports, the social implications associated with new architectural places and spaces -- are often more difficult to grasp because the evidence that illuminates them is relatively scant. Although some scholars have examined recent cases related to these processes (Watson, 1997), further research needs to be conducted to shed light on a broader palette of examples.

Concrete was a complementary building material to the steel frame and, as the twentieth century began, those complements yielded yet another significant American technology for export: reinforced concrete. I suggested in Chapter 2 that by the end of World War I steel and concrete had helped create a foundation for a system of contracting abroad. However, I also explained that the materials did not magically configure such a foundation without the deft (and some might argue 'devious') intervention of either human ingenuity or guile. Truscon and Ideal were two of the companies that engaged in significant operations. The challenge of the Panama Canal, the passing of the Federal Reserve Act, the establishment of the National Association of Manufacturers and the U.S. Chamber of Commerce were some of the critical developments related to the U.S. government in the first two decades of the twentieth century.

World War I marked a watershed in American architectural exporting, as it did in so many aspects of architectural change, from the establishment of the Bauhaus in 1919 to the implications of the Russian Revolution in 1917. In Chapter 3, I suggested that some U.S. exporters involved in construction-related ventures had to face challenging decisions about whether to take shorter or longer 'roads' in order to succeed in those ventures. Some chose short-term gain over potential long-term pain, while others invested more time (and, of course, money) in understanding the fuller social, political and economic dimensions of the construction dramas in which they had become enmeshed. One reflection of this longer-term vision was the National Federation of Construction Industries' establishment of a Foreign Trade Committee; another was American contractors' participation in the International Federation of Building and Public Works. And indeed, in the early 1920s many U.S. construction companies began proactively to seek a wider range of commissions overseas. They were able to do so, in part, because of the increasing presence of U.S. bank branches which, thanks to changes in U.S. laws permitting them to market their services abroad, were also among the most significant U.S. clients who launched commissions that employed U.S. architects and builders. Architects were generally led into foreign work either by their clients or by other professionals involved in construction: contractors, building material suppliers or engineers. Shortly after World War I, in an action that demonstrated how some U.S. architects were beginning to see the potential of work abroad, the A.I.A. established a Foreign Building Cooperation Standing Committee. Although the scope of that Committee's activities was mostly concerned exclusively with Latin America, one of the more curious, broader-based conclusions from that Committee concerned its urging that new 'mental angles of approach' be adopted where international practice was concerned.

Time was needed to understand different ethical codes, languages and building needs. The Committee implied that transferring U.S. practices to non-U.S. contexts was far from simple, because geographical distances usually implied cultural differences. That observation held true as much at the end of the twentieth century as it did nearer the beginning.

Between the two World Wars the scale of American architectural exporting widened from individual, sporadic building projects to ones which encompassed the city as a whole. Although some U.S. planners had engaged in city-wide ventures in the first years of the twentieth century (e.g., Daniel Burnham in the Philippines), it was not until the 1920s that U.S. planners, engineers, contractors, real estate developers and architects began to win a more amplified range of commissions for either the modernizing or establishment of cities, from South America to East Asia. As I showed in Chapter 4, as U.S. practitioners propagated their own paradigm of progress in the 1920s and 1930s, they brought materials, methods and urban infrastructure that complemented U.S.-derived spaces of production and places of consumption. Subsequently, because of the damage wrought by World War II, U.S. architectural exporters benefited from economic, political and cultural conditions that facilitated their activities overseas.

In Chapter 5 I mapped many of those activities. To frame them more coherently, I suggested that although some were due to 'private hands', others were found within 'public gloves' of the U.S. government, which became increasingly active after World War II in promoting U.S. construction through its foreign aid programmes. Ward (1998) has suggested that the diffusion of planning during the twentieth century be considered within a matrix of possibilities, from 'imposition' and 'borrowing' to 'synthetic innovation'. My research about a range of American AEC professionals during the period 1945 to 1975 corroborates what Ward has suggested about how to conceptualize a typology of city planning diffusion: that although the range of their options was broad, the scope of their involvement was variable. Despite that variation, however, it is possible to see shifting foci of attention from U.S. architectural exporters, as Europe, South America and the Middle East became increasingly significant for those exporters during this period. However, they also experienced increasing construction-related competition. And as they exported what I termed 'the architectural tools of war and peace', they found that hybrid situations (with an increasingly complicated cast of partners and challenges) were more commonplace than direct, word-for-word 'translations' of U.S. forms and spaces.

American architectural exporting during the final quarter-century of the twentieth century demonstrated both a fusion of salient trends and

a profusion of diverse examples. U.S. government initiatives have continued to provide incentives for American AEC professionals to become involved in overseas work, from U.S. Department of Commerce advisors providing assistance about business practices abroad, to foreign aid projects which stipulate that contracts be awarded to U.S. firms. However, many AEC professionals from the U.S. either proactively find foreign commissions on their own, or they are eagerly sought after by clients from abroad, because of 'brand-name recognition' as well as for other reasons explained at the beginning of this book. However, as was suggested by the case of the Cheung Kong Center, because of increasing globalization of hybrid AEC firms, 'American' is increasingly an elusive adjective to pinpoint.

I began this book by asserting that U.S. design and construction abroad was a confused mosaic

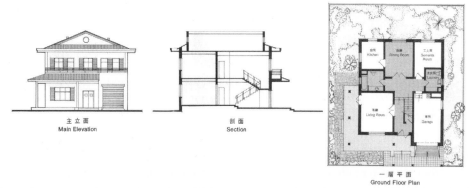

Figure 6.10. Developers using a grab-bag of architectural elements to evoke American-ness in Beijing. (*Source:* Promotional brochure for Rose Garden Villas, 1993)

that called out to be examined in greater detail and explained with fuller clarity. The pieces of that mosaic have resided in places both familiar and obscure. Underlying much of what I have presented has been the suggestion that we pay far greater attention than we have heretofore to lesser-known architectural works worldwide, many of which hold keys – in their forms, structures and contexts – to greater realities than meet the eye. I also suggested that in the course of my analysis I had reached three major conclusions: (1) that as the transplanting of American architecture occurred, it did so in complex ways; (2) that the exporting of American architecture occurred earlier than many have assumed, and (3) that the evidence suggested an advantage for both the importer and exporter of American architecture to be more fully cognizant of the culture from which the architecture came as well as more sensitive to the culture in which the architecture would be existing.

In bringing closure to this work, I now share a fourth conclusion: that more research is required before that mosaic can be understood even more deeply. The social dynamics of architectural acceptance or rejection need to be examined more fully, and the hybrid cases in between those two poles need to be found and scrutinized. Issues related to architectural diffusion, and the relationships between building, economics, politics and culture need to be placed under a microscope with greater magnification. This book has taken some initial steps in these directions, but any work such as this that purports to examine 'American architecture' over the course of 130 years, and that ranges across vast geographies, is necessarily just opening a Pandora's box of intriguing cases and arguments about a stimulating topic. Now that the box has been opened, the book is about to be closed.

NOTES

1. The subtitle is adapted from a statement by Ada Louise Huxtable (1986, p. 297), in which she was referring to a housing project by the Eggers Group in Dammam, Saudi Arabia: 'That's exporting an image and a technology with a vengeance. The disembodied and discredited clichés keep right on rolling along'.

2. This information about HOK was provided by Cameron Hestler, Business Development Manager for HOK's Hong Kong office; and by King Graf, Vice Chairman of HOK who, by 1990, had worked for the firm since 1966, often as 'project management principal' (Graf, 1990). I thank both gentlemen for sharing their insights with me.

3. The engineering firms were Dames & Moore, Syska & Hennessy and Caudill Rowlett Scott (CRS).

4. The *Guide* was a prelude to several other publications, most based upon conferences sponsored by the A.I.A. during the 1980s and 1990s. For a summary of one of those conferences, see 'Global Architecture Examined in New York', *Architecture*, 1991, **80**(2), pp. 18–20. Among the most important of these publications was an entire issue of *Architecture* (the journal of the A.I.A.) devoted to 'American Architects Abroad', (1990, **79**(9)), and five publications by the A.I.A.'s International Committee: *International Design and Practice, Europe* (1991); *International Trends in World Markets* (1992); *International Design and Practice, the Pacific Rim; Global Architecture: New Markets, New Opportunities;* and *International Committee Member Survey*.

5. Specifically, the IECIC urged executive and legislative action on the following: provide more competitive methods of financing overseas projects by expanding the lending authority of the Export-Import Bank; support more effective export promotion policies and reduce international protectionist policies; simplify anti boycott laws; pass export trading company legislation; increase the funding authorization for the Commerce Department's trade and development programme; and continue to improve that Department's Foreign Commercial Service.

6. Cheung Kong (Holdings) is another of Li Ka-shing's major companies and it is that company which gives the Center its name.

7. I gratefully acknowledge the assistance of Mr. Ray Zee, former Design Director of Leo A. Daly Pacific Limited, who kindly answered my questions about this case study. For further information in the public domain, see www.cheungkongcenter.com

8. For other published commentaries about the Cheung Kong Center, see *Building Journal*, 1998; Hammond, 1999; Mooney, 1999; Tam, 1999; and Thomas, 1999.

9. This quotation is from Ray Zee; see note 7 above. However, for a broader discussion of similar issues, also see Dandekar, 1998 and Tombesi, 2001.

Bibliography

Adas, Michael (1989) *Machines as the Measure of Men: Science, Technology, and Ideologies of Western Dominance.* Ithaca and London: Cornell University Press.

AIA (American Institute of Architects) *Annuaries* (1914–1931). Washington, D.C.: AIA Archives.

AIA Foreign Relations Committee Papers (1925–1928) Washington, D.C.: AIA Archives.

AIA Proceedings of the Annual Conventions (1921–1935) Washington, D.C.: AIA Archives.

AIA Office Files (1924–1928) Washington, D.C.: AIA Archives.

Albrecht, Donald (ed.) (1995) *World War II and the American Dream: How Wartime Building Changed a Nation.* Washington, D.C. and Cambridge, Mass.: National Building Museum and MIT Press.

Alsayyad, Nezar (ed.) (1992) *Forms of Dominance: on the Architecture and Urbanism of the Colonial Enterprise.* Avebury: Aldershot.

Alsayyad, Nezar (ed.) (2001) *Consuming Tradition, Manu-facturing Heritage: Global Norms and Urban Forms in the Age of Tourism.* London and New York: Routledge.

American Institute of Architects (1978) *Architect's Guide to International Practice.* Washington, D.C.: AIA.

Amin, Samir, Arrighi, Giovanni, Gunder, Andre, Wallerstein, Frank and Wallerstein, Immanuel (1990) *Transforming the Revolution: Social Movements and the World-System.* New York: Monthly Review.

Anders, Ray Leslie, Jr. (1954) A History of the Construction of the Ledo Road by the United States Corps of Engineers. Unpublished PhD dissertation, University of Missouri, Columbia.

Angel, Juvenal (comp.) (1955–56) *Directory of American Firms Operating in Foreign Countries*, 1st ed. New York: World Trade Academy Press, Inc.

Angel, Juvenal (comp.) (1959–60) *Directory of American Firms Operating in Foreign Countries*, 3rd ed. New York: World Academy Press.

Angel, Juvenal (comp.) (1966) *Directory of American Firms Operating in Foreign Countries*, 6th ed. New York: World Academy Press.

Angel, Juvenal (comp.) (1979) *Dictionary of American Firms Operating in Foreign Countries*, 9th ed. New York: Uniworld Business Publications.

Appadurai, Arjun (1996) *Modernity at Large: Cultural Dimensions of Globalization*. Minneapolis: University of Minnesota Press.

Appy, Christian G. (ed.) (2000) *Cold War Constructions: The Political Culture of United States Imperialism, 1945–1966*. Amherst: University of Massachusetts Press.

Arrarte, José Maria Bens (1956) El Malecón de la Habana. Su reconstrucción actual. Datos históricos. El primer proyecto hecho en 1901. *Arquitectura*, 262, pp. 34–38.

Atherton, John (1985) Culture and context. *Revue française d'études américaines*, **10**, pp. 213–24.

Atterbury, Paul (2001) Steam and speed: industry, transport and communications, in Mackenzie, J.M. (ed.) *The Victorian Vision: Inventing New Britain*. London: V & A Publications, pp. 147–172.

Austin, Allan S. (1931) Communism builds its city of utopia. *New York Times Magazine*, 9 August, pp. 10–11.

Austin Book of Buildings, 7th ed, (1922) Cleveland: Austin Company.

Bacevich, Andrew J. (2002) *American Empire: the Realities and Consequences of U.S. Diplomacy*. Cambridge, Mass.: Harvard University Press.

Baden-Powell, Francis (1993) *Building Overseas: Butterworth Architecture Management Guide*. Oxford and Boston: Butterworth Architecture.

Baker, Paul R. (1980) *Richard Morris Hunt*. Cambridge, Mass.: MIT Press.

Balbiani, Andrew S. and Brown, Robert M. (eds.) (1983) *Partnership to a Planet: 40 Years of TAMS*. New York: Tippetts-Abbett-McCarthy-Stratton.

Banham, Reyner (1989) *A Concrete Atlantis: U.S. Industrial Building and European Modern Architecture, 1900–1925*. Cambridge, Mass: MIT Press.

Bergère, Marie-Claire (1986) *L'age d'or de la bourgeoisie chinoise*. Paris: Flammarion.

Bennett, John (1991) *International Construction Project Management: General Theory and Practice*. London: Butterworth-Heinemann.

Bernstein, Barton J. (ed.) (1970) *Politics and Policies of the Truman Administration*. Chicago: Quadrangle.

Bickers, Robert, A. (1999) *Britain in China: Com-munity, Culture and Colonialism, 1900–1949*. Manchester: Manchester University Press.

Blair, John G. (2000) First Steps toward globalization: nineteenth-century exports of American entertainment forms, in Wagnleitner, Reinhold and May, Elaine Tyler (eds.) *Here, There and Everywhere: The Foreign Politics of American Popular Culture*. Hanover and London: University Press of New England, pp. 17–33.

Bleifuss, D.J. (1951) Ceylonese learn American methods quickly on Gal Oya Dam. *Civil Engineering*, **21** (September), pp. 45–48.

Boase, Arthur J. (1944) South American building is challenging. *Engineering-News Record*, **133**, 19 October, pp. 121–128.

Boase, Arthur J. (1945) Construction practices in South America. *Engineering-News Record*, **135**, 6 September, pp. 96–102.

Bobrick, Benson (1985) *Parsons Brinckerhoff: the First 100 Years*. New York: Van Nostrand Reinhold.

Booker, John (1990) *Temples of Mammon: The Architecture of Banking*. Edinburgh: Edinburgh University Press.

Bostwick, A. (1926) Municipal Progress in China. *American City*, 35, p. 36.

Bowen, Ralph H. (1985) American cultural imperialism reconsidered. *Revue française d'études américaines*, **10**, pp. 179–193.

Boyer, E. and Mitgang, L. (1996) *Building Community: A New Future for Architecture Education and Practice*. Princeton: Carnegie Foundation for the Advancement of Teaching.

Bregenzer, C.E. (1920) *Iron Age Catalogue of American Exports*, Vol. 1. New York: Iron Age Publishing Company.

Brock, W.H. (1981) The Japanese connexion: Engineering in Tokyo, London, and Glasgow at the end of the nineteenth century. *The British Journal for the History of Science*, **14**, pp. 227–244;

Broehl, Wayne G., Jr. (1968) *The International Basic Economy Corporation*. Washington, D.C.: National Planning Association.

Brumfield, William C. (1990) Russian perceptions of American architecture, 1870–1917, in Brumfield,

William C. (ed.) *Reshaping Russian Architecture: Western Technology, Utopian Dreams*. Cambridge and New York: Cambridge University Press and Woodrow Wilson International Center for Scholars.

Building Journal (1998) Skyline shift: Cheung Kong Centre. **25**(2), pp. 13–15.

Bunge, Robert P. (1958) Exporting: Here's how to do it successfully. *American Business*, **28** (February), pp. 10–14.

Calhoun, D. (1973) *The Intelligence of the People*. Princeton: Princeton University Press.

Cantor, Norman F. (1997) *The American Century: Varieties of Culture in Modern Times*. New York: HarperCollins.

Cardoso, Fernando H. and Faletto, Enzo (1979) *Dependency and Development in Latin America*. Berkeley: University of California Press.

Castells, Manuel (1996) *The Rise of the Network Society (The Information Age: Economy, Society and Culture*, vol. I). Oxford: Blackwell.

Castells, Manuel (1997) *The Power of Identity (The Information Age: Economy, Society and Culture*, vol. II). Oxford: Blackwell.

Castells, Manuel (1998) *The End of Millennium (The Information Age: Economy, Society and Culture*, vol. III). Oxford: Blackwell.

Castillo, Greg (1992) Cities of the Stalinist empire, in Alsayyad, Nezar (ed.) *Forms of Dominance: on the Architecture and Urbanism of the Colonial Enterprise*. Avebury: Aldershot, pp. 261–288.

Çelik, Zeynep (1997) *Urban Forms and Colonial Confrontations: Algiers Under French Rule*. Berkeley, CA: University of California Press.

Chan, A. (1996) *Li Ka-shing: Hong Kong's Elusive Billionaire*. Toronto: Macmillan.

Chan, K. (1995) Cheung Kong gets go-ahead. *Hong Kong Standard*, 28 April, p. F-2.

Chandler, Alfred (1990) *Scale and Scope: The Dynamics of Industrial Capitalism*. Cambridge, Mass.: Harvard University Press.

Chapman, William (1995) Irreconcilable differences: urban residences in the Danish West Indies, 1700–1900. *Winterthur Portfolio*, **30**, pp. 129–172.

Clarke, Thomas Curtis (1901) European and American bridge-building practice. *Engineering Magazine*, **24**, April, pp. 43–58.

Cleveland, Harlan, Mangone, Gerard J. and Adams, John Clarke (1960) *The Overseas Americans*. New York: McGraw-Hill.

Cleveland, Harold van B. and Huertas, Thomas F. (1985) *Citibank, 1812–1970*. Cambridge, Mass.: Harvard University Press.

Cody, Jeffrey W. (1983) The Pan-American Exposition of 1901: City Beautiful and City Imperial. Unpublished paper.

Cody, Jeffrey W. (1995) Nous vous vendrons le terrain, nous construirons vos habitations: l'immobilier résidentiel à Shanghai de 1911–1937, in Henriot, Christian (ed.) *Les Métropoles Chinoises au XXe Siècle*. Paris: Editions Arguments, pp. 73–86.

Cody, Jeffrey W. (1996*a*) Erecting monuments to the god of business and trade: the Fuller Construction Company of the Orient, 1919–1926. *Construction History*, **12**, pp. 67–77.

Cody, Jeffrey W. (1996*b*) American planning in Republican China. *Planning Perspectives*, **11**, pp. 339–377.

Cody, Jeffrey W. (1996*c*) Striking a harmonious chord: foreign missionaries and Chinese-style buildings, 1911–1949. *Architronic: The Electronic Journal of Architecture*, **5**(3). http://www.saed.kent.edu/Architronic

Cody, Jeffrey W. (1997) Site unseen: American portable buildings for export, 1879–1945, in *Proceedings of the 1996 ACSA European Conference, Copenhagen: Construction of Tectonics for the Post-industrial World*. Washington, D.C.: Association of Collegiate Schools of Architecture, pp. 275–281.

Cody, Jeffrey W. (1999*a*) Remnants of power behind the bund: Shanghai's IBC and Robert Dollar Buildings, 1920–22. *Architectural Research Quarterly*, **3**(4), pp. 335–350.

Cody, Jeffrey W. (1999*b*). Columbia circle: an obscured Shanghai suburb, 1928–1932. *Dialogue: Architecture + Design + Culture*, **23**, February/March, pp. 130–135.

Cody, Jeffrey W. (2000). The woman with the binoculars: British architects, Chinese builders, and Shanghai's skyline, 1900–1937, in Campbell, Louise (ed.) *Twentieth-Century Architecture and its Histories: Millennial Volume of Architectural History*. Otley: Society of Architectural Historians of Great Britain, pp. 251–274.

Cody, Jeffrey W. (2001) *Building in China: Henry K. Murphy's 'Adaptive' Architecture, 1914–1935*. Hong Kong and Seattle: Chinese University Press and University of Washington Press.

Cohen, Jean-Louis (1995) *Scenes of the World to Come: European Architecture and the American Challenge, 1893–1960*. Paris and Montreal: Flammarion and the Canadian Centre for Architecture.

Cohen, Jean-Louis and Damisch, Hubert (1993) *Américanisme et Modernité: l'idéal américain dans l'architecture*. Paris: EHESS, Flammarion.

Cohen, Jean-Louis (1993) L'Oncle Sam au pays des Soviets: le temps des avant-gardes, in Cohen, J.-L. and Damisch, H. (eds.) *Américanisme et Modernité: l'idéal américain dans l'architecture*. Paris: Flammarion, pp. 403–435.

Collins, Peter (1998) *Changing Ideals in Modern Architecture, 1750–1950*, 2nd ed. Montreal: McGill-Queens University Press.

Commons, J.R. (1903–04) The New York building trades. *Quarterly Journal of Economics*, **18**, p. 414.

Costello, Vincent (1998) Planning on the colonial fringe: land use planning in Iran. Proceedings of the 8th International Planning History Conference, Sydney, Australia, July 1998, pp. 103–108.

Covell, Jeffrey L. (1996) Brown & Root, Inc, in Grant, Tina (ed.) *International Directory of Company Histories*, Vol. 13. Chicago and London: St. James Press.

Covell, Jeffrey L. and Salamie, David E. (2000) Fluor Corporation, in Pederson, Jay (ed.) *International Directory of Company Histories*, Vol. 34. Chicago and London: St. James Press.

Cox, Kevin R. (1997) *Spaces of Globalization*. London and New York: Guilford Press.

Crain, Edward E. (1995) *Historic Architecture in the Caribbean Islands*. Gainesville: University of Florida Press.

Crimes, Mike (1991) *Civil Engineering 1839–1889: A Photographic History*. Phoenix Mill, Gloucestershire: Sutton Publishing. Crinson, Mark (1996) *Empire*

Building: Orientalism and Victorian Architecture. London: E & FN Spon.

Crinson, Mark (1997) Abadan: planning and architecture under the Anglo-Iranian Oil Company. *Planning Perspectives*, **12**(3), pp. 341–359.

Cuff, Dana (1991) *Architecture: the Story of Practice*. Cambridge, Mass.: MIT Press

Dalal, P. (2000) Internet use at firms accelerates. *AIArchitect*, June, n.p.

Daly, R.C. (1957) *Seventy-five Years of Construction Pioneering: George A. Fuller Company (1882–1957)*. New York: Newcomen Society in North America.

Dan, I. (1932) The reconstruction of Tokyo and aesthetic problems of architecture. *Far Eastern Review*, **28**, pp. 39–43.

Dandekar, H. (ed.) (1998) *City, Space + Globalization: An International Perspective*. Ann Arbor: College of Architecture and Urban Planning, University of Michigan.

Daniels, Walter (ed.) (1950) *The Point Four Program*. New York: H.W. Wilson.

Darnell, Victor C. (1984) *Directory of American Bridge-Building Companies 1840–1900*. Washington, D.C.: Society for Industrial Archeology.

Davidson, Joel (1995) Building for war, preparing for peace: World War II and the military-industrial complex, in Albrecht, Donald (ed.) *World War II and the American Dream*. Washington, D.C. and Cambridge, Mass.: National Building Museum and MIT Press, pp. 184–229.

Davis, Allen F. (ed.) (1981) *For Better or Worse: The American Influence in the World*. Westport, Ct. and London: Greenwood Press.

Davis, Philip K. (1932) The building of Molotov: where Russian Fords will be produced. *Journal of Worcester Polytechnic Institute*, April, pp. 83–88.

Dayer, Roberta A. (1981) *Bankers and Diplomats in China, 1917–1925: the Anglo-American Relationship*. London: Frank Cass & Company, Ltd.

De Grazia, Victoria (1985) Americanism for export. *Wedge*, no. 7–8 (Spring), pp. 74–85.

Dean, Andrea O. (1990) European forecast. *Architecture*, **79**(9), pp. 58–63.

Delhumeau, Gwenaël (1992) Hennebique, les

architectes et la concurrence, in *Culture constructive: les cahiers de la recherche architecturale* issue no. 29. Paris: Editions Parenthèses, pp. 33–52.

Delhumeau, Gwenaël (1999) *L'invention du Béton Armé: Hennebique, 1890–1914*. Paris: Editions Norma, Institut Français d'Architecture.

Diefendorf, Jeffry M. (1993) *In the Wake of War: the Reconstruction of German Cities After World War II*. New York and Oxford: Oxford University Press.

Dietsch, Deborah K. (1990) Americans in London. *Architecture*, **79**(9), pp. 64–71.

Dirks, Nicholas (1992) *Colonialism and Culture*. Ann Arbor: University of Michigan Press.

Dixon, John Morris (1995) Exporting architecture. *Progressive Architecture*, **76**(1), pp. 25–28.

Doane, Ralph (1919) The story of American architecture in the Philippines. *Architectural Review*, **8**, pp. 25–32; 115–22.

Dolan, Patric (1990) The global approach. *Real Estate Forum*, **45**(7), pp. 72–103.

Domosh, Mona (1996) *Invented Cities: The creation of Landscape in 19th-Century*. New Haven: Yale University Press.

Drummond, Wallace (1926) Construction of Public Works in Peru. *American Exporter*, **99**(4), pp. 16–17, 133–135.

Dulles, Eleanor (1944) *The Export-Import Bank of Washington; the First 10 Years*. Washington: U.S. Government Printing Office.

Eakin, Emily (2002) 'It takes an empire,' say several U.S. thinkers. *International Herald Tribune*, 2 April, p. 1.

Eaton, Leonard (1972) *America Comes of Age: European Reaction to H.H. Richardson and Louis Sullivan*. Cambridge, Mass: MIT Press.

Ehlers, Joseph H. (1966) *Far Horizons: The Travel Diary of an Engineer*. N.Y.: Carlton Press.

Ellin, Nan (1999) *Postmodern Urbanism*. New York: Princeton Architectural Press.

Ellwood, Donald M. (1992) *Rebuilding Europe: Western Europe, America and Postwar Reconstruction*. London: Longman.

Ellwood, Donald M. (1993) The Marshall Plan. *Rassegna*, **54** (June), pp. 84–88.

Esherick, Joseph W. (1987) *The Origins of the Boxer Uprising*. Berkeley: University of California Press.

Euromarket (1959) The shopping center comes to France. March, pp. 22–23.

Fairbank, Wilma (1994) *Liang and Lin: Partners in Exploring China's Architectural Past*. Philadelphia: University of Pennsylvania Press.

Farhi, Paul and Rosenfeld, Megan (1998) The world welcomes America's cultural invasion. *International Herald Tribune*, 26 October, p. 1.

Featherstone, Mike, Lash, Scott and Robertson, Roland (1995) *Global Modernities*. London: Sage.

Fédération Internationale du Batiment et des Travaux Publics (1929–1932) Notes périodiques.

Feliu, Eugenio (2000) The Atacama desert's last nitrate cities. *Architectural Research Quarterly*, **4**(4), pp. 337–347.

Ferguson, Charles J. (ed.) (1931) *Anderson, Meyer & Company, Limited of China*. Shanghai: Kelly and Walsh.

Feuerwerker, Albert (1967) Industrial enterprise in twentieth-century China: the Chee Hsin Cement Company, in Feuerwerker, Albert, Murphey, Rhoads and Wright, Mary (eds.) *Approaches to Modern Chinese History*. Berkeley: University of California Press, pp. 304–341.

Finn, D. (1995) *Meiji Revisited: the Sites of Victorian Japan*. N.Y. and Tokyo: Weatherhill.

Fluor, J. Robert (1978) *Fluor Corporation: A 65-Year History*. New York: Newcomen Society.

Forestier, Jean Claude Nicolas (1906) *Grandes Villes et Systèmes de Parcs*. Paris: Hachette.

Frank, Andre Gunder (1967) *Capitalism and Underdevelopment in Latin America*. New York: Monthly Review.

Frank, Andre G. (1998) *Reorient: Global Economy in the Asian Age*. Berkeley, CA: University of California Press.

Friedman, Thomas L. (2000) *The Lexus and the Olive Tree: Understanding Globalization*. New York: Anchor.

Fruehauf, Heinrich (1993) Urban exoticism in modern and contemporary Chinese literature, in Widmer, Ellen and Der-wei Wang, David (eds.)

From May Fourth to June Fourth: Fiction and Film in 20th Century China. Cambridge, Mass.: Harvard University Press, pp. 133–164.

Fuller, George A. Co. (1910) *Fireproof Building Construction: Prominent Buildings Erected by the George A. Fuller Company (1910)*. New York: George A. Fuller Company.

Fuller, George A. Co. (1923) *Third Annual Report of the Managing Director of the George A. Fuller Construction Company of the Orient Ltd*. Privately printed.

Fuller, George A. Co. (1924) *Fourth Annual Report of the Managing Director of the George A. Fuller Construction Company of the Orient Ltd*. Privately printed.

Fuller, George A. Co. (1952) *Office Buildings*. n.p.: George A. Fuller Company.

Fuller, Larry P. (1996) Going global. *World Architecture*, **42**, January, pp. 24–31.

Furlough, Ellen (1993) Selling the American way in interwar France: Prix Uniques and the Salons des Arts Menagers. *Journal of Social History*, **26**(3), pp. 491–520.

Galmiche, Xavier (2001) *Havana: Districts of Light*. Paris: Vilo.

Gelabert-Navia, Jose A. (1996) American architects in Cuba: 1900–1930. *Journal of Decorative and Propaganda Arts*, **22**, pp. 132–149.

Gelb, Michael (1991) *An American Engineer in Stalin's Russia: the Memoirs of Zara Witkin, 1932–1934*. Berkeley: University of California Press.

Gibbs, Kenneth T. (1984) *Business Architectural Imagery in America, 1870–1930*. Ann Arbor: UMI Press.

Giberti, Bruno (2002) *Designing the Centennial: A History of the 1876 International Exhibition in Philadelphia*. Louisville: University of Kentucky Press.

Gitlin, Todd (1992) World leaders: Mickey et al. *New York Times*, 3 May, Section II, pp. 1 *et seq.*

Goldstein, Carl (1989) Stronger foundations. *Far Eastern Economic Review*, **144**(18), pp. 37–58.

Gonzalez, Lorenzo (1996) Modernity and the City: Caracas 1935–1958. Unpublished Ph.D. dissertation, Cornell University.

Goodrich, Ernest P. (1930) Some experiences of an engineer in China. *Michigan Engineer*, vol. 48, p. 15.

Gordon, Douglas E. (1991) EC92, the Market of Tomorrow Open Today. Memo (American Institute of Architects) (April), p. 27.

Gould, Kira (1999) American architects export collaboration as a means to sustainability. *AIArchitect*, (November), p. 23.

Gournay, Isabelle (1998) Prestige and professionalism: the influence of American architects, in Gournay, Isabelle and Vanlaethem, France (eds.) *Montreal Metropolis 1880–1930*. Montreal: Canadian Centre for Architecture, pp. 113–132.

Gournay, Isabelle (2001) Romance, prejudice and Levitt's Americanization of the middle class in France, in Chew, William L. (ed.) *National Stereotypes in Perspective: Americans in France – Frenchmen in America*. Amsterdam: Rodopi.

Gournay, Isabelle (2002) Levitt France et la banlieue a l'américaine: premier bilan. *Histoire Urbaine*, **5**, pp. 167–188.

Graf, King (1990) International Design and Practice. Unpublished transcript of a discussion at American Institute of Architects, Washington, D.C.

Grant, Kerry S. (2001) *The Rainbow City: Celebrating Light, Color and Architecture at the Pan-American Exposition*. Buffalo: Canisius College Press.

Greenhalgh, Paul (2001) The art and industry of mammon: international exhibitions, 1851–1901, in Mackenzie, J.M. (ed.) *The Victorian Vision: Inventing New Britain*. London: V & A Publications, pp. 265–280.

Greensfelder, Albert P. (1930) The International Building Congress. *Constructor*, **12**(8), pp. 34–36.

Greif, Martin (1978) *The New Industrial Landscape: the Story of the Austin Company*. Clinton, New Jersey: Main Street Press.

Greig, Doreen (1971) *A Guide to the Architecture in South Africa*. Cape Town: Howard Timmins.

Gutiérrez, Ramón (2002) Buenos Aires, a great European city, in Almandoz, Arturo (ed.) *Planning Latin America's Capital Cities, 1850–1950*. London and New York: Routledge, pp. 45–74.

Gutiérrez, Ramón and Tartarini, Jorge (1996) *El Banco de Boston: La Casa Central en la Argentina, 1917–1997*. Buenos Aires: Fundación Banco de Boston.

Haddow, Robert H. (1997) *Pavilions of Plenty: Exhibiting American Culture Abroad in the 1950s*. Washington and London: Smithsonian Press.

Hamilton, S.B. (1956) New civil engineering projects in colonial countries. *Civil Engineering*, **26** (September), p. 102.

Hammond, S. (1999) Cheung Kong Center: prestige. *Building Journal* (Hong Kong), July, pp. 36–45.

Hanagan, Michael (2002). States and capital: globalizations past and present, in Kalb, Don, van der Land, Marco, Staring, Richard, van Steenbergen, Bart and Wilterdink, Nico (eds.) *The Ends of Globalization: Bringing Society Back In*. Lanham, Maryland: Rowman & Littlefield, pp. 67–86.

Hannigan, John (1998) *Fantasy City: Pleasure and Profit in the Postmodern Metropolis*. London and New York: Routledge

Hannerz, Ulf (1996) *Transnational Connections: Culture, People, Places*. London and New York: Routledge.

Hannigan, John (1998) *Fantasy City: Pleasure and Profit in the Postmodern Metropolis*. London and New York: Routledge.

Hardt, Michael and Negri, Antonio (2000) *Empire*. Cambridge, Mass. And London: Harvard University Press.

Harvey, David (1989) *The Condition of Postmodernity*. Oxford: Blackwell.

Hays, Samuel P. (1995) *The Rise of Industrialism, 1885–1914*, 2nd ed. Chicago and London: University of Chicago Press.

Headrick, Daniel (1988) *The Tentacles of Progress: Technology Transfer in the Age of Imperialism, 1850–1940*. Oxford: Oxford University Press.

Hebdige, Dick (1988) *Hiding in the Light: On Images and Things*. London and New York: Routledge.

Heikkila, Eric J. and Pizarro-O'Byrne, Rafael (eds.) (2002) *Southern California and the World*. Westport, Ct.: Greenwood Press.

Hietkamp, Lenore (1998) The Park Hotel (1931–1934) and Its Architect, Laszlo Hudec (1893–1958): 'Tallest Building in the Far East' as Metaphor for Pre-Communist Shanghai. Unpublished MA thesis, University of Victoria, Canada.

Hildebrand, Grant (1974) *Designing for Industry: The Architecture of Albert Kahn*. Cambridge, Mass: MIT Press.

Hodge, Raymond J. (1982) Design/construction exports: IECIC's role. *Business America*, **5**, 1 November, pp. 24–25.

Hogan, Michael (1989) *The Marshall Plan: America, Britain and the Reconstruction of Western Europe, 1947–1952*. New York: Cambridge University Press.

Hoggson, Noble F. (1920) World cooperation in business. *Bulletin of the Associated General Contractors*, **11**, pp. 18–21.

Home, Robert (1997) *Of Planting and Planning: The Making of British Colonial Cities*. London: E & FN Spon.

Hopkins, Alfred (1922) Some ideas on bank buildings – artistic and practical. *Architectural Forum*, **36**(1) p. 1.

Horwitz, Richard, (ed.) (1993) *Exporting America: Essays on American Studies Abroad*. New York: Garland.

Hough, B. Olney (1909) *Elementary Lessons in Exporting*. New York: Johnston Export Publishing Company.

Hough, B. Olney (1921) *Practical Exporting: a Handbook for Manufacturers and Merchants*, 7th ed. New York: Johnston Export Publishing Company.

Hounshell, David A. (1984) *From the American System to Mass Production, 1800–1932*. Baltimore and London: Johns Hopkins University Press.

Howell, Herbert P. (1920) The International Market for Iron and Steel, *Commerce Weekly* [National Bank of Commerce], **2**(3), pp. 3–12.

Howenstine, E. Jay (1972) Social considerations in promoting overseas construction work in developing countries. *Construction Review*, **18**, June, pp. 4–8.

Hunt, M.H. (1972) The American remission of the Boxer Indemnity: a reappraisal. *Journal of Asian Studies*, **31**, pp. 539–559.

Hutchinson, William K. (1986) Regional exports of the United States to foreign countries: a structural analysis, 1870-1910. *Research in Economic History*, **10**, pp. 131–154.

Huxtable, Ada Louise (1986) Americans abroad,

in Huxtable, A.L. *Architecture Anyone?* New York: Random House.

Ibelings, Hans (1997) *Americanism: Dutch Architecture and the Transatlantic Model*. Rotterdam: NAi Uitgevers.

Irving, John (1989) *A Prayer for Owen Meany*. New York: Morrow/Avon.

Israel, Jerry (1971) *Progressivism and the Open Door: America and China, 1905–1921*. Pittsburgh: University of Pittsburgh Press.

Jacobs, Jane (1996) *Edge of Empire: Postcolonialism and the City*. London: Routledge.

Jacobson, Matthew Frye (2000) *Barbarian Virtues: The United States Encounters Foreign Peoples at Home and Abroad, 1876–1917. New York*: Hill & Wang.

Johnston, W.J. (1906) Commerce and industries of Argentina. *American Exporter*, **58**(5), pp. 147–152.

Joseph, S.B. (1918) A ready market overseas. *System*, **34**(1), pp. 70–78.

Judis, John B. (1992) *Grand Illusion: Critics and Champions of the American Century*. New York: Farrar Straus & Giroux.

Judis, John B. (2002) Forget about the American Century. *New York Times*, 20 August, p. A27.

Kahler, H.M. (1914) The paradox of architecture. *Export American Industries*, vol. **13**(6), pp. 37–42.

Kahn, Albert, Inc. (1937) *Industrial and Commercial Buildings Detroit*. Privately published.

Kalb, Don (2002) Localizing flows: power, paths, institutions, and networks, in Kalb, Don, van der Land, Marco, Staring, Richard, van Steenbergen, Bart and Wilterdink, Nico (eds.) *The Ends of Globalization: Bringing Society Back In*. Lanham, Maryland: Rowman & Littlefield, pp. 1–28.

Kanigel, Robert (1997) *The One Best Way: Frederick Winslow Taylor and the Enigma of Efficiency*. New York: Viking.

Kai, T. (1922) Public Service Engineering in Canton. *Journal of the Association of Chinese and American Engineers*, **3**, April–May, pp. 9–10.

Kaplan, Amy and Pease, Donald E. (eds.) (1993) *Cultures of United States Imperialism*. Durham and London: Duke University Press.

Kaplan, Robert (2001) *Warrior Politics: Why Leadership Demands a Pagan Ethos*. New York: Random House.

Katz, Paul (1999) Global trends in Commercial Architecture. Unpublished paper delivered at an 'Architectural Seminar' of the American Chamber of Commerce, Hong Kong, China, 17 November.

Keller, David Neal (1989) *Stone & Webster, 1889–1989: A Century of Integrity and Service*. N.Y.: Stone & Webster, Inc.

Keith, O. (1922*a*) Commission Government in Canton. *Far Eastern Review*, **18**, pp. 101–103.

Keith, O. (1922*b*) The New Canton. *Far Eastern Review*, 18, March, p. 146.

Khvostovsky, L.G. (1931) Construction in Soviet Russia: Possibilities for American contractors to sell their services in U.S.S.R. *The Constructor*, **13**(12), pp. 16–18.

King, Anthony D. (1995) *The Bungalow: the Production of a Global Culture*, 2nd ed. New York: Oxford University Press.

King, Anthony D. (1997) *Culture, Globalization and the World-System: Contemporary Conditions for the Representation of Identity*. Minneapolis: University of Minnesota Press.

Klein, Julius (1929*a*) *Frontiers of Trade*. New York and London: Century Company.

Klein, Julius (1929*b*) 'Adaption' for markets abroad – to what extent is it necessary? *Manufacturing Industries*, **17**(2), pp. 89–92.

Knevitt, Charles (1990) American Firms in Britain: a report card. *Architectural Record*, **178**, November, pp. 53–54.

Koch, R. (1959) American influence abroad, 1886 and later. *Journal of the Society of Architectural Historians*, **18**(1), pp. 66–69.

Kopp, Anatole (1970) *Town and Revolution: Soviet Architecture and Town Planning, 1917–1935*. London. Thames & Hudson.

Koshino, T. (1979) *West Meets East: the Japanese Introduction to Western Architecture in the 19th and 20th Centuries*. Tokyo: Sanseido.

Kotkin, Steven (1988) *Magnetic Mountain: City Building and City Life in the Soviet Union of the 1930s*. Unpublished PhD dissertation, University of California, Berkeley.

Kramer, Michael and Roberts, Sam (1976) *I Never Wanted to be Vice-President of Anything*. N.Y.: Basic Books.

LaFeber, Walter (1963) *The New Empire: An Interpretation of American Expansion, 1860–1898*. Ithaca, N.Y.: Cornell University Press.

Laird, Warren P. (1928) *Our Sister Continent, General Magazine and Historical Chronicle*. n.p.: University of Pennsylvania.

Landau, H. Lad (1918) Steel exports in the light of the new licensing regulations. *Export American Industries*, **21**(3), pp. 73–74.

Langley, Lester D. (1976) *Struggle for the American Mediterranean: United States-European Rivalry in the Gulf-Caribbean, 1776–1904*. Athens: University of Georgia Press.

Larkin, R.N. (1949) Overseas consultants wins contract for $650-million Iran development. *Engineering-News Record*, **143**, 20 October, p. 25.

Le Dantec, Jean-Pierre (1994) Forestier aujourd'hui, in Leclerc, Bénédicte (ed.) *Jean Claude Nicolas Forestier, 1861–1930: du jardin au paysage urbain*. Paris: Picard.

Leary, Thomas and Sholes, Elizabeth(1998) *Images of America: Buffalo's Pan-American Exposition*. Charleston, S.C.: Arcadia.

Lechner, Frank J. and Boli, John (eds.) (2000) *The Globalization Reader*. Oxford: Blackwell.

Lee, E. Bing-shuey (1936) *Modern Canton*. Shanghai: Mercury Press.

Lee, J. and Walters, D. (1989) *International Trade in Construction, Design, and Engineering Services*. Cambridge, Mass.: Ballinger Publishing Company.

Lee, M.C. (1930) Public construction in Canton. *Far Eastern Review*, **26**, May, pp. 217–219.

Lejeune, Jean-Francois (1996) The city as landscape: Jean Claude Nicolas Forestier and the great urban works of Havana, 1925–1930. *Journal of Decorative and Propaganda Arts*, **22**, pp. 151–185.

Lerner, Max (1957) *America as a Civilization: Life and Thought in the U.S. Today*. New York: Simon & Schuster.

Lewis, Arnold (1997) *An Early Encounter with Tomorrow: Europeans, Chicago's Loop and the World's Columbian Exposition*. Urbana: University of Illinois Press.

Lewis, Miles (1988a) *Two Hundred Years of Concrete in Australia*. Sydney: Concrete Institute of Australia.

Lewis, Miles (1988b) *The Domed Reading Room*. Melbourne: State Library of Victoria.

Lewis, Miles (1993) The Asian trade in portable buildings, fabrications. *Journal of the Society of Architectural Historians, Australia and New Zealand*, **4**, pp. 31–55.

Liang Ssu-ch'eng [Sicheng] (Fairbank, Wilma (ed.)) (1984) *A Pictorial History of Chinese Architecture*. Cambridge, Mass. and London: MIT Press.

Lin, Shirley S. (ed.) (1990) *Citicorp in China: A Colorful, Very Personal History since 1902*. Hong Kong: Citicorp.

Liscombe, R.W. (1991) A 'new era in my life': Ithiel Town abroad. *Journal of the Society of Architectural Historians*, **50**, pp. 5–17.

Llanes, Lilian (1985) *Apuntes Para una Historia Sobre los Constructores Cubanos*. Havana: Editorial Letras Cubanas.

Loeffler, Jane C. (1998) *The Architecture of Diplomacy: Building America's Embassies*. New York: Princeton Architectural Press.

Logcher, R.D. and Levitt, R.E. (1979) Organization and control of engineering design firms. *Journal on Issues in Engineering, ASCE*, **105**, pp. 7–13.

Longstreth, Richard (1997) *City Center to Regional Mall: Architecture, the Automobile, and Retailing in Los Angeles, 1920–1950*. Cambridge, Mass. and London: MIT Press.

Lougheed, A.G. and Kenwood, A.L. (1982). *Technological Diffusion and Industrialization before 1914*. New York: St. Martin's Press.

Luce, Henry R. (1959) *The Dangerous Age of Abundance*. New York: Newcomen Society in North America.

Lui, Alex (1999) American architects in Hong Kong. *China Business Review*, **26**(16), pp. 46–48.

Macmillan, Allister (1911) *The West Indies Illustrated*. London: W.H. & L. Collingridge.

MacPherson, Kerrie L. (1987) *A Wilderness of Marshes: the Origins of Public Health in Shanghai, 1843–1893*. Hong Kong: Oxford University Press.

MacPherson, Kerrie (1990) Designing China's urban future: the Greater Shanghai Plan, 1927–1937. *Planning Perspectives*, **5**, pp. 39–62.

Marashian, O.M. (1958) Construction spotlight shifts to Iran. *Engineering-News Record*, **156**, 25 September, pp. 51–60.

Marlin, William (1975) America's impacts on the arts: architecture. *Saturday Review*, 13 December, pp. 74–80.

Marx, Leo and Smith, Merrit R. (eds.) (1994) *Does Technology Drive History? The Dilemma of Technological Determinism*. Cambridge, Mass. and London: MIT Press.

Mattelart, Armand (1983) (David Buxton, trans.) *Trans-nationals and the Third World: the Struggle for Culture*. South Hadley, Mass: Bergin & Garvey.

Mayer, Robert (1973) The origins of the American banking empire in Latin America: Frank A. Vanderlip and the National City Bank. *Journal of InterAmerican Studies and World Affairs*, **15**(1), pp. 60–76.

Mays, Vernon (1991) A test of values. *Landscape Architecture*, **81**, September, pp. 50–55.

Mazuzan, George (1974) Our new gold goes adventuring: the American International Corporation in China. *Pacific Historical Review*, **43**(2), pp. 212–232.

McCartney, Laton (1988) *Friends in High Places: the Bechtel Story, the Most Secret Corporation and How it Engineered the World*. New York and London: Simon and Schuster.

McCormick, Thomas J. (1967) *China Market: America's Quest for Informal Empire, 1893–1901*. Chicago: Quadrangle.

McCullough, David (1977) *The Path Between the Seas: the Creation of the Panama Canal, 1870–1914*. New York: Simon and Schuster.

McElderry, Andrea L. (1976) *Shanghai Old-Style Banks (chien-chuang), 1800–1935: A Traditional Institution in a Changing Society*. Ann Arbor: Center for Chinese Studies, University of Michigan.

McLuhan, Marshall (1962) *The Gutenberg Galaxy: the Making of Typographic Man*. Toronto: University of Toronto Press.

McMenimen, William V. (1945) Construction Prospects at Home and Abroad. *Engineering-News Record*, **134**, 5 April, pp. 101–102.

McQuade, Walter (1980) An expatriate builder's changing frontiers. *Fortune*, **102**, 30 June, pp. 96–102.

Meinig, D.W. (1986) *The Shaping of America: A Geographical Perspective on 500 Years of History*. Volume 1: *Atlantic America, 1492–1800*. New Haven and London: Yale University Press.

Melosi, Martin (1999) *The Sanitary City: Urban Infrastructure in America from Colonial Times to the Present*. Baltimore: Johns Hopkins University Press.

Misa, Thomas (1995) *A Nation of Steel: The Making of Modern America, 1865–1925*. Baltimore and London: Johns Hopkins University Press.

Mitchell, W. (1999) *E-topia: 'Urban life, Jim – But Not As We Know It'*. Cambridge, Mass.: MIT Press.

Montalvo, Maria Lobo, Luisa (2000) *Havana: History and Architecture of a Romantic City*. San Francisco: Monacelli Press.

Mooney, T. (1999) Constructing a landmark. *Asian Architect & Contractor*, October, pp. 14–17.

Mote, David (1997) J.A. Jones, Inc, in Grant, Tina (ed.) *International Directory of Company Histories*, Vol. 16. Chicago and London: St. James Press.

Moudry, Roberta M. (1995) Architecture as Cultural Design: The Architecture and Urbanism of the Metropolitan Life Insurance Company. Unpublished Ph.D. dissertation, Cornell University.

Muschamp, Herbert (1992) The Niña, the Pinta and the fate of the 'White City'. *New York Times*, 8 November, p. II–32.

Muller, E.J. (1904–1905) Reinforced concrete. *Proceedings of the Shanghai Society of Engineers and Architects*, pp. 121–148.

National Research Council (1989) *Building for Tomorrow: Global Enterprise and the U.S. Construction Industry*. Washington, D.C.: National Academy Press.

Notoji, Masako (2000) Cultural transformation of John Philip Sousa and Disneyland in Japan, in Wagnleitner, Reinhold and May, Elaine Tyler (eds.) *Here, There and Everywhere: The Foreign Politics of American Popular Culture*. Hanover and London: University Press of New England, pp. 219–226.

Norberg-Shulz, Christian (1988) *New World Architecture*. New York: Princeton Architectural Press and the Architectural League of New York.

Nye, David E. (1996) *American Technological Sublime*. Cam-bridge, Mass. and London: MIT Press.

Olwig, Karen F. and Hastings, Kirsten (1997). *Siting Culture: the Shifting Anthropological Subject*. London: Routledge.

Oncu, Ayse and Weyland, Petra (1997). *Space, Culture and Power*. London: ZED Books.

Orth, Myra Dickman (1975) The Influence of the 'American Romanesque' in Australia. *Journal of the Society of Architectural Historians*, **34**(1), pp. 3–18.

Oszuscik, Philippe (1988) The French Creole cottage and its Caribbean connection, in Roark, Michael (ed.) *French and Germans in the Mississippi Valley: Landscape and Cultural Traditions*. Cape Girardeau: Center for Regional History and Cultural Heritage, Southeast Missouri State University, pp. 61–78.

Parsons, Kermit C. (1992) American influence on Stockholm's post World War II suburban expansion. *Planning History*, **14**(1), pp. 3–14.

Pedersen, W (1999) Practicing in Asia. Unpublished lecture at 'American Architects in Asia' symposium, University of Virginia, Charlottesville, October.

Pells, Richard (1997) *Not Like Us: How Europeans have Loved, Hated and Transformed American Culture since World War II*. New York: Basic Books.

Pencoyd Iron Works (1900) *Steel in Construction*, 12th ed. Philadelphia: A. & P. Roberts Company.

Persico, Joseph (1982) *The Imperial Rockefeller*. New York: Simon & Schuster.

Peters, Tom (1996) *Building the Nineteenth Century*. Cambridge, Mass.: MIT Press.

Phelps, C.W. (1927) *The Foreign Expansion of American Banks*, New York: Ronald Press.

Phillips, James R. (1984) Capital goods and international construction. *Business America*, **7**, 30 April, pp. 6–7.

Pickworth, J.W. and W. H. Weiskopf (1927) Tokyo bank building designed to resist earthquakes. *Engineering News-Record*, **98**, pp. 1010–1014.

Picton-Seymour, Desiree (1989) *Historical Buildings in South Africa*. Cape Town: Struikhof.

Placzek, Adolph (ed.) (1982) *Macmillan Encyclopedia of Architects*. New York: Free Press.

Polk, Benjamin (1961) *Architecture and the Spirit of the Place*. Calcutta: Oxford Book and Stationery.

Polk, Benjamin (1985) *India Notebook: Two Americans in the South Asia of Nehru's Time, Benjamin and Emily Polk*. Salisbury, Wiltshire: M. Russell.

Pomeranz, Kenneth (2001) *The Great Divide: China, Europe and the Making of the Modern World Economy*. Princeton: Princeton University Press.

Préstamo, Felipe (1995) *Cuba: arquitectura y urbanismo*. Miami: Ediciones Universal.

Préstamo, Felipe J. (1996) The architecture of American sugar mills: the United States Fruit Company. *Journal of Decorative and Propaganda Arts*, **22**, pp. 62–81.

Proudfoot, Peter, Maguire, Roslyn and Freestone, Robert (eds.) (2000) *Colonial City, Global City: Sydney's International Exhibition 1879*. Darlinghurst, NSW, Australia: Crossing Press.

Pugach, Noel H. (1997) *Same Bed, Different Dreams: A History of the Chinese American Bank of Commerce, 1919–1937*. Hong Kong: Centre of Asian Studies, University of Hong Kong.

Pugh, Olin (1957) *The Export-Import Bank of Washington*. New York: Columbia University School of Business Administration.

Rabinow, Paul (1990) *French Modern*. Cambridge, Mass. and London: MIT Press.

Rasmussen, O.D. (1925) *Tientsin: An Illustrated Outline History*. Tientsin: Tientsin Press.

Rassweiler, Anne D. (1988) *The Generation of Power: The History of Dneprostroi*. Oxford and New York: Oxford University Press.

Reade, Charles G. (1928) *Town Planning in the Philippines*. Kuala Lumpur: n.p.

Rebori, A.N. (1917) The work of William E. Parsons in the Philippine Islands. *Architectural Record*, **41**, April, pp. 305–324.

Reinink, A.W. (1970) American influences on late nineteenth-century architecture in the Netherlands. *Journal of the Society of Architectural Historians*, **29**(2), pp. 163–174.

Reinsch, Paul S. (1914) American handicaps in

reaching Chinese Trade. *Daily Consular and Trade Reports*, vol. 195, pp. 984–985.

Reybold, E. (1943) Construction gets its passport. *The Constructor*, 25 (July), pp. 100–103.

Ricard, Serge (ed.) (1990) *An American Empire: Expansionist Cultures and Policies, 1881–1917*. Aix-en-Provence: Université de Provence.

Ricks, Thomas E. (2001) U.S. urged to embrace an 'imperial' role. *International Herald Tribune*, 22 August, p. 1.

Rimmer, P.J. (1988) The internationalisation of engineering consultancies: problems of breaking into the club. *Environment and Planning A*, **20**, pp. 761–788.

Roberts, A. & P., Company (1900) *Steel in Construction: Pencoyd Iron Works*, 12th ed. Philadelphia: The Company.

Robin, Ron (1992) *Enclaves of America: the Rhetoric of American Political Architecture Abroad, 1900–1965*. Princeton: Princeton University Press.

Rockwell, John (1994) The new colossus: American culture as power export. *New York Times*, 30 January, Section II, pp. 1 *et seq.*

Rosenberg, Emily S. (1982) *Spreading the American Dream: American Economic and Cultural Expansion, 1890–1945*. New York: Hill and Wang.

Ross, Lee (1943) Building Brazil. *Foreign Commerce Weekly*, **11**, 3 July, p. 6.

Rowe, Peter (1996) Design in an increasingly small world, in Saunders, W. (ed.) *Reflections on Architectural Practice in the Nineties*. New York: Princeton Architectural Press, pp. 220–230.

Rowell, C. Current (undated) Comment. Typed manuscript. Henry K. Murphy Papers. Murphy Family, Branford, Connecticut.

Rundt, Stefan Jean (1960) When in Rome . . .: the importance of understanding customs, manners and mores in doing business abroad. *Management Review*, February, pp. 4, 113.

Russett, Bruce (1985) The mysterious case of vanishing hegemony; or, is Mark Twain really dead? *International Organization*, **39**(2), pp. 207–231.

Ruthven, Malise (2002) *A Fury for God: The Islamist Attack on America*. London and New York: Granta.

Rydell, Robert W. (1984) *All the World's a Fair: Visions of Empire at American International Expositions, 1876–1916*. Chicago and London: University of Chicago Press.

Rydell, Robert W., Findling, John E. and Pelle, Kimberley D. (2000) *Fair America: World's Fairs in the U.S.* Washington, D.C.: Smithsonian Institution Press.

Said, Edward W. (1978) *Orientalism*. New York: Vintage.

Said, Edward W. (1993) *Culture and Imperialism*. New York: Alfred A. Knopf.

Sassen, Saskia (1998) *Globalization and its Discontents*. New York: The New Press.

Sassen, Saskia (2000) *Cities in a World Economy*, 2nd ed. Thousand Oaks and London: Pine Forge Press.

Saunders, David A.L. (1959) The reinforced concrete dome of the Melbourne Public Library, 1911. *Architectural Science Review* (Australia), **2**(1), pp. 39–46.

Saunders, Mary (1987) Conference focuses on the architecture, engineering, and construction industry's global competitiveness. *Business America*, **10**, 7 December, pp. 12–13.

Saunders, Richard E. (1945) Report from the Pacific. *Architectural Forum*, **83**, August, pp. 124–125.

Saunders, William S. (ed.) (1996) *Reflections on Architectural Practices in the Nineties*. New York: Princeton Architectural Press.

Schinz, A. (1989) *Cities in China*. Berlin and Stuttgart: Gebruder Borntraeger.

Schmertz, Mildred F. (1990) Japanese imports. *Architecture*, **79**(9), pp. 72–75.

Schubert, Dirk and Sutcliffe, Anthony (1996) The 'Hauss-mannization of London? The planning and construction of Kingsway-Aldwych, 1889–1935. *Planning Perspectives*, **11**(2), pp. 115–144.

Schoonover, Thomas D. (1988) Metropole rivalry in Central America, 1920s–1930, in Woodward, Ralph Jr. (ed.) *Central America: Historical Perspective on the Contemporary Crisis*. Westport, Connecticut: Greenwood.

Schoonover, Thomas D. (1991) *The United States in Central America, 1860–1911: Episodes of Social Imperialism and Imperial Rivalry in the World System*. Durham: Duke University Press.

Schultz, Stanley (1989) *Constructing Urban Culture: American Cities and City Planning, 1800–1920.* Philadelphia: Temple University Press.

Scobie, James, R. (1974) *Buenos Aires: Plaza to Suburb, 1870–1910.* New York and Oxford: Oxford University Press.

Scoon, Robert (1970) Those communist model A's. *The Restorer,* **14**(6), pp. 1–14.

Scoon, Robert (1971) More about those communist model A's. *The Restorer,* **15**(6), pp. 1–6.

Scott, Allen J. (1998) *Regions and the World Economy: the Coming Shape of Global Production, Competition and Political Order.* Oxford: Oxford University Press.

Scott, John (1942, 1989) *Behind the Urals: An American Worker in Russia's City of Steel.* Boston: Houghton Mifflin, 1942; Bloomington, Indiana: University of Indiana Press, 1989.

Scott-Stevens, S. (1987) *Foreign Consultants and Counterparts: Problems in Technology Transfer.* Boulder, CO and London: Westview Press.

Seidensticker, E. (1990) *Tokyo Rising: The City since the Great Earthquake.* New York: Knopf.

Service, Alastair (1979) *London 1900.* New York: Rizzoli International.

Seymour, Howard (1987) *The Multinational Construction Industry.* London: Croom Helm.

Shannahan, J. (1908) The Gokteik Viaduct. *The Book-Keeper,* **21**(1), pp. 1–5.

Shirk, Charles A. (1978) *The Austin Company: A Century of Results.* New York: Newcomen Society of North America.

Siegfried, André (1952) Can Europe use American methods? *Foreign Affairs,* **30**, July, pp. 660–668.

Sih, P.C.W. (1993) *Fax Power.* New York: Van Nostrand Reinhold.

Simpson, Pamela H. (1995) Cheap, quick and easy. Part II: Pressed metal ceilings, 1880–1930, in Cromley, Elizabeth C. and Hudgins, Carter L. (eds.) *Gender, Class, and Shelter: Perspectives in Vernacular Architecture, V.* Knoxville: University of Tennessee Press, pp. 151–163.

Skillings, D. N. & D.B. Flint's *Illustrated Catalogue of Portable Sectional Buildings* (1861) Boston and New York: n.p.

Smith, Lyndon P. (1908) The new building for the National City Bank. *American Architect and Building News,* **94**(1713), pp. 1229–1231.

Smith, Michael Peter (2001) *Transnational Urbanism: Locating Globalization.* Oxford: Blackwell.

Stallworthy, E.A. and Kharbanda, O.P. (1985) *International Construction.* Aldershot: Gower.

Starr, Peter (2002). *Citibank: A Century in Asia.* Singapore: Editions Didier Millet.

Starrett, William A. (1923) New construction in an ancient empire. *Scribner's Magazine,* **74**, pp. 273-274.

Starrett, William A. (1928) *Skyscrapers and the Men Who Build Them.* New York: Scribners.

Stein, Joel and Levine, Caroline (eds.) (1990) *Money Matters: A Critical Look at Bank Architecture.* New York: McGraw-Hill.

Stewart, David B. (1987) *The Making of a Modern Japanese Architecture: 1868 to the Present.* New York and Tokyo: Kodansha International.

Stoddard, William B. (1924) Selling Yankee home ideas to the Oriental. *Building Age,* **46**, September, pp. 78–79.

Stone, Edward Durell (1962) *The Evolution of an Architect.* New York: Horizon Press.

Strassmann, W. Paul and Wells, Jill (eds.) (1988) *The Global Construction Industry: Strategies for Entry, Growth and Survival.* London: Unwin Hyman.

Strike, James (1991) *Construction into Design: The Influence of New Methods of Construction on Architectural Design, 1690–1990.* Oxford: Butterworth Architecture.

Sumka, Howard J. (1989) Global urbanization: mobilizing international H/CD partnerships. *Journal of Housing,* **46**(5), pp. 221–228.

Sun, Yat-sen (1922) *The International Development of China.* New York and London: G.P. Putnam's Sons, Knicker-bocker Press.

Sutton, Antony (1968) *Western Technology and Soviet Economic Development.* Vol. 1. *1917–1930.* Stanford: Stanford University Press.

Takaki, Ronald (1993) *A Different Mirror: A History of Multicultural America.* Boston: Little, Brown & Co.

Tam, A. (1999) Hong Kong's linen lantern. *Asian Architect & Contractor,* **28**(10), pp. 10–13.

Tetlow, Karin (1990) Foreign exchange. *Architecture*, **79**(9), pp. 101–108

Thomas, Nicholas (1994) *Colonialism's Culture: Anthropology, Travel and Government*. Princeton: Princeton University Press.

Thomas, R. (1999) Something special for Mr Li. *Space* (Hong Kong), October, pp. 108–117.

Thomas, W.T. (1937) Faith working by love in Japan. *Missionary Review of the World*, **60**, pp. 584–586.

Thomson, J.C. Jr. (1969) *While China Faced West: American Reformers in Nationalist China, 1928–37*. Cambridge, Mass.: Harvard University Press.

Thornburg, Max (1949) The Middle East and the American engineer. *Journal of Engineering Education*, **39**, March, pp. 332–333.

Tignor, Robert *et al.* (2002) *Worlds Together, Worlds Apart*: New York and London: W.W. Norton.

Tipson, Frederick S. (1997) Culture clash-ification: a verse to Huntington's cause. *Foreign Affairs*, March-April, pp. 166–169.

Tombesi, Paolo (2001) A true south for design?: the new international division of labour in architecture. *Architectural Research Quarterly*, **5**(2), pp. 171–179.

Tomlinson, John (1991) *Cultural Imperialism: A Critical Introduction*. London: Pinter.

Tomlinson, John (1999) *Globalization and Culture*. Chicago and London: University of Chicago Press.

Trueheart, Charles (1998) U.S. culture abroad finds foes and imitators. *International Herald Tribune*, 28 October, p. 1.

Truman, Harry S. (1949) Inaugural Address, 20 January 1949.

Trumpbour, John (2002) *Selling Hollywood to the World: U.S. and European Struggles for Mastery of the Global Film Industry, 1920–1950*. Cambridge: Cambridge University Press.

Tselos, Dimitri (1970) Richardson's influence on European architecture. *Journal of the Society of Architectural Historians*, **29**(2), pp. 156–162.

Twain, Mark (1901) To the Person Sitting in Darkness, *North American Review*, February.

Twombly, Robert (1995) *Power and Style: A Critique of Twentieth-century Architecture in the United States*. New York: Hill & Wang.

Tyau, M.T.Z. (1930) Planning the new Chinese national capital. *Chinese Social and Political Science Review*, **14**, pp. 372–388.

Underwood, David K. (1991) Alfred Agache, French sociology, and modern urbanism in France and Brazil. *Journal of the Society of Architectural Historians*, **50**, pp. 130–166.

Upton, Dell (1998) *Architecture in the United States*. Oxford and New York: Oxford University Press.

Upton, Dell and Vlach, John Michael (eds.) (1986) *Common Places: Readings in American Vernacular Architecture*. Athens: University of Georgia Press.

Van Dormael, Armand (1978) *The Bretton Woods Conference: Birth of a Monetary System*. London: Macmillan.

Van Zanten, David (1969) Jacob Wrey Mould: echoes of Owen Jones and the high Victorian styles in New York, 1853–1865. *Journal of the Society of Architectural Historians*, **28**, pp. 41–57.

Venegas Fortias, Carlos (1996) Havana between two centuries. *Journal of Decorative and Propaganda Arts*, **22**, pp. 13–34.

Vonier, Françoise (1997) A view through European eyes. *AIArchitect*, August, p. 23.

Vories, William M. (1931) In this office every drafts-man is boss. *American Architect*, **141**, pp. 30–31.

Wadell, John A.L. (1897) To build bridges in Japan. *American Exporter*, **40**, p. 18.

Wagnleitner, Reinhold (1986) Propagating the American dream: cultural policies as means of integration. *American Studies International*, **24** (1), pp. 61–84.

Wagnleitner, Reinhold and Tyler May, Elaine (eds.) (2000) *Here, There and Everywhere: The Foreign Politics of American Popular Culture*. Hanover and London: University Press of New England.

Wallerstein, Immanuel (1974) *The Modern World-System*. New York: Academic Press.

Wallerstein, Immanuel (1980) *The Modern World-System II*. New York: Academic Press.

Ward, David and Zunz, Olivier (eds.) (1992) *The Landscape of Modernity: Essays on New York City, 1900–1940*. New York: Russell Sage Foundation.

Ward, Stephen (1998) Re-examining the international diffusion of planning. *Proceedings of the 8th In-*

ternational Planning History Conference, Sydney, Australia, pp. 935–940.

Warf, Barney (1991) The international construction industry in the 1980s. *Professional Geographer*, **43**(2), pp. 150–162.

Watson, James L. (1997) *Golden Arches East: McDonalds in East Asia*. Stanford: Stanford University Press.

Waxman, Sharon (1998) What sells abroad influences U.S. pop culture. *International Herald Tribune*, 27 October, p. 1.

Wehler, Hans-Ulrich (1974) *Der Aufstieg des amerikanishen Imperialismus: Studien zur Entwicklung des Imperium Americanum*. Gottingen: Vandenhoeck und Ruprecht.

Weiss, Marc (1987) *The Rise of the Community Builders: The American Real Estate Industry and Urban Land Planning*. N.Y.: Columbia University Press.

Wells, Jill (1986) *The Construction Industry in Developing Countries: Alternative Strategies for Development*. London: Croom Helm.

Wermiel, Sara E. (2000) *The Fireproof Building: Technology and Public Safety in the Nineteenth-Century American City*. Baltimore and London: Johns Hopkins University Press.

Wharton, Annabel Jane (2001) *Building the Cold War: Hilton International Hotels and Modern Architecture*. Chicago and London: University of Chicago Press.

Wheeler, Harry (1918) Speech at the opening of the First Conference of the National Federation of Construction Industries, Proceedings of the First National Conference.

White, Donald W. (1999) *The American Century: the Rise and Decline of the United States as a World Power*. New Haven and London: Yale University Press.

Whyte, William F. and Holmberg, Allan R. (1956) Human problems of U.S. enterprise in Latin America. *Human Organization*, **25**(3), pp. 20–40.

Wiggins, J.R. (1921) International aspects of construction: Study of world's construction activities approved. *Bulletin of the Associated General Contractors*, **12**, pp. 23–25.

Wilkins, Mira and Hill, Frank E. (1964) *American Business Abroad: Ford on Six Continents*. Detroit: Wayne State University Press.

Wood, Arthur Prescott (1902–1903) The President's Address. *Proceedings of the Shanghai Society of Engineers and Architects*.

Worcester, Dean C. (1914) *The Philippines: Past and Present*. New York: Macmillan.

World Bank (1999) *Entering the 21st Century: the Changing Development Landscape*. Washington, D.C.: The World Bank.

Wright, Arthur and Cartwright, H.A. (eds.) (1908) *Twentieth Century Impressions of Hongkong, Shanghai, and other Treaty Ports of China*. London: Lloyd's Greater Britain Publishing Company.

Wright, Gwendolyn (1991) *The Politics of Design in French Colonial Urbanism*. Chicago and London: University of Chicago Press.

Wright, Gwendolyn (2002) Building global modernisms. *Grey Room*, no. 07, pp. 124–134.

Wu Lien-teh (1931) A Visit to Modern Amoy. *China Critic*, vol. **4**, pp. 103–104.

Wyman, Walter F. (1914) What American manufacturers are doing to earn foreign trade – II. *Export American Industries*, **13**(2), pp. 47–48.

Yeung, Yue-man (2000) *Globalization and Networked Societies: Urban-Regional Change in Pacific Asia*. Honolulu: University of Hawaii Press.

Zevi, Bruno (1981) The influence of American architecture and urban planning in the world, in Davis, Allen J. (ed.) *For Better or Worse: the American Influence in the World*. Westport, Ct. and London: Greenwood Press, pp. 27–38.

Zukin, Sharon (1993) *Landscapes of Power: From Detroit to Disney World*. Berkeley, CA: University of California Press.

Zunz, Olivier (1998) *Why the American Century?* Chicago and London: University of Chicago Press.

Zwick, Jim (1992) *Mark Twain's Weapons of Satire: Anti-Imperialist Writings on the Philippine-American War*. Syracuse: Syracuse University Press.

Index